IMAGE, WORD
EARLY CHRISTIAN

Christianity proclaims Christ and the incarnate word of God; the Bible is described as the Word of God in both Jewish and Christian tradition. Are these usages merely homonymous, or would the ancients have recognized a more intimate relation between the word incarnate and the word proclaimed? This book investigates the concept of *logos* in pagan, Jewish and Christian thought, with a view to elucidating the polyphonic functions which the word acquired when used in theological discourse. Edwards presents a survey of theological applications of the term Logos in Greek, Jewish and Christian thought from Plato to Augustine and Proclus. Special focus is placed on: the relation of words to images in representation of divine realm, the relation between the *logos* within (reason) and the *logos* without (speech) both in linguistics and in Christology, the relation between the incarnate Word and the written text, and the place of reason in the interpretation of revelation.

Bringing together materials which are rarely synthesized in modern study, this book shows how Greek and biblical thought part company in their appraisal of the capacity of reason to grasp the nature of God, and how in consequence verbal revelation plays a more significant role in biblical teaching. Edwards shows how this entailed the rejection of images in Jewish and Christian thought, and how the manifestation in flesh of Christ as the living word of God compelled the church to reconsider both the relation of word to image and the interplay between the *logos* within and the written *logos* in the formulation of Christian doctrine.

ASHGATE STUDIES IN PHILOSOPHY & THEOLOGY IN LATE ANTIQUITY

Series Editors

Dr Mark Edwards, Oxford University, UK
Dr Lewis Ayers, Emory University, USA

The Ashgate Studies in Philosophy & Theology in Late Antiquity series focuses on major theologians, not as representatives of a 'tradition', whether Christian or classical, but as individuals immersed in the intellectual culture of their day. Each book concentrates on the arguments, not merely the opinions, of a single Christian writer or group of writers from the period AD 100–600 and compares and contrasts these arguments with those of pagan contemporaries who addressed similar questions. By study of the political, cultural and social milieu, contributors to the series show what external factors led to the convergence or divergence of Christianity and pagan thought in particular localities or periods. Pagan and Christian teachings are set out in a clear and systematic form making it possible to bring to light the true originality of the author's thought and to estimate the value of his work for modern times. This high profile research series offers an important contribution to areas of contemporary research in the patristic period, as well as providing new links into later periods, particularly the medieval and reformation.

Other titles published in this series:

Clothed in the Body
Asceticism, the Body and the Spiritual in the Late Antique Era
Hannah Hunt

The Spirit of Augustine's Early Theology
Contextualizing Augustine's Pneumatology
Chad Tyler Gerber

Evagrius and Gregory
Mind, Soul and Body in the 4th Century
Kevin Corrigan

Dionysius the Areopagite and the Neoplatonist Tradition
Despoiling the Hellenes
Sarah Klitenic Wear and John Dillon

Image, Word and God in the Early Christian Centuries

MARK EDWARDS
University of Oxford, UK

ASHGATE

Published by
Ashgate Publishing Limited
Wey Court East
Union Road
Farnham
Surrey, GU9 7PT
England

Ashgate Publishing Company
110 Cherry Street
Suite 3–1
Burlington, VT 05401–3818
USA

www.ashgate.com

British Library Cataloguing in Publication Data
Edwards, M. J. (Mark J.)
   Image, word and God in the early Christian centuries. – (Ashgate studies in philosophy & theology in late antiquity)
   1. Logos (Christian theology) 2. Word of God (Christian theology) 3. Logos (Philosophy) 4. Philosophy, Ancient. 5. Rhetoric, Ancient. 6. God – Knowableness – History of doctrines – Early church, ca. 30–600. 7. God (Judaism) – Knowableness – History of doctrines. 8. Revelation – Christianity – History of doctrines – Early church, ca. 30–600. 9. Revelation – Judaism – History of doctrines. 10. Bible – Criticism, interpretation, etc. – History – Early church, ca. 30–600.
   I. Title II. Series
   220.1'3–dc23

Library of Congress Cataloging–in–Publication Data
Edwards, M. J. (Mark J.)
   Image, word, and God in the early Christian centuries / by Mark Edwards.
      p. cm.—(Ashgate studies in philosophy & theology in late antiquity)
   Includes bibliographical references and index.
   ISBN 978-1-4094-0645-7 (hbk)—ISBN 978-1-4094-0671-6 (pbk.)—
ISBN 978-1-4094-0646-4 (ebook) 1. Logos (Philosophy) 2. Philosophy, Ancient.
3. Logos (Christian theology)—History of doctrines—Early church, ca. 30–600.
4. Incarnation. 5. Christianity. 6. Judaism. I. Title.

   B187.L6E39 2013
   232'.2—dc23
                                                                2012026626

ISBN 9781409406457 (hbk)
ISBN 9781409406716 (pbk)
ISBN 9781409406464 (ebk – PDF)
ISBN 9781409473527 (ebk – ePUB)

Printed and bound in Great Britain by the
MPG Books Group, UK.

For my mother

Contents

Introduction

Christianity is, as everyone knows, a religion of the word. This means, in the first place, that it purports to be grounded not in human instinct or conjecture, but in the self-disclosure of God through covenant, prophecy and their written attestations. The claims of the divine command, so thunderously urged by Barth,[1] have been acknowledged in the late twentieth century not only by the churches of ancient pedigree and the heirs of the Reformation, but by self-styled revolutionaries, liberators and apostles of the coming age.[2] Second – and this, too, Barth has forced upon the conscience of the Church after a long interim of deafness[3] – Christianity proclaims that this same word, becoming vulnerable in the ministry of Jesus Christ, was proved victorious in his resurrection. In him, the God whom no one has seen at any time (John 1.18) became visible to his contemporaries, though only for a season. This season being past, the knowledge of him is available to obedient hearers of a new word, delivered this time not through the law and the prophets, but through the recorded memories of those who knew him. The image of God – for so Christ is supposed to have been, as the paradigm and perfection of humanity, survives the incarnation, or remains incarnate, in the written Gospel.

Are words, then, the only medium of the 'good news' which is denoted by the term 'gospel'? The longest and most imperious of the Homilies of the Church of England urges that a picture cannot explain itself with the unambiguous clarity of a sermon, that the laity are apt to be more enamoured of the image than of the truth that it purportedly betokens, and that patrons of the image have proved bad subjects both to God and to his human deputies.[4] Yet Gregory the Great, the founder of the English Church, was among these patrons, and is credited with the aphorism that images are the scripture of the unlearned.[5] In the East, more prolix defenders of the use and worship of images maintained that when the Word became the flesh, he showed us an image of God that was at once amenable to representation and worthy of reverence. The iconophile contends that we cannot put away the image without denying either that the Word is God or that the man Jesus is identical with the Word.[6]

---

[1] For example, Barth (1975), 125–247.
[2] See, for example, von Balthasar (1982), 435–462; Millbank (1997), 55–122.
[3] Barth (1975), 399–447 and *passim.*
[4] Griffith (1864), 179–283.
[5] Ouspensky (1992), 132–133.
[6] See Louth (2002), 193–222, on John of Damascus.

More commonly heard in ancient than in modern times is the argument that those who set the Bible against the icon have merely substituted a graphic image for a graven one. The nineteenth century coined the term 'Bibliolatry', while the puritan in Swift's *Tale of a Tub* takes to punctuating his clothes with his favourite texts.[7] Suspicion of the book as a voiceless artefact can be traced back to Plato, who, modern critics argue, ought to have brought the same suspicion to the very use of words and to every attempt to elicit a fixed an irreducible deposit of meaning from our own utterances or those of others.[8] On this view there is always an uncultivated space between the seeker and the promised land of meaning, which is never simply given to the audience along with the act of speech. The reification of meaning as a correlate of the word would be, on this view, a product of the same metaphysics that led superstitious nations to impose a form on God.

Both iconoclasm and the discourse employed against it in the Orthodox and Catholic communions have their roots in the deliberations of an age without icons – or more accurately, when we speak of the latter half, an age in which the multiplication of physical icons had received no commentary in theological literature. The material culture of polytheism was not yet extinct even in the late fifth century, and believers were not permitted to forget that God has dispensed a sovereign antidote to idolatry in the Word incarnate, written and proclaimed. The word written showed that, while it was not impossible for God to take a visible form, such apparitions were transient and interpretable only because of the speech that accompanied or succeeded them. The more distinct the epiphany, the less apt it was to be recognized as an epiphany. This law was repeatedly confirmed when the Word assumed a more permanent body: it was not those with eyes to see but those with ears to hear who discovered him to be greater than he seemed.

The first chapter of the present study illustrates the primacy of being over seeing as a mode of revelation in the Old Testament, though I have also taken account of apparent departures from this principle in the text and in the Judaism of the Roman era. The saying that humanity is made in the image of God supplies a tentative charter for anthropomorphic visions of the Deity in the Old Testament; in Chapter 2 I shall argue that it functions in the New Testament as a hermeneutic canon, explaining both how God can be in Christ and how the reader, as man addressed by Man, can find in himself the clue to the hidden pattern of the Gospel. Chapter 3 examines the diverse notions of *logos* held by Greek philosophers, giving pride of place (as most early Christian writers did) to Plato, who would seem to have forgotten his disdain for the graphic image when he speaks of the world as an icon of the paradigm, and of his own mythopoeic writing as an icon of the soul's ascent from shadows to the contemplation of immaterial forms. In Chapter 4 we see that his admirers took two paths. Philo the Jew could accept the iconic character of the scriptures and could imagine the creative word as a adumbration in God's mind of the things that he was to make visible; the plastic

---

[7]   Newman (1882), 39; Swift (1976), 342.

[8]   Derrida (1981).

representation of the divine, on the other hand, was no less abhorrent to him than to the least philosophical of his co-religionists. Pagan defence of the image, by contrast, becomes a familiar exercise among sophists, and particularly among those who are most conversant with Plato's thought, although they are adepts in a trade that he professes to despise.

These apologies coincide in date with the first publication of Christian texts in which the idols of the forum are contrasted with the true image of God in humanity, and sometimes with the manifestation of the consummate image in the man Jesus. While (as we shall observe in Chapter 5) these writings seldom fail to assert the superiority of the scriptures over every pagan representation of divinity, they achieve no synthesis of anthropology, hermeneutics and Christology. Origen's completion of this synthesis gives him a right to the lion's share of Chapter 6, although Tertullian and Clement, who appear in this chapter only as his harbingers, would be handled less summarily had I been allowed to inflict a larger volume upon the public. In Chapter 7, further Platonic experiments will fall under review: the differentiation of the icon from the image in Plotinus, the qualified vindication of divine statues in Porphyry, and Iamblichus' demonstration that, while sensible epiphanies may be real, they become delusive when they are taken for epiphanies of real gods. We appear to witness a temporary dissolution of Origen's synthesis in Chapter 8, which follows the efforts of theologians in the fourth century to prove that the divinity of Christ is a corollary of his biblical character as the Father's image. In Chapter 9, on the other hand, we discover in the works of Proclus a more comprehensive philosophy of symbols than had hitherto been advanced by any Platonist, combined with a rediscovery of the didactic and exemplary role of Socrates in the dialogues. Augustine shares the tenth chapter with Dionysius the Areopagite. The former attempts, more diligently than anyone since Origen, to show that the expression 'Word of God', when used of scripture, is not a mere homonym for the same expression when applied to Christ.

Augustine himself was guilty of an uncharacteristically facile judgment on the Neoplatonists when he wrote that they could affirm everything in the prologue to the Fourth Gospel up to the point where the Word becomes flesh (*Confessions* 7.9). This gospel begins, as the sacred canon begins for Jews and Christians, with the creation of all from nothing by the Word and its culmination in humanity. From the communication of the image to the first humans, with the promise of the likeness, Christians believed that they could deduce the necessity of the incarnation as the capstone to God's plan for the divinization of his earthly surrogates. This plan was understood to embrace the body, whether or not the body was included in the image; any representation of God in a form that he had not chosen as his image was idolatry, and so was the adoration of the creature itself in place of the Creator (Romans 1.19–21). For Plato, on the other hand, the origin of the human race is only one theme among many, and the creation of the world – which cannot be known except by myth and may not even be an event in time – is not the source of transcendental knowledge or of the philosopher's conviction that we are greater than we seem. The form of the Good would beckon eternally even if the Demiurge of the *Timaeus* were as fanciful as the deities of Homer. Any object in the sensible world may serve the philosopher as a shadow or an icon of the real; the enemy of emancipation is not so much the plastic image as the body which is attached to every soul in the present world as its *eidôlon*, and which all too often supplants the soul in our interests and affections.

Platonism is not, as we understand that term, a theology. The doctrine of ideas, where it is entertained, is not revealed, and is not a testimony to the impotence of human understanding. It builds itself, without the intervention of a superhuman architect, from the logic of experience – or rather from the apparent contradiction between the fragility of our sensory experience and the permanence of language. Immutable truth can be predicated only of intelligible objects; the permanence of these objects entails the existence at all times of an intelligence to perceive them; in calling this divine, however, a Platonist does not mean to deny that the *logos* in each of us can aspire to the apprehension of the same forms that are already perceived by the god in whose train the soul drives its celestial team. An embodied soul may dwell in the intelligible sphere, saying with Plotinus 'it is the gods who should come to me, not I to them' (Porphyry, *Life of Plotinus* 10.35). Lesser intellects may receive intimations from the same sphere, but not such as would violate the axioms of philosophical reasoning or invite us to believe that what is naturally impossible becomes 'certain' when attributed to God.[9]

Platonism imposes less of a tax on our credulity. Christianity has exhibited a more universal power to reform the conscience. It is not the purpose of this study to judge between them, or to explain why one still flourishes widely in every part of the world but Europe while the other is all but extinct. My hope is rather, by juxtaposing them, to throw into relief what is peculiar to each, and in particular to show that the contrasts noted in the last paragraph spring from dissonant valuations of the image, which are rooted in turn in dissonant understandings of the relation between the human and the divine.

---

[9]   Tertullian, *On the Flesh of Christ* 5 – a logical deduction from divine omnipotence, not a forensic commonplace, as proposed.

Chapter 1

Seeing and Hearing God in the Old Testament

The Septuagint – the Greek version of the Hebrew Torah, augmented by original compositions – was a common treasury of revelation for Jews and Christians of the early Roman Empire. And not only for Jews and Christians: educated Greeks, it appears, were familiar with those verses in which 'the Lawgiver of the Jews' ascribes the origin of all things to the simple command of God (Genesis 1.2–3). These verses, while they may not be the earliest in date of composition, have stood for centuries at the beginning of the Torah, and it is fitting that they should be the most widely known because they illustrate that primacy of hearing over seeing which the present chapter will demonstrate to be generally, if not ubiquitously, characteristic of the whole corpus. This is to not to say that ocular revelations are rare or illusory, but that speech affords stronger evidence than any visual sign of the presence of God, and imparts a clearer understanding of his will. Authors who do not hesitate to credit God with an audible voice are apt to represent what is seen as something other than God himself – a fire, an angel, the vague similitude of a human form. As fear of anthropomorphism becomes more acute, the word, the voice or the name may become grammatical substitutes for the tetragrammaton, the unpronounceable name of God himself; as we shall see, however, this verbal proxy seldom acquires the substance of an angel or active deputy, let alone of a second god, in works that have not been deeply coloured by Greek or Christian traditions. If palpable existence could be accorded to the word as a thing distinct from God himself, that was because of the palpability of the scriptures, which to their latter-day interpreters were what God had been to their forebears, now that even vocal prophecy was as much a miracle of yesterday as the burning bush.[1]

Creation by the Word

'And God said, Let there be light' (Genesis 1.3).[2] These are the most famous of God's words in a book the whole of which is traditionally revered, by Jews and

---

[1]   Cf. Josephus, *Against Apion* 1.141.

[2]   The King James version of the Bible is quoted throughout this book, except where the argument requires the quotation or retranslation of the Greek text of the Septuagint or New Testament. The editions quoted from are *Septuaginta*, ed. Rahlfs and Hanhart (2012) and *Novum Testamentum Gracae*, ed. Garrod (1963).

Christians alike, as the Word of God. By 'the whole' we may mean simply the work that in Greek and most European tongues is entitled 'Genesis'; we may mean the corpus of literature that Jews call the Torah or Tanakh, though where Christians predominate the Greek is known as the Septuagint and the Hebrew as the Old Testament; or we may mean the uneasy but fruitful coupling of two canons which forms the scripture of the Church, and for which the usual designation is the Bible, derived from the Greek for 'book'. Such terms were not available to the author of the Greek treatise *On the Sublime* or *On the Grand Style*, who, while drawing all his other illustrations from pagan literature, concludes from this one passage that the 'Lawgiver of the Jews' can have been no ordinary man. A more shallow judgment is expressed by Galen, a physician to us but in his own day a philosopher, who considers it more rational to imagine the Creator as an artisan working on matter than to take refuge, as the Jews and Christians do, in the notion of an omnipotent fiat curbed by no antecedent laws.[3] Galen's name for this divine artificer is Demiurge; biblical literature, as we shall see, reserves this term for a manufacturer of idols, while the appellation that Jews and Christians came to of God in his role was *ktistês*, a rarer term in Greek, and one that was held consistently, if not invariably, to be applicable to no being but God himself.

But is it to be presumed that God, as *ktistês*, effects his purposes without a material substrate? The first sentence of the book proclaims that 'in the beginning, God created the heaven and the earth'. Immediately we hear that 'the earth was without form and void' and that 'the Spirit of God moved upon the face of the waters'. The prophet Jeremiah appears to know the first half of this text, since he envisages the future ruin of Israel as a return to this primordial *tohu-bohu*, or state of chaos. Allusions in Gnostic writings and in the work of the philosopher Numenius suggest that the words describing the motion of the Spirit, which challenge comparison with Plato's account of the animation of matter by the world-soul, were as notorious in some circles as the following verse, which records the creation of light.[4] But did the *tohu-bohu* originate, like the light itself, in the unconditioned will of God, or was this inchoate mass coeternal with him, as a Platonist like Galen would have urged? If we take the first view, we must postulate two creations, first of the substrate, then of the world itself; if we adopt the second, the opening sentence ('in the beginning God created') must be construed not as the exordium to the narrative, but as a rubric: the true narrative commences, on this view, with the creation of light, and the intermediate verse describes a state anterior to this creation.[5] There is in fact no passage of the Septuagint which plainly attests the creation of the world from nothing, unless it be 2 Maccabees 7.28, where the power of God to bring things into being from 'that which is not' is cited as evidence of his ability to restore life to his elect. But 2 Maccabees is a work preserved only in Greek, an item in the 'apocryphal' or 'deuterocanonical'

---

[3]   Walzer (1949), 11–13.

[4]   Numenius, Fr. 30, Des Places; see May (2004), 48n.

[5]   Cf. 2 Corinthians 3.4–6.

portion of scripture, and in any case the locution *ex ouk ontôn* ('from things which are not') may as easily refer to an indeterminate substrate as to an absolute state of non-existence.[6] In conclusion, therefore, we cannot say with confidence whether the author of Genesis 1, or any of his readers before the Christian era, held that creation by the Word of God was incompatible with the existence of a primordial chaos upon which this divine utterance imposed the present contours of the world.

An utterance, we may say: but is there a voice? Audible speech is addressed to the ear, but no interlocutor is mentioned in the text or in any Jewish or Aramaic exegesis of the early Christian era. Nor does the text encourage us to reify God's word as a thing distinct from himself: that, as we shall see, was left to a later and more philosophical generation. Genesis 1.3 was understood by the rabbis to mean that the world was created without a coadjutor,[7] and for some it became a dogma that it was created out of nothing, though the strength with which they assert this attests the credibility of the opposing doctrine. We read at Psalm 33.6 that the heavens were made by the word of God, where the Greek is *logos* and the Hebrew *dabar*: in neither language, however, is the word even an instrument, let alone a person. The expression is circumlocutory, a symptom of the same diffidence that caused Hebrew writers to say that it was not God, but his name, that possessed the sanctuary, not God but his glory that will fill the earth.[8]

We have seen that God was not to be conceived as an artisan; it was not, for all that, unlawful to describe the world as a piece of architecture. For those who held, with Hillel against Shammai, that the earth was created before the heavens, the former represents the foundation, the latter the superstructure.[9] The edifice most suited to the comparison was the Temple in Jerusalem not because it was fashioned with the same ease, but because it was unique and a consummate specimen of the builder's art. It was always to be remembered that this earthly house was built for the sake of the worshipper, not as a domicile for the uncontainable God, and that its predecessor, the tabernacle carried by the Israelites in the wilderness, was merely the simulacrum of a heavenly archetype revealed to Moses. The relation between the world and the Temple is one of prolepsis rather than of analogy; in the language of hermeneutics it is typological rather than allegorical, where the former term connotes the adumbration of one event by another, the latter a figurative expression of an atemporal truth. More accurately, we see here an inversion of the typological principle as this is commonly understood by Christians, for in this case it is the paradigm that comes first, while what follows is the ectype, realizing only the shadow of its original.

---

[6]   May (2004), 16–18.

[7]   Or rather with no coadjutor but the Torah: Freedman (1977), 1.

[8]   Moore (1922).

[9]   Freedman (1977), 13–14.

The Image of God

Heaven and earth are God's creation, not his likeness. This is an obvious point but not a barren one, for no book was more often compared to Genesis in antiquity than Plato's *Timaeus*, the closing sentence of which declares that the cosmos is the unique (*monogenes*) image of its eternal paradigm. We shall see later, in Chapter 7, that some Platonists held the Demiurge and the paradigm to be one entity, and for such thinkers it would follow that the world exhibits not only the power, but the lineaments of its maker. The 'priestly writer' whom most scholars hold responsible for the narrative of creation in six days does not suggest that God is visible in any of his works before the sixth day. Only then, and adopting the plural pronoun for the first time, does he proclaim 'Let us create man in our image and likeness'. Forthwith he appears to do something less than this, for we are told that man was created in the image of God, as though man were a single entity, and nothing is said of the likeness. An appended clause, which states that 'he created them male and female' seems, if anything, to indicate an unlikeness between the creature and the one God who is commonly spoken of in the masculine gender. To the male and female together the Creator issues an ordinance to populate the earth, attaching to this a promise of dominion over all the other inhabitants of water, land and air.

This enigmatic passage raised as many questions for the ancient as for the modern reader. What does it mean to speak of an image of God, and is this the same thing as a likeness? There are scholars of high authority who maintain that the words mean here what they would signify in any other context, which is to say that the author imagined the first human being to be a replica of his Maker.[10] Physical similarity is undoubtedly implied in the occurrence of the phrase at Genesis 5.3, where a different author, who probably antedates the priestly writer, speaks of Seth as the image and likeness of his father Adam. If man resembles God, it follows that God resembles man, and we learn from both rabbinic and Christian sources in antiquity that this anthropomorphic tenet was widely held. In all our sources, however, it is the error of someone else, the untenable alternative which an author must ceremoniously repudiate to secure a hearing for his own position. There are scholars, again of good repute, who cannot believe that even the narrator of Genesis 1 was so ingenuous;[11] some, looking for a gloss in the ambient text, propose that the meaning of the term 'image' is conveyed in the words investing man with authority over the denizens of the three elements. God's vicegerent, on this view, is the image of God insofar as he is the sole representative of their common Author to the fish of the sea, the fowls of the air and the four-footed beasts of the land.

This is one of the readings entertained in ancient sources. Both ancient and modern exegetes are apt to ignore a third occurrence of the term 'image' at Genesis 9.6, where it is stipulated that one who sheds the blood of his human neighbour

---

[10]   Von Rad (1966), 56; cf. Barr (1993), 158.

[11]   Westermann (1974), 55–56; cf. Jónsson (1988), 13; Barr (1993), 157–159.

must pay with his own because man was made in the image of God. Here the thought appears to be that a human being is God's must precious chattel, so that to say that man is made in the image of God is to say that he bears God's seal as a mark of ownership and affection. Yet, though this sealing is predicated in biblical texts of Israel, of the Christian elect and of Christ himself, it has not been so frequently invoked in the elucidation of Genesis 1.26 as other notions which are grounded not in parallel with cognate texts from the scriptures, but in received beliefs concerning the nature of God. Since God is supposed to be eminently rational, it may be surmised that the image consists in the exercise of reason or in the possession of a capacity for free decision, not vouchsafed to any other creature. Or, again. it may be urged that, as God is supremely good, his image is retained so long as we persevere in rectitude. No resemblance in corporeal attributes is posited here; on the contrary, the usual view is that, if there is any natural affinity between God and man, it is grounded in man's possession of an incorporeal soul. This is a philosophical, not a biblical, hypothesis, a legacy of the Greek occupation of the Jewish world after Alexander – though it would not be good philosophy to infer that it is therefore an unlawful speculation for a Christian, or an inauthentic belief when embraced by Jews.

So far we have only begun to broach the difficulties that arise from the gnomic style of the priestly writer. If (for example) God undertakes to make man in his image and likeness, but goes on to create in the image alone, does this entail that likeness and image are one, as both fourth-century and twentieth-century critics have opined, or is it rather that the likeness is a gift to be superadded to the image, but provisionally withheld? This speculation seems to be confirmed by the asseveration at Genesis 9.6, which was quoted above, that every man is the image of God, without any mention of the likeness. The next question is, if the likeness has been withheld, how are we to acquire it? Righteousness is a universal duty, but if this means the virtue that is perfected by resistance to odds and the conquest of temptation, it can find no mirror in God, whom we must presume to be incapable of failure or of being less than he is. One answer might be that humans live under two ordinances: to manifest the image in such attributes as wisdom and benevolence, which appertain also to God; and to realize the likeness in those attributes which set us apart from God but admit of perfection in their own kind. Yet, even if we grant that God and man share such a commonwealth of properties, we may doubt whether any such casuistry was imagined by the author of this text.

Enigma succeeds enigma when we are told that the man in the image of God was created male and female. Greek and English renderings imply a collective rather than an individual subject, but according to an early rabbinic construction of this verse the first created human was a hermaphrodite. This, one might maintain, was a necessity, since no being of either sex could possess the image of a Creator who has none. By a naive inversion of the same conceit one might conclude that, if his image is literally bisexual, God himself must be not so much sexless as androgynous.[12] Any such hypotheses, however, will prove baseless if we assume that the same event is represented in the narrative which we now describe as the second chapter of Genesis. According to this account, the protoplast, or first created human entity, is not the species but a solitary male, who receives the designation Adam (man) as a proper name. He is not summoned out of nothing by a word, but fashioned from the clay of the earth, and is not said to bear the image of his Maker. The female is not coeval with the male, but is fashioned later from his rib because it is deemed 'not good that man should be alone'. Both man and woman fall so far short of God in wisdom that it is the hope of 'becoming like gods' that tempts them to violate his ordinance and pluck the fruit of knowledge. It is only when they have both acquired the knowledge of good and evil that God says, with a curious permutation of singular and plural, 'the man is become as one of us'.

If we regard the first episode as a proleptic abbreviation of the second, we shall understand 'God created man' to mean 'God fashioned man', and 'male and female' to signify 'first the male, then the female'. As the second omits, but does not deny, the bestowal of the likeness, we are free to guess that image, likeness or both reside in the inner man, or even in the body; on the other hand, we may wonder what addition or amercement it may have received from the desire to 'be as gods'. But is it necessary to educe one narrative from discordant passages? Might one not argue, rather, that there are indeed two subjects, two distinct though not unrelated works of God? Let us suppose, for example, that the first creation is that of the soul, the mind or the inner man, who is common to all, invisible as God is and subject to no differentiation of the sexes; the second creation, on this view, would be that of the outward frame, with its solid texture and differentiated organs. A corollary might be that the image is that which is present in all by divine endowment, while the likeness is that which each attains according to the measure of his or her efforts and capacities. Neither this hypothesis of two creations nor the proposed corollary will entail that the inner man has ever existed without a body. It is possible, since an inspired text can accommodate every artifice known to literature, that what is conveyed historically is to be understood analytically – in other words, that the inner man precedes the outer man only as the essence or species precedes the individual, in the order of logical presupposition but not in the order of time. Even the implied superiority of the inner man would not entail that the outer man is an afterthought or excrescence, for, as it can plausibly be maintained that essence cannot exist except in the particular, so it can be urged that a disembodied soul is no more the human being that God intended to create than a soulless body. If it is true, on the one hand, that our carnal organs set us apart from God and, on the other, that we are required to achieve the likeness of God by the exercise of these organs, it is as reasonable to suppose that we reach the likeness by perfecting the bodily form as by transcending it. After all, the creation is not that of an image but of a being 'in' or 'according to' the image, and the premature ambition of Adam and Eve was not to be God but to be 'as gods'.

---

[12]   Freedman (1977), 54.

The modern scholar, of course, is unlikely to attempt any synthesis of the two chapters, whether by postulating one creation or two. The preferred opinion is that the first account is from the hand of the priestly writer, the second from the Jahwist, that both were constructing myths from older myths, and as they differ no less in their ends than in their materials, we have nothing to gain by attempting to reconcile them. This is the historico-critical method, which, by crediting the text itself with a history, deprives it of all historiographic value. To the ancients this expedient would have seemed more frigid than the most laboured allegory, for if one thing was certain, it was that God had disclosed the truth through his human instruments, whatever the situation and purpose of each, and that he would not have failed to vouchsafe us a true and consistent account of human origins.

That man was made in the image of God is so much a cardinal doctrine of Christian thought that it may surprise us to find it receiving only a fleeting commentary in the classic midrash. It records just one rabbinic animadversion – that, whereas the angels bear the image of God but do not procreate, animals procreate but lack the image.[13] Humanity, created in the image and at the same time in both sexes, occupies the equator between two hemispheres, but is not a privileged denizen of either. There is no redeemer in Jewish thought, who, being the incarnate image of God, could be set in antithesis to Adam; and there is no indication in the Mosaic scriptures, or in the writings of the prophets, that the Creator evinces any predilection for the human form when he makes himself known to Israel. As we shall see in the following section, the scriptures imply, and the rabbis believed, that the deity who can assume the guise of a pillar of fire, an angel or a radiant cloud is never in fact so perfectly apprehensible by vision as by hearing. Perhaps we should say that he manifests himself to the ear within; or, more precisely still, to the inward ear assisted by the eye.

Divine Intermediaries

God's first communications to man in Genesis – the command to multiply and the prohibition of the fruit – are not accompanied by any reference to the medium of speech or to a particular addressee. It is after his trespass that Adam is apostrophized by the 'voice of the Lord God walking in the garden'. The syntax was as ambiguous to ancient commentators on the Hebrew as to the modern English reader. To believe without qualification that it was God who walked was a dangerous anthropomorphism; one palliative was to take the verb metaphorically (whatever this may entail), another was to seek an alternative referent for the noun. One rabbinic comment preserved in the midrash adopts this second device, though obliquely;[14] the Aramaic targums, or paraphrases, speak of the voice of the *memra*,

---

13   Freedman (1977), 62.
14   Freedman (1977), 153 n.2.

that is, of the word of God imagined as an agent.[15] It may be that the walking of God's deputy remains as metaphorical as that of God himself, but if it should be taken literally, no sacrilege ensues. We have seen that the word before the world, the word of creation, is barely conceived as an instrument, let alone as a separate agent; the word within the world, the word of intercourse, becomes the surrogate of the God who utters it for fear that he himself will otherwise be circumscribed by his own creation.

The voice cries 'Adam, where art thou?' (Genesis 3.8), and the transgressors come forth; in what form they see God we do not learn, though nothing could be clearer than the words of reproof and prophecy that follow. So it is when God imposes a penalty on Cain for the murder of Abel (Genesis 4.10–12): we hear all that the murderer hears, but are not told how he hears it or whether hearing is accompanied by vision. We are soon informed of two divine resolutions – to spare our pains by shortening life and to send the Flood as a punishment for iniquity – which God confided only to himself. He communicates his intention to Noah, with precepts for the building of the ark (Genesis 6.3–7); if the narrative once again says nothing of any vocal or visual medium, it is not jejune but purposely elliptical, since in its Sumerian and Babylonian prototypes the shipwright overhears a warning secretly imparted by the god Ea to the reeds around his home.[16] God's subsequent blessing of Noah and his deliberations before he overthrows the Tower of Babel are related with the same economy (9.9, 11.6). After God chooses Abraham to be the father of a great nation (12.3), the two are in regular communion, and on certain occasions God 'appears' to Abraham, who invariably prostrates himself, perhaps to hide his face or to avoid that of his interlocutor. Yet at times there is simply a call, to which he replies (in contrast to Adam) 'here I am'. The great covenant, broached in a vision (15.1), is cemented under a 'horror of great darkness' (15.12), but it cannot be said that dreams are the characteristic mode of his intercourse with God. Once we see with his eyes, when he perceives three men at the door of his tent in Mamre (18.1), and is conscious at once of the presence of the Lord. Nevertheless, this one example of lucid vision is also the only instance of dissent, for Sarah laughs when she discovers that she is to bear a child in her ninetieth year (18.12), while Abraham, when he learns of the intended annihilation of Sodom, is bold enough to ask that the many be spared for the sake of ten (18.32).

There are not ten righteous men in Sodom, but one. The emissaries who come to Lot are received as men; when Lot later adopts 'my Lord' as a style of address, we cannot be sure that 'Lord' is a synonym for 'God'. Hagar, when she is driven forth to make way for Isaac, is reassured by a angel, whom she retrospectively takes to be God 'who seeth me' (16.11–13). Abraham's grandson Jacob encounters angels not in his own house, but in solitude and exile. At the place which he names Bethel, or house of God, he sees them in a dream, ascending and descending by a ladder, above which God (who is not further described) delivers an epilogue to his

---

[15]   Boyarin (2001), 256, citing Klein (1980), 145–146.

[16]   George (1999), 89.

promise to Abraham (28.12–15). Wrestling with an unknown man by night, Jacob is told at dawn that he has power with God, and having asked in vain for the name of his adversary, concludes that he has looked on the face of God (32.24–30). Only at 35.9 is it said expressly that God 'appeared' to him. He appears again to Jacob in a vision at 46.2; on the other hand, while the latter's son Joseph is a prolific dreamer who grows prosperous with the help of the Lord (39.2), we nowhere hear that God appeared, or even spoke to him. It would seem, then, that persons other than Abraham seldom have the privilege of conversing directly with God, that dreams are now a more usual means of intercourse than waking apparitions, and that sometimes his identity is apparent only after he has spoken. While we cannot say of Jacob, as one might say of Abraham, that the more he sees the less he is willing to hear, it remains true that the apparition of God, when recounted at all, is always the barest of preambles to the message that he imparts.

In the other four books of the Pentateuch, on the other hand, the word of God is reinforced and verified by ocular phenomena. It is the spectacle of the burning bush that first makes Moses aware of his presence; as is common in such scenes, the voice that addresses him is at first said to be an angel's, though (as again is common) God and his angel seem to be identified as the narrative proceeds. Moses must be convinced by signs, and when he himself becomes *theos* ('god') to Pharaoh at Exodus 7.1, it is only by conspicuous violations of the natural order that he at last prevails. If signs by themselves are mute, they are not superfluous as concomitants to divine speech even after the deliverance from Egypt. The descent of God on Sinai is advertised by fire and tempest; while this may be for the benefit of the multitude (who 'saw no form and heard no words', according to Deuteronomy 4.12), Moses himself is not content to hear God's proclamation of the Law unless he can also see his face. Advised that he can bear no more than the vision of God's hindquarters, he nonetheless interprets this as a seeing 'face to face', and in this he is hardly deceived, as God declares that he spoke with him 'as a man speaks with his friend'. Because they have received no such disclosure, the Israelites presumptuously fashion a golden calf as their image of God; they were not to know that idolatry was forbidden in the Decalogue which Moses was about to bring down from the summit, but his wrath when he discovered their trespass caused him to break the tablets, thus destroying the one graven image by which God had consented to make himself known to Israel. The tablets of the reconstituted law, proscribing graven and molten images alike, were kept in the ark, which in turn was housed in the tabernacle, where Moses and Aaron alone could speak with God. For the Israelites, however, the divine presence was signified by the fiery pillar which went before the ark in its forty years of wandering. Nor were they entirely cheated of a direct epiphany: after the promulgation of the Law, 'they saw the God of Israel, and there was under his feet as it were a paved work of sapphire stone'. On another occasion they were permitted something very like an idol: the sole antidote to the venom of the serpents which had been sent to chastise their mutterings was to look on the brazen serpent which Moses fashioned at God's behest. The story does not now represent this as the image of God, yet a brazen serpent was worshipped in the Temple until Hezekiah removed it; it was about this time that God – appointing prophecy rather than imagery as his medium in order to reach those who were not within sight of Jerusalem – began to proclaim 'look unto me, all ye ends of the earth, and be saved'.

Temple and Prophets

After the death of Moses it remains true that the Israelites do not see the form of God or hear his voice. There is no one else in the host to whom he speaks as directly as he spoke to Balaam, a pagan diviner, who was later identified with Zoroaster. Balaam, being no Israelite, is inclined to temporize after the first command, and hence receives another, contradictory one, which proves to be his undoing. At no time are we told what he saw when he prayed for counsel, or by what means he received it. At Judges 2.1 an angel upbraids the whole people because they have formed mixed unions with the indigenous Canaanites. What form he took we are not told, but he appears to be recognized as a plenipotentiary of God without being taken for God himself. No command is issued, and those who listen have only the opportunity to repent of their irremediable sin. Ehud professes to bring a word of God to King Eglon (Judges 3.20), but this is merely the ruse by which he contrives his assassination. In chapters 6 and 7 the word of God comes frequently to Gideon, but the angel who delivers it on the first occasion is greeted with incredulity until he vouchsafes a sign (Judges 6.37). The spirit of the Lord is also said to fall upon Gideon, as later on Jephtha and Samson (11.29, 15.14); it may be, therefore, that ecstasy has become the usual medium of divine communication with individuals. The birth of Samson, however, is announced with great solemnity by an angel, who is perceived as such by Manoah when he departs. He is the one character in the Book of Judges who declares that he has seen God (13.22), and his belief is not expressly corroborated by the author. His inference, erroneous as it proves, that he is bound to die in consequence of this vision implies that direct traffic between God and his creatures is now no longer to be expected or desired.

It appears that God continues to speak to the foes of Israel, as he spoke to Balaam. When the Philistines capture the ark, but then discover that it is a vessel of uncontrollable power and a termagant to their own deity, the remedy is found by priests and diviners, who are surely their own, though they act as conduits for the voice of God (1 Samuel 4–6). It is at this time, however, that we see the inauguration of a new guild, that of the *nabiim* or prophets,[17] who enjoy such regular commerce with God that we never hear of angelic mediators or of a confirmatory vision. The first of the line is Samuel, who initially hears the summons as the voice of a man, mistaking it for that of Eli, the priest with whom he resides. Eli, while he discerns the source of the call, has experienced no such communications and no doubt acquires his knowledge of God's will through the mysterious apparatus of Urim

---

[17]   Dodd (1960), 1952–1960.

and Thumim (Exodus 28.30, for example). Samuel, for his part, receives the word of God henceforth at intervals, by direct though unexplicated means (1 Samuel 3). Under divine authority he anoints Saul, then deposes him, placing David on the throne. Although both Saul and David have bouts of ecstasy, God generally addresses them through such instruments as Samuel and Nathan, and under their successors in the northern kingdom of Israel a corporation of prophets is formed around the throne. The northern monarchs, however, being strangers to God, make enemies of the true prophets, banishing Isaiah to the wilderness and excluding Micaiah ben Imlah from the court (1 Kings 22.6–12). Elijah is comforted by miracles and occasionally by audible reassurance (1 Kings 17); Micaiah owes his intelligence to a vision not of God, but of the defeat which awaits King Ahab at Ramoth-Gilead and the mystification of the court-prophets by a lying spirit (1 Kings 22.17). In the writings of those prophets who denounced the northern kingdom we note the same pattern: Amos recounts a series of visions, but never of God, while Hosea's inspiration is apt to take the form of prophecy or command.

In the southern kingdom of Judah, God is represented to the kings by a superior order of prophets; at the same time the kings have their own way of representing God. It is David's project to build a house for God that will be more opulent than his own (2 Samuel 7.2). He is told in a dream that a building made with hands cannot contain the Almighty (Chronicles 17.4); the enterprise is not, however, abandoned but postponed to the reign of Solomon, who completes it with the aid of the Phoenicians. These allies – who are in some accounts the sole masons of the Temple – could not be held to a strict observance of the Decalogue, even if the Decalogue was in force at that time in Israel.[18] In any case, the furniture of the tabernacle, according to the histories that have come down to us, included two gold cherubim above the mercy-seat (Psalm 99.1); since this had been copied from a heavenly archetype, it was natural that the Temple, too, should accommodate these lieutenants of God, whom we first encounter in the Mosaic scriptures as the sentinels at the gate of Eden after the expulsion of Adam and Eve. A psalmist says of God himself that he sits above the cherubim (Psalm 80.1), while a prophet who cannot be accused of connivance with idolatry appears to detect no blasphemy in the notion that God may be present in his own house (Isaiah 6.1). Isaiah sees him enthroned above the seraphim, a different species of angel, whose name, in the opinion of some scholars, shares a root with the Hebrew word for a serpent.[19] It is possible that the being who tempts Adam and Eve to betray God in the extant account of the Fall was once conceived as an agent of God himself, as Satan is in surviving passages of the Hebrew scriptures.[20] As we also read in Ezekiel of a cherub who fell from Eden (Ezekiel 28.16), it may be a general rule that the servants of God become his adversaries whenever they give way to pride – that is

---

[18] On the furnishing of the Temple, see Vaux (1961), 312–330.

[19] Eichrodt (1967), 204–205; Ringgren (1966), 100, is more reserved.

[20] For example, in Job 1. See now Gordon and Rendburg (1997), 259.

to say, whenever the representative mistakes himself, or is mistaken by others, for his invisible Sovereign.

The vision in Isaiah is transitory, since the Lord is not a permanent inhabitant of the Temple. It is also, since a picture alone cannot edify, the prelude to the commissioning of Isaiah, which he accepts when a burning coal is placed on his lips (Isaiah 6.6). Isaiah delivers oracle after oracle, without alluding to any new encounter; his continuator, whom we call Second Isaiah, does not witness any epiphany of the God whom he has lifted 'above the circle of the earth' (Isaiah 40.22); when Third Isaiah dresses God in the panoply of a man of war, he is writing not as a seer but as a poet (Isaiah 59.17). A different kind of circumspection is evident in Habakkuk, to whom the Lord appears in a conflagration of glory tipped with horns and fire-coals, leaving the prophet conscious of the 'hiding of his power' (Habakkuk 3.4). Ezekiel is accosted, in the wake of a cloud, a whirlwind and a fire, by four winged creatures, which tax the reader's eidetic faculties by combining a human form with the attributes of three other beasts. The rabbis who forbade the recitation of his exordium and his final vision, however, were perhaps offended most of all by two elusive visions of God – as the likeness of the similitude of a man at 1.28 and as 'the glory' whose voice was as that of many waters at 43.2. Yet in both these instances, it will be noted that Ezekiel is careful not to draw a naive comparison between God himself and any of his created works; he also refrains from describing the spirit who carries him to a new province of the imagination in chapter 37, and elsewhere it is simply the 'word of the Lord' that comes upon him. Daniel is, by contrast, pictographic: the angels who minister to him are in appearance 'sons of men' (Daniel 8.15, for example); this figure is a symbol of the nation in contradistinction to the beasts who oppress it at 7.13, but no promise of redemption in older canonical texts had prepared the reader of Daniel for his depiction of the Ancient of Days as a white-clad figure whose hair was as wool, dispensing judgment from his fiery throne.

Among the major prophets, Jeremiah is the least inclined to visions. God's revelation to him is always verbal and, for all we know, apprehensible only to the inner ear. He is wary, as Isaiah is, too, of popular faith in the indestructibility of the Temple. Instead he takes his stand upon the Law – above all, on the Law enshrined in the book of Deuteronomy. 'Enshrined' is no idle term here, for it is likely that we are intended to take this book, or its prototype, for the one that King Josiah, in conjunction with Hilkiah the priest, the prophetess Huldah and Shaphan the scribe, recovered from the Temple a generation before the time of Jeremiah.[21] The reading of this book, to universal consternation and repentance, was almost a replica of the event at Sinai; less tangible than the tables of the Law, the book was nonetheless a more portable memento of the first covenant as its contents were not sequestered within the ark but published to all. While God can speak to a prophet, and the prophet to his neighbours, there are no limits to the audience which can be reached

---

[21]   For a classic statement of the (contested) view that the book discovered in 2 Kings 22 is Deuteronomy, see Wellhausen (1957), 402–410.

by a book through an interdependent chain of reciters and amanuenses. The Law exhorts the Israelite fathers to make themselves phylacteries, or mnemonics, of its ordinances and recite them to their children (Deuteronomy 6.4–8); the new teaching of Deuteronomy is that the written statutes ought to cherished inwardly, as precepts of the heart (30.6, 30.14). Josiah's public reading and the penitence that it evoked attest to the indivisibility of the written and the oral; they are also a foretaste of the consummation foreseen by Jeremiah, when God will write his Law in the hearts of his people (Jeremiah 31.33). The exile proved to Ezekiel that in preparation for this it would be necessary for God to 'remove the heart of stone and give them a heart of flesh' (Ezekiel 36.26).

Wisdom and Law

From what has been said above, it should be clear that the relation between the image and the word in biblical literature is not entirely homologous with that between sight and hearing, since speech and writing frequently conspire in the propagation of the word. Nor, for that matter, can a strict antithesis be drawn between the word as a vehicle of divine revelation and the image as the talisman of false piety. There is such a thing as the image of God in humanity, though it would not be agreed by all that this implies resemblance, either in inward or in outward properties. It is also possible for God to be visibly manifest to his interlocutors, though we never hear that the vision becomes habitual even for those who are habitually receptive to his word. What is seen is not described, or is adumbrated only in similes, in the period before we can suspect Greek influence on the prophetic idiom. More often it is an angel that it is seen, though its features are clearly delineated only when it is not identified with God. Those visitants who are identified with God himself are often manlike in aspect; where the resemblance to man is most perfect, however, the obvious inadequacy of the visual form would seem to impair belief in the thing revealed. Often the word precedes the recognition of the angel as God, and certainly one would have to be an idolater to imagine that the vision alone, without concomitant speech, could impart any knowledge of God's character or his will. In the texts that survive, it is never admitted that God was represented in the furnishings of the Temple, though we hear of at least one effigy that was worshipped (2 Kings 18.4). At best he can be seen there in a prophetic rapture; the tables of the Law are, however, the only graven artefact that abides there as a permanent testimony to his covenant with Israel (1 Kings 8.3). The supersession of these chiselled heirlooms by the Book of the Law makes it possible to distribute a chastened history of the first Israelites, which remembers the cult of images as a perennial backsliding into the errors of the Canaanites or the Egyptians. The last, and the most ineluctable, exhibition of God's presence in the Temple, in the hour when its treasures were already being looted, is a prophecy of woe to the usurpers, communicated not by any angelic or human avatar, but by a hand of unseen origin, tracing four words on the wall (Daniel 5.5).

We have noted above that, rather than encumber God with legs, some readers of Genesis 3.8 chose to personify his word. We discovered no such propensity to imagine the word of creation as a discrete intermediary, since, before it was uttered, there was no being but God, and hence no need of mediation. Nevertheless, the more ardently the oneness of God is proclaimed – and that is a presupposition, if not a stated axiom, of all but a handful of verses in the scriptures of Israel – the more impossible it will appear to the worshipper that there should be two divine economies, one extrinsic to the world and one within it. Creation and revelation are not so easily sundered if one comes to perceive the fabric of the world itself as a standing testimony to the prepotence and benign wisdom of its author.[22] It is the positive revelation of the Law that draws the eye to an antecedent revelation in the natural order: 'The heavens declare the glory of God, and the firmament showeth his handiwork' (Psalm 19.1). In its present form this eulogy gives a voice to the sun and moon; it also goes on to intimate that there is, if not an identity, at least a strict analogy, between the law of God which converts the soul and the inscription of his glory in the heavens. The cultivation of wisdom in the young is the goal of the sapiential literature – conventionally, if perfunctorily, attributed to Solomon – which dates from an era succeeding that of the prophets and legislators. The keynote of this literature is the saying 'in wisdom hast thou made all things', but wisdom is more than the power of creation. In the longest work of the corpus, purportedly a translation from the Hebrew of Jesus ben Sirach, the mighty works of wisdom are recounted, from the time when she 'came forth from the mouth of the Most High' (Sirach/Ecclesiasticus 24.5) to the last effects of her omnipresent working in the human realm (24.31); at last – after her catalogue has already subsumed the creation of the heavenly tabernacle, the gift of rulers to every nation and the enthronement of God in Zion – it is proclaimed that 'all these things are the book of life and the covenant of the Most High' (24.32). The next verse indicates that this is the patrimony which Israel received from Moses as her Law.[23]

One novel characteristic of this sapiential literature is that Wisdom herself is frequently her own eulogist, unveiling herself in every revelation of historical truth or cosmic origins. She makes her first appearance at Proverbs 8.22, asseverating 'the Lord possessed [or, as Greeks preferred, 'created'] me in the beginning of his way'. She does not expressly claim a part in the making of the depths, the heights and the heavens, but she can boast that she was conceived before them and present when they were formed. One reading of the text (perhaps not the best) suggests that she regards herself as the daughter of the Almighty. It has often been suggested that in this figure we see a vestige of an ancient cult of the wife of God, which is otherwise attested in a lone inscription to Yahweh and his Asherah. It lies outside the scope of the present book to determine whether Asherah was indeed a personal being, or whether she was identical with the Ashtaroth of the

---

[22]   Von Rad (1972), 144–176.

[23]   See further Davies (1955), 162–176.

Canaanites;[24] it is plain enough that in the wisdom literature, as it survives today, there is no hint that God ever had a consort, and that this conceit of a heavenly wisdom is only the preamble to the much longer accounts of her actions on behalf of, or in the hearts of, the elect. Hence, in the passage quoted above from Sirach, she passes quickly from her own birth to her activities in the care of the world and the dispensation of justice. In Proverbs her soliloquy is followed by an account of her erection of a house with seven pillars and her invitation to turn aside and sup with her (9.1ff). Her antitype is the fallen woman – not only because fornication is the most seductive of vices in the young, but because the bond between Israel and God is commonly represented as a marriage which the female partner is all too prone to sully by her adultery with false gods. For all her sins, it is Israel who is properly the bride of God; Wisdom participates in this union only insofar as she is teacher of the Law by which adherence is sustained.

In the latest specimen of the tradition, the Wisdom of Solomon, which was composed in Greek, the personal traits of Wisdom are enhanced, though she is no longer permitted to speak on her own account. She now becomes the ambassador of providence, carrying God's admonitions to those whom he means to exempt from his wrath; we must also presume that she is that almighty word which, at 18.15–16 leaps down from the royal throne to wield the 'sharp sword of the unfeigned commandment' against the dissidents in the wilderness, spanning the gap between earth and heaven and filling all things with death. Before the creation she is the emanation of God and his radiance; she is not merely God's delight, as at Proverbs 8.30, but his mirror and the image of his goodness. More perspicuously than any other verse in a canonical text, this implies that God has a form, but it does not justify the Gentiles in their efforts to reproduce that form in idols of wood and stone. Idolatry, forbidden by Noah to all his descendants, is nonetheless the chronic and ubiquitous error of those who live without the Law; the strictures of the prophets become progressively more choleric and satirical, no doubt because the danger of Israel's succumbing increased as she fell under the sway of other nations. The arguments are repetitive and formulaic: the work of the hands can never be superior to the workman; it is vain to fashion ears and eyes for inanimate lumps that can neither see nor hear, and impious to represent the invisible under a visible form. The error of the Gentiles, then, is primarily one of vision, whereas the sin of Israel proceeds above all from her failure to hear the Law. It is possible that the Gentiles, who do not have the Law, are incapable of hearing the proclamation of God in the heavens, since the witnesses to this proclamation are themselves men of the covenant; yet one means of illumination has certainly been vouchsafed to them, for Israel herself is appointed as their light. Their blindness is initially a privation to be remedied; it becomes a sin when they attempt to cure it by devising counterfeit images of the invisible. In Isaiah's first song of the servant, where he is called a light to the Gentiles, it is said that he will not raise his voice, though his attributes in a later song – if this is indeed the same figure – resemble those of the

---

[24]   See further Smith (2002), 47–53.

word in the Wisdom of Solomon (Isaiah 49.2). The Gentiles are therefore not in the position of Job, who had known of God by hearing before he saw (Job 42.5); there is no direct communication to them, but an opportunity to see and imitate those who have heard.

Can we argue, from the example of Job, that seeing is the consummation of hearing? It is not, in fact, evident that Job sees anything but the whirlwind from which God speaks, though he has certainly prayed to confront his adversary, and this encounter is the frustration of Satan's wager that Job will curse God to his face.[25] The vision of God in Daniel and Ezekiel is the occasion of prophecy, rather than its content or its goal. It appears to be truer to say that vision may be explained and purified by hearing; we have seen that it is speech that reveals the character of an angel, explains his mission or dissipates incredulity. It is the hearing of the Law which enables the psalmist to say 'when I see the heavens, the work of thy fingers' (Psalm 8.4), without the temptation of worshipping the heavens or of attributing human organs to God. Again, it is because the Law shapes our comprehension of the natural order that the letters of the Hebrew alphabet could be imagined to be the tools of the first creation.[26] The rabbis who entertained this trope were not in danger of vesting magical properties in the letters, but were conscious that it was by the reduction of ephemeral sounds to enduring symbols that the word which framed the tabernacle of heaven had been preserved and propagated on earth – preserved and propagated, when the need arose, independently of the Temple or the ark.

Job may hope that after death he will see God (19.25–26), but the verse is not representative of the Old Testament, and in common life it is not the knowledge but the fear of him that is wisdom (28.28). 'The depth saith, it is not in me, and the sea saith, it is not with me' (28.14). There is a sibling to this passage at Deuteronomy 30.11–14: 'This commandment that I command thee this day is not above thee, nor far off from thee. Nor is it in heaven ... nor is it beyond the sea ... But the word is very nigh unto thee, in thy mouth and in thy heart.' It is not the pursuit of a glory beyond all worlds, but the quotidian exercise in the present world of a God-given faculty that renders us acceptable to God. Is this the same as realizing his likeness? The metaphor is foreign to wisdom literature, but if wisdom above is the mirror of God and the wise man below his most perfect image, there is nothing obscure in the handful of apocalyptic texts in which the image of God below descries his archetype in heaven as a figure resembling a son of man or the likeness of a man's similitude.

---

[25]   Leibowitz (1992), 52, is one of the few to see that this epiphany is the last test for Job, the crux and not the climax of his drama.

[26]   Freedman (1977), 10–11; Ginzberg (1998), 4–8.

Epilogue

After AD 70 there was to be no temple in Israel and no tolerance of images in the traditions that retained their authority among the Jews. The icon represents the king, but only in his absence;[27] if man himself is the icon of God,[28] he has all the less reason to forge his own counterfeits. The sole medium of divine communication in this world was the written Torah, to its last jot and tittle, together with the oral interpretation of the rabbis. The rabbi brought his own powers of divination to the text, making no appeal to any auxiliary witness: when Eleazar prayed that a voice from heaven would verify his ruling on a legal precept, the voice obliged, but his fellow-exegetes reminded him that the word 'is not far off from thee, nor above thee, nor in heaven … but close by thee'.[29] To aspire in the present life to knowledge of that which lay behind the Law was both arrogant and perilous: of three who entered paradise, only Rabbi Akiba escaped with his sanity,[30] if indeed a man who gave his blessing to bar Kochba's insurrection can be deemed sane.

Was it always thus? We are told by Origen and Jerome that the rabbis of their time forbade the young to study either the prologue of Ezekiel, where the descent of a chariot bearing four winged creatures is succeeded by an apparition of God enthroned in the semblance of a man, or the conclusion of the same work, which anticipates the creation by divine fiat of an everlasting temple to replace the short-lived masonry of Solomon.[31] These reports suggest that they had seen the first specimens of Merkavah literature, in which the seer, performing a celestial reconnaissance in the chariot, becomes privy to the secrets of creation.[32] The most heterodox of these texts record an ascent through seven Hekhalot, or palaces, each surpassing the last in the splendour and calculated incongruity of its visual symbolism. If the face of God himself is never disclosed, the sage can encounter him by proxy in his angels: the name Metatron, if Greek suggests proximity to the Throne, while its mock-Hebrew counterpart Yahoel   hints at the inexpressible Name.[33] If the rabbis scented blasphemy here, they do not seem to have been uniformly averse to the visual decoration of the synagogue. In an enigmatic passage of his *Homilies on Exodus*, Origen says that the Jews in recent times had forgotten the prohibition of images and had repented only when they saw

---

[27]   Unattributed citation from *Song of Songs Rabbah* in Neusner (1991), 138.

[28]   Joshua ben Levi (*Deuteronomy Rabbah* 4.4), cited by Kochan (1997), 116. See Feldman (1927), 22, for Hillel's simile from the facsimile: if we polish a statue because it is the king's, should we not take more care with our own bodies, which are made in the likeness of the King of Kings?

[29]   Nadich (1994), vol. 2, 61–62.

[30]   Scholem (1995).

[31]   *Prologue to Commentary on Song of Songs*, pp. 62.24–63.2 Baehrens.

[32]   Scholem (1995), 40–67.

[33]   Scholem (1995), 67–70, though few other scholars would now assign a date before the fifth century to the extant Hekhalot literature.

Gentiles abandoning their idols to join the Church.[34] The friezes of a synagogue discovered at Dura-Europos on the Euphrates may not suffice to vindicate the charge of idolatry, since it cannot be proved that worship was ever paid to them;[35] the spirit of the Decalogue, however, was certainly not observed if the mighty hand outstretched in one of the paintings symbolizes the omnipotence of God.[36]

If there was one artefact that commanded the devotion of every rabbi, it was the letter of the Torah. To Rav, who described its characters as the letters of creation,[37] it was no artefact but the autograph of the same God who had carved the Decalogue on tablets of stone and inscribed Belshazzar's doom on the wall of the Temple (Daniel 5.5). One enumeration of the sacred texts, attested by Josephus, reduced them to 22, the number of letters in the Hebrew alphabet (*Against Apion* 1.138); in the strange apocalypse which we know as 4 Ezra, the Greek alphabet serves as a canon, and the seer brings 24 volumes down from heaven. Pictures show that physical devotions were addressed to the scrolls;[38] if this was not idolatry in the biblical sense, the same could be said of Gentile veneration of the image. In targums, or paraphrases of the scriptures, authority is frequently ascribed not directly to God, but to his word of command, the Memra, and it is not he but the Shekinah, his presence or glory, that is said to engage in commerce with his creatures. G.F. Moore's proviso that a lexical surrogate is not a 'personal intermediary' should be heeded;[39] nevertheless, these terms provide a verbal bridge between scriptural monotheism and the Christian theology of Christ as Second Person of the Trinity. A verbal bridge cannot be merely verbal where the written word is regarded as the one permanent tabernacle of the Law, which is all that has been made known of God.

---

[34]   *Homilies on Exodus* 2.4, pp. 160.20–161.2 Baehrens.

[35]   Goodenough (1988), 177–265, maintains that much of the iconography is pagan in origin; Nasrallah (2010), 219–221, doubts that Rabbi Gamaliel spoke for all Jews when he urged that such pictures could only be ornamental.

[36]   On this possibility see Goodenough (1988), 253, and Goodman (2003).

[37]   Urbach (1975), 312.

[38]   Goodenough (1988), 185.

[39]   Moore (1958), 418–421.

Chapter 2
Seeing and Hearing God in the New Testament

The documents which make up our New Testament were composed by men who, using Greek as an everyday tongue, appear to have no model for writing but the Septuagint. Their prose admits, as all prose does, of rhetorical analysis, but they have evidently not attended any school where such analysis would have guided them in the imitation of Lysias or Plato.[1] Nor could they have held their own in philosophy with the dilettantes of the pagan world, although their ethical precepts often coincide, like those of all sane men, with the teachings of at least one classical school. It can hardly be denied that the primitive Christians were indebted to Philo's concept of the Logos or to some kindred speculation;[2] it is only in Philo, however, not the New Testament, that the term *logos* denotes the reason of God without reference to his speech. Christ, as the speaking emissary of the Father, had none of the eloquence that a Gorgias or a Philostratus deemed essential to a *logos*; as the image of the Father, he came to make the invisible visible, not through the static heraldry of the plastic arts, nor (as Plato imagined) by direct illumination of the intellect, but by mingling power with obedience in a short life, voluntarily concealing his glory under a veil of flesh. The precedents both for his miracles and for his ministry are more easily discovered in the Septuagint than in Hellenistic literature before the Roman era;[3] yet, even in the Septuagint, the vision of God takes a different form, and if one can say without absurdity that ocular knowledge of God is claimed more often in the New Testament than the Old, it must be added that in the New Testament there is a more consistent occlusion of his glory. For this reason the image never supersedes the word in these seminal texts of the Christian tradition; the word remains the indispensable vehicle of the image.

It will be obvious already that I intend in this chapter to treat the New Testament as a single work by many hands, and not as a forced collation of hermetic and heterogeneous 'Christianities'. For my purposes here no justification of this method is necessary, for, whether or not the higher criticism is as high as it purports to be, it flourishes at an altitude that was never scaled in antiquity by Christian or pagan critics of the New Testament. The canon, once established, was simply the canon, whatever its history: to Christians it was part of the Word of

---

[1] Classen (2002); Edwards (2006).

[2] Dodd (1968), 54–73.

[3] Kee (1986), esp. 129–130.

God, and the incarnation of the Word was its pervasive subject even if some of its authors never used the title 'Logos' or made any allusion to the divinity of Christ. The critical historian would agree in this at least with the systematic theologian, that the present chapter ought to begin with Paul, whom former regards as the author of the most primitive Gospel and the latter as a privileged exponent of the eternal Gospel which is implicit in the canonical four.

Christ, Image and Likeness in Paul

The noun *homoiôma* (likeness) occurs three times in Paul's Epistle to the Romans, and in none of these instances is any honour derived from the object of comparison. Every trespass among the Gentiles flows from the first, which was to worship creation rather than the Creator. The absurdity betrayed itself at once in their attempts to portray the invisible God, in defiance of reason and the second commandment, under the likeness of four-footed beasts (Romans 1.23). Here there is double imposture, since the beast does not resemble God and the idol bears only a specious similarity to the beast; hence it is that Paul can pronounce elsewhere that the idol represents a demon rather than God, but at the same time that to a believer it is 'nothing in the world' (1 Corinthians 8.4; cf. 10.19), not so much pernicious as inane. When he employs the term 'likeness' again in Romans, it is to say that death is the universal lot for Adam's offspring, even for those who had not sinned 'after the likeness' of the first transgression (Romans 5.14). The redemption is effected, as Paul goes on to proclaim, by the advent of the Son of God 'in the likeness of sinful flesh' (Romans 8.3). Here it may be debated whether Paul means to say that the flesh of Christ was a simulacrum, or rather, as the author of the Epistle to the Hebrews explains it, that he had true flesh, resembling ours in all but sin. The common presupposition of these texts is that the mere likeness is an abuse of the natural order, a thing that, in better circumstances, would not have been.

Twice in the Pauline letters we meet a reference to the *eikôn* (image) of God. In the first letter to the Corinthians, the authenticity of which is commonly held to be indisputable, the capstone to his argument that a woman should wear a veil when she prays or prophesies is that, whereas she is the glory of man, the man is the image and the glory of God (1 Corinthians 11.7). Paul does not say that the woman is the image of either God or man, nor does he add the caveat that the man is, properly speaking, not God's image but his handiwork according to the image. No personal resemblance to God and no representative function are explicitly assigned to the man; he exemplifies the image here by the exercise of a hegemonic role. That Paul means to invest him with authority over his spouse cannot be doubted, since he goes on to assert that the man was not created for the woman but the woman for the man (11.9); at the same time, this invocation of Genesis 2 suffices to prove that neither subsists without the other (11.11).

The Epistle to the Colossians, if genuine, is a later work, displaying some characteristics of an encyclical and affording a more comprehensive view of Christ as the object of belief. After a long effusion of exhortation and thanksgiving, the apostle declares that the Son whom God has appointed as the minister of our redemption is 'the image of the invisible God, the firstborn of every creature' (1.15), adding that 'in him' all things were created (1.16) and concluding that he is the 'firstborn from the dead, that in all things he may hold the primacy' (1.18). Although the reading 'invisible image of the invisible God' is attested in some early quotations, the less paradoxical variant is endorsed in all modern editions. The primacy which accrues to Christ in 1.18 is, if not the result, at least a concomitant of the resurrection; the recurrence of the term 'firstborn' (*prôtotokos*) in 1.15 and 1.18 has been thought to warrant the inference that the subject of the former verse is also the incarnate, not the pre-existent, Christ.[4] The asseveration that 'all things were created in him' can be understood to mean that he was the end for which all things were destined; 1.15 would then be an adumbration of the good news that is proclaimed in 1.18, conveying the assurance that the miracle was not an abrupt or anomalous breach of natural law but a consummation of the natural order. It is difficult, nonetheless, to refrain from comparing the phrase 'in him' with the 'in the beginning' of Genesis 1.1, or to shake off the impression that this eulogy is modelled on the personification of Wisdom in the Solomonic writings. Early Christian readers never doubted that this passage in Colossians commemorates the work of Christ before the ages, even when they construed Proverbs 8.22 as a veiled prefigurement of his coming in the flesh.

These, as has been remarked, are the only two instances of the term 'image' in the corpus. In the Greek world, however, where an *eikôn* would most commonly be a statue, its form or superficies is denoted by the term *morphê*, and *morphê* would appear to be almost a synonym for *eikôn* in the famous celebration of Christ's ministry at Philippians 2.6–12. 'Let that mind be in you', he writes, 'which was also in Christ Jesus; who, being in the form [*morphê*] of God, did not think it a robbery [*harpagmos*] to be equal with God, but emptied himself, assuming the form [*morphê*] of a slave and coming to be in a human likeness', the consequence being that he was 'found in fashion [*skhêmati*] as a man'. It is almost a commonplace that in this willing renunciation of the form of God, we see the antidote to that presumption which caused Adam to forfeit the image of God; the *harpagmos* is best interpreted as the theft which Adam committed in the false belief that he would become like God.[5] While *morphê* answers to *eikôn*, *skhêma* appears to be a synonym of *homoiôma*, which once again connotes some aberration from the course ordained by God. In this case, the aberration is only apparent, since the natural course has already been compromised by Adam's sin, and the grand design is not subverted but fulfilled by the apparently preternatural obedience of Christ.

---

[4] For discussion see Dunn (1989), 189–194.

[5] Dunn (1989), 115–116, against Glasson (1974–1975).

This reading is corroborated by texts in indisputably Pauline letters which present Christ as the antitype to Adam. Thus, at 1 Corinthians 15.45, the first man becomes a living soul, the second a life-giving spirit, while at Romans we are informed that as through one man all died, through another were all made alive. As these passages intimate, to say that Christ is the second Adam is not to deny that he is more than Adam. The 'Philippians hymn' appears to be recounting not only an act of perfect obedience, but also the sublime condescension of one who, had he wished, might have remained free of our infirmities. Markus Bockmuehl adduces a number of passages from Philo and the rabbis which suggest that the form of God is a visible envelope which he assumed on those occasions when he is said to have revealed himself to humans, an accommodation of superabundant power to our indigent faculties.[6] It is sound exegesis, therefore, to suppose that this exemplar of the human was also an ectype of the divine. At the same time, as we noted with regard to Colossians 1.18, we must take account of the fact that the exaltation of Christ appears to follow his 'obedience unto death' (2.8). It was in consequence of this, says the apostle – the Greek is 'wherefore' (2.9) – that God gave him 'the name above all names', decreeing that every knee should bow at the name of Jesus and every tongue confess him Lord (2.10–12).

What had Paul seen of Christ, the image of the invisible deity? He makes no claim in his letters to have met him in the course of his earthly ministry; when he urges that 'we no longer know Christ after the flesh', he means that he and his correspondents have come to perceive that in Christ which is greater than man. Not to know Christ after the flesh is to honour the testimony of those by whom he was seen (ôphthê) in the wake of his death. Among these the apostle numbers himself at 1 Corinthians 15.6, yet the import of the verb ôphthê becomes uncertain when we peruse the three accounts of Paul's conversion in the Acts of the Apostles.[7] According to the first, he was encompassed by a brilliant light and heard a voice crying, 'Saul, Saul, why do you persecute me?' When he asked 'Who are you, Lord?', the voice replied 'I am Jesus whom thou persecutest' (Acts 9.3–4). We are told that his eyes were opened, but that (in contrast to Adam and Eve) he saw nothing; the bystanders, in the meantime, heard a voice but saw no man (Acts 9.5–7). The story does not imply that the words were distinctly audible to anyone other than the intended recipient nor that Paul himself was aware of any definite form. The blindness is healed by a Christian in Damascus, Ananias, who receives a command in a 'vision' (9.10), though again we learn what he heard, not what he saw. Paul's own account of the miracle at Acts 22 differs only in one particular: he affirms that his companions saw the light but heard no voice. The narratives concur if we assume that the crowd was aware of a light and a voice, but picked out neither form nor words, being in the position of the Israelites who witnessed but could not comprehend the gift of the Law to Moses on Mount Horeb. A third report at Acts 26.13–18 imparts the new information that

---

[6]   Bockmuehl (1997).

[7]   Marxsen (1978), 106–107; Schillebeeckx (1974), 360–397.

the light was of the brightness of the sun, that the voice addressed Paul in Hebrew, and that the mission enjoined upon him was to open the eyes of the nations. It is in keeping with the usage of the Old Testament that Paul the Israelite should hear more than he saw, while the effect of his preaching was to make others see.

It is possible, then, that when Paul claims at 1 Corinthians 15.6 to have seen Christ, he means only that he has known him by acquaintance and not through an intermediary, just as Job could profess to have seen God when the latter spoke to him from the whirlwind (Job 42.5). At Acts 22.17–18, where Paul speaks of a trance which he experienced in the Temple, he remembers it not as a visual manifestation but as the vehicle of a divine command to quit Jerusalem. There is no cause to identify this event with the rapture described at 1 Corinthians 12.2–5, which is expressly said to have carried another man into the third heaven, and to a paradise where he heard words that it would be sacrilege to utter. Once again the sense to which God appeals is not sight but hearing, though 'whether in the body or out of the body I know not' (1 Corinthians 12.3). According to Romans 11.17, it is by hearing that faith is engendered, and, although it might seem incongruous that the argument throughout this portion of Romans should be sustained by appeals to prophecies 'written' for Israel before the resurrection, Paul applies an ingenious trope to the text which had once proclaimed the omnipresence of the law to make it speak instead of its own consummation and supersession in Christ. '*Say not in thy heart, Who shall ascend into heaven?* – that is, to bring Christ down; or, *Who shall descend into the deep?* – that is, to bring up Christ again from the dead. But what saith the scripture? *The word is nigh thee, even in thy mouth and in thy heart*' (Romans 10.6–8). As is evident from the sequel, Christ is present not by vision but by faith, and to those who call upon his name. Even the scriptural text in Paul is not so often an alphabetic document as a living exhortation: we do not so often read that 'it is written' as that a prophet says or cries.

Paul cannot maintain, of course, that believers in his own day could maintain an intercourse with Christ through the organs of sight and hearing which had sufficed for spectators of his earthly ministry. Some ancient readers divined from Galatians 1.16, where Paul speaks of a revelation 'in me' rather than 'to me', that the external faculties played no part in his own encounter with Christ, which was in any case vouchsafed to him as to one 'born out of time' (1 Corinthians 15.8). Quotidian knowledge, as Paul insists repeatedly, is that of 'Christ in me', and the mark of his presence is the regenerate and sacrificial life of the believer, the exhibition of that 'mind which was in Christ Jesus' (Philippians 2.5). This entails not merely a conformation of the will to that of Christ, but also the fashioning of the resurrection body into the likeness of his body (Philippians 3.21) – a rare case in which the term *homoiôma* implies neither falsification nor indignity. Such a usage is possible when the last things come and the old have passed away, when God is known to us as we have been known eternally to him, and when the things that we have glimpsed darkly as in a mirror are at last seen 'face to face' (1 Corinthians 13.12).[8]

Logos and Light in the Gospel of John

Paul, as we have observed, makes Christ the true referent of a text which was initially a scriptural affidavit to the sufficiency of scripture. He offers no hermeneutic justification of this manoeuvre, and does not adopt *rhēma* (word) as a title of Christ. An appellative force is given to the noun *logos* – which in common Greek denotes a reason, principle, account or discourse, but seldom a word – in three books of the New Testament. In the Apocalypse or Revelation, the work of a certain John, the exclamation that 'the testimony of Jesus is the spirit of prophecy' (Revelation 19.10) is followed immediately by a rending of the heavens and the appearance of a rider on a white horse whose flaming eyes (19.12), together with the two-edged sword that proceeds from his mouth (19.15) recall the depiction of the Son of Man at Revelation 1.14–16. The rider, though he possesses a name 'which none knows but himself' (19.12), is styled in the next verse the Word of God – aptly enough, as the two-edged sword at Hebrews 4.12 represents the divine interrogation of the sinful heart. It is in fact an angel, not the Word, who proceeds to muster the saints, though, when they are forced into war, it is the two-edged sword that extirpates those who venerated the image of the beast (Revelation 19.21). If we may identify this champion with the Christ who bears the 'name above all names' at Philippians 2.10, we can recognize in his victory an extension of the principle that the godless are overcome by testimony (Revelation 12.11); we can also detect a foreshadowing of this coercive proclamation in chapters 2 and 3, where the Son of Man dispatches letters of counsel and reproach to the seven churches of the Troad. While John does not hesitate to attire the Son of Man (or Lamb, or Logos) in a variety of grotesque and arresting symbols, the result is often a purely eidetic medley, which could not be translated into a physical medium. It is the beast who requires his worshippers to grovel before an image, and who engraves upon them the number 666. Although he utters blasphemies (13.6), and unclean spirits proceed from the mouths of his allies (16.13), intelligible speech is the prerogative of the Son of Man and his acolytes. He is the Alpha and Omega (1.8),[9] but the written characters come to life in the efficacious play of the two-edged sword.

Ancient readers differed as to whether Revelation should be ascribed to John the Apostle or to a certain John the Elder; they had no doubt that it was John the Apostle who testified, in the opening verse of the epistle known as 1 John, that he had seen with his eyes and handled with his hands the Logos of life. For the elucidation of this they inevitably turned to the anonymous record of the 'beloved

---

[8]   Seaford (1984) sees an allusion to the Dionysian mysteries.

[9]   Cf. *Damascus Document* 15 at Vermes (1995), 106.

disciple' which appears to be a product of the same hand. The first verse of this is commonly translated in English, after the Latin Vulgate, as 'In the beginning was the Word'. The alternative offered here does not pretend to greater authority, but is designed to show that the text can be read with no prepossession in favour of orthodoxy, or even of dogmatics:[10]

> In the beginning there was speech, and the speech belonged to God, and what God was the speech was. This belonged to God in the beginning. Everything came to be [or came to pass] through it, and without him came into being [or came to pass] not a single thing. What came to be [or pass] in it was life, and the life was the light of humanity. And the light shines in the darkness [or simply 'light shines in darkness'], and the darkness [or simply 'darkness'] has not captured [or 'comprehended'] it. (John 1.1–5)

There is a clear allusion to Genesis in the exordium and hence some probability that the 'beginning 'is the creation of the world. The statement of God's relation to his Logos in the second clause echoes language which occurs in earlier personifications of Wisdom. Coming to be (or coming to pass) may be predicated strictly of the first creatures, or of all that has been done or initiated in the world to the present day. The light which is coeval with the Logos would be that of the first creation if we continue to read the entire text as a scholium on the opening chapter of Genesis; the darkness which has failed to capture or comprehend the light would then be that which, according to some interpretations of Genesis 1.3, was also its cradle: 'God, who made the light to shine out of darkness', says Paul, 'has shone forth in our hearts' (2 Corinthians 4.6). But, just as Paul is speaking of a continuing illumination, visible to the saints but hidden from those whose eyes are blinded by the God of this world (2 Corinthians 4.4), so the evangelist uses the present tense (not 'shone' but 'shines') to show that the subject of his prologue is a light which has outlived the first effulgence to become a perennial source of revelation. The intrusion of John the Baptist in the verse following our quotation ('there came to be a man, sent from God, whose name was John') might tempt one to surmise that he embodies the light, and it may be that he was the hero of a lost prototype. In the extant work, however, we are assured that he was but a witness to the light that 'was coming in to the world to illumine everyone', or perhaps 'which illumines everyone who comes into the world'. Its apparition is finally announced at John 1.14: 'the Word became flesh'. This is the second and last occurrence of Logos as a cognomen of the person who in the Gospel is henceforth the 'Son of Man' and the 'Son of God', though, as we have seen, the First Epistle of John attributes properties to the Logos which would not have been manifest but for the incarnation.

It has often troubled scholars that, in the body of the Gospel, Christ twice styles himself the light of the world (John 8.12, 9.4), and twice yokes life with other

---

[10]   Cf. Ashton (1994), 26–31.

predicates in an 'I am' saying (11.25; 14.6), but never declares 'I am the Logos'.[11] It is true nonetheless, as most scholars now acknowledge,[12] that the prologue is the soul of the entire narrative, for Christ throughout this Gospel is the walking Logos, not only the prophet but the proclamation, whose very presence divides the world into those who believe and those who are obdurate to the Word of God. Although he refuses to verify his claims by appeal to particular texts of scripture (7.42), and his purported quotations are often hard to trace (7.38), he accuses his critics of defying Moses and assures them that will find his testimonials in their own Law (5.39–47). He adduces a text from the Law (in fact from Psalm 82.6), in which his own designation 'Son of God' is shown to have been conferred on those to whom the 'word of God' (the *logos tou theou*) had come in former times (10.34–35); the analogy could be pressed to imply that the Pharisees, at the time of speaking, are in the same position and that their interlocutor is not merely the Son of God but his Word. He bears witness to himself, though the Law forbids it (8.18), and cites the Father as a second witness (5.36), though there is no other testimony than his own to the Father's suffrage. On the one occasion when God speaks from heaven to comfort him, the bystanders are unable to distinguish the words and mistake the noise for the voice of an angel or a thunderclap (12.28–29). When others desert him, Peter remains, because 'you have the words of eternal life' (6.69).

It is, of course, Christ's task as light of the world to make others see; he differs from his prophetic forerunners only in that the blind to whom he preaches are not the heathen but his own people. The healing of the man born blind is a deed unprecedented since the creation of light, dividing the spectators as the first word had divided light from darkness (9.32). But what can be seen without faith? Miracles may be granted, but with a reprimand to those who ask for signs (4.49), and it is more creditable to believe the words of the prophet than his works (10.38). 'We beheld his glory', exclaims the evangelist (1.18), but there is no transfiguration in this Gospel, and from his own dictum – 'I, if I be lifted up, shall draw all unto me' (12.31) – it appears that his ignominy in the face of the world is his glory in the eyes of the elect. Abraham may have seen Christ's day (8.56), but those in the present world who wish to live must 'keep his word' (8.51). While he consents to show his wounds to Thomas (20.27), it is his voice, not his appearance, which reveals him to Mary Magdalen (20.16), and the higher blessing is pronounced on those who, like the disciple who deduced the resurrection from the abandoned clothes (20.8), have not seen but believed (20.29).

Hearing eclipses sight because words abide, whereas anything that is seen is doomed to perish (cf. 2 Corinthians 4.18). It is not only that the words of the Mosaic law are indelible, but that those of Christ, the everlasting object of the Law and its sole interpreter, can be sown anew in any community of true believers by the indwelling of the Paraclete, or Spirit, whom he has sent to take his place. It is well known that the Fourth Gospel contains many sayings which are not

---

[11]   See further Ball (1996), 60–160.

[12]   For example, Robinson (1983); Bultmann (1965), 59–70.

attested in the other three; it has also been observed that the sayings are apt to break free of the context to which the narrative has ostensibly assigned them.[13] The words spoken in confidence to one interlocutor may be overheard by another, or explicitly directed to absent parties. 'We speak of what we know', says Jesus to Nicodemus at 3.13, as though he were representing a community, but 'you' – and here he uses the plural pronoun, not the singular – 'have not believed our report'. Nicodemus has nothing to say when he is informed that 'The Son of Man' must be lifted up (3.19); it is in another time and place that the crowd demands 'who is this Son of Man?', though he has uttered no such prophecy in their hearing. We may wonder how the midnight colloquy with Nicodemus came to be known to the evangelist, or whether there was some dragoman at hand to recall what passed between Christ and Pilate (18.33–38). Such questions are as little to the purpose as a wholesale accusation of mendacity: The Spirit is a second paraclete, therefore a second Christ (1John 2.1), and any words that are spoken by the community at his prompting are the words of Christ himself.

And yet, while Christ is barely an object of vision in this Gospel, it is he who makes the Father visible. Hiding himself at will (5.59), unknown by face to the guards who perform his arrest (18.4–5) and barely recognizable after the resurrection even to his intimates, he can nonetheless tell the inquiring Greeks that 'he who has seen me has seen the Father' (14.9). The evangelist (or the Baptist) is merely faithful to the biblical deposit when he asseverates at 1.18 that 'no one has seen God at any time'. But if the Son who reveals him is himself invisible to us since his ascension, we seem to be on the heels of an antinomy. Once again, the gloss can be found in the First Epistle of John, where, as in Paul, the contemplation of glory is an eschatological consummation of faith in things unseen. In both, the vision of Christ and the realization of his likeness are one event. 'Dearly beloved', writes 'John' (1 John 3.2), 'we are now the sons of God, and it hath not yet appeared what we shall be. When we see him, we shall be like him, for we shall see him as he is.'

Not Seeing and not Hearing in the Gospel of Mark

The Christ of the Fourth Evangelist, then, is the Logos made flesh, the revelation embodied in the Revealer. But what does he reveal? The kingdom of heaven, we may answer; but who would not exchange his cryptic signposts – 'be born from water and spirit' (John 3.5) and 'unless one eats the flesh of the Son of Man and drinks his blood' (6.53) – for the bald imperatives of the Sermon on the Mount or the unfathomable simplicity of the commandment to 'love the Lord with all thy heart' and to 'love thy neighbour as thyself' (Mark 12.30–31)? The burden of Christ's teaching in the Fourth Gospel is not so often love or forgiveness of sins

---

[13] To Fortna (1988) this indicates maladroit redaction; to Hoskyns (1947) it is the mark of a gospel that never comes to rest.

as simply belief, which is characteristically represented under symbols connoting vision. Yet the object of vision seems, in the majority of sayings, to amount to little more than faith in faith, belief in the inculcator of belief. Christ's epithets are legion: he is the way, the truth, the life, the resurrection, the door, the light by which believers see, the vine in which they abide, the shepherd whose voice they follow, the Messiah who will reveal all things. Yet all these pregnant metaphors tell us merely that if we know the way we shall be able to follow it, if we have the light we shall see, if we hear we shall know. The title 'Son of God' may mean no more than 'children of God' at John 1.13, or it may convey the ineffable claim that is implicit in the repeated iteration of 'I am' (cf. 5.18); it is, in any case, a designation given to him by others. Under his own description, 'Son of Man', he affirms that he came from heaven, that he must be raised up like the serpent in the wilderness, and that some will enjoy a vision of angels ascending and descending upon him; but each new confidence darkens the enigma, and when the crowd – having heard more than was said to it – asks 'who is this Son of Man?' (12.34), it is dramatizing the perplexity of the reader, to whom everything has been said and nothing explained.

The Gospels of Luke and Matthew strike most readers as simpler texts, but the work that is still commonly supposed to be the prototype of both is like a shadow that recedes from every torch. Positive teaching never takes the form of a sermon in the Gospel of Mark, and the few injunctions that Jesus utters at the prompting of insincere or hostile postulants – 'sell your goods to feed the poor', 'if thy hand offend thee, cut it off' (Mark 9.42), 'if a man divorces his wife and marries another, he is guilty of adultery against her (10.11)' – are often deemed too harsh for universal application. Such aphorisms as 'beware the leaven of the Pharisees' (8.15), or 'why dost thou call me good? No one is good but God' (10.18), have been found not merely harsh but impenetrable. The second is all the harder to elucidate because Jesus hears so much about himself and says so little in this Gospel. He hears the Father say 'this is my beloved Son, in whom I am well pleased' at 1.11; he is addressed by demons as the Son of God and as the Holy One of God (1.24); he is 'King of the Jews' to Pilate (15.2, 15.9, 15.12, 15.26), but to Peter, the most prominent of his apostles, simply 'the Christ', or anointed one (8.29). But he silences the demons whenever they testify (3.12), tosses back the words of the governor (15.2), and, in the wake of Peter's confession, simply 'charges' his disciples 'to say nothing about him to anyone' (8.30). When he performs a healing, he forbids it to be known (5.43). These admonitions, however, have no consequences even within the Gospel; the fame of his miracles burgeons, and the question which secures his condemnation before the Sanhedrin is 'are you the Christ?' (14.61).

In a study which is often misrepresented,[14] William Wrede perceived that the 'Messianic secret' (that is, the purposeful evasion of the question of Christ's identity) is not so much an element in the plot as a revelation, in dramaturgic form,

---

[14]   For criticisms and appreciations of Wrede (1971), see Tuckett (1983).

of the impossibility of mere revelation. The title 'Son of God' is not perspicuous, as is evident from the fact that, when Jesus finally accepts it at 14.62, his inquisitors draw the wrong inference and pronounce him worthy of death. No interpretation of his ministry can be drawn from the taunts of the crowd at his crucifixion – 'Let the Christ, king of Israel, descend from the Cross' (15.32) – or from the centurion's exclamation 'surely this man was a son of a god' (15.39). Plain enough to us, the command to say nothing of the transfiguration until the Son of Man be risen from the dead is incomprehensible to his most intimate disciples (9.9); when he bids them beware of the leaven of the Pharisees (8.15), their confusion is so profound that he taxes them with blindness, deafness and hardness of heart (8.17–18). We ought not to surmise, however, that the author is mocking the hebetude of these particular followers of Jesus in order to cry up the superior understanding of his own sect;[15] if the book were intended to convey a single lesson or uphold a particular estimate of Jesus, this would surely not have eluded the world of scholarship. As it is, the most expert readers cannot even agree as to whether it was Jesus, the evangelist or a forgotten intermediary who threw in the ironic exhortation at 13.14: 'let the reader understand'.

The work of elucidation is in all cases left to the reader. It is surely for this reason that, although the resurrection in plainly foretold in passage after passage, the Gospel of Mark is the only one of the four which contains no account of Christ's appearances after his death. The closing sentence states that the women to whom the good news of the resurrection had been entrusted told to it no one else, 'for they were afraid' (16.8).[16] Their silence (which, had it been maintained, would have left the Gospel itself stillborn) must be weighed against the equally unseasonable garrulity of Peter at the midpoint of the Gospel. Having witnessed the glorification of Jesus – in the company of Moses and Elijah, who had ascended to heaven before him and who stand respectively for the Law and the prophets – Peter ejaculates, 'Let us build three tabernacles', only to be silenced by the author himself, with the judgment that 'he knew not what he was saying, for he was afraid' (9.5–6). He speaks when he ought to be reticent, as the women fail to promulgate the tidings that cannot be hidden. On the same principle, a leper who is ordered not to say anything of his healing 'broadcasts many things and publishes the *logos*' (1.45), while a liberated demoniac, charged to tell everyone in the Gentile Decapolis 'what the Lord has done for him', attributes the miracle instead to Jesus (5.20). In every revelation there is a measure of occultation, because both the preaching of Jesus and the preaching about him have a supernatural content which cannot be faithfully proclaimed in a human tongue.

This is Jesus' own account of his ministry in the parable of the sower.[17] Having described the different results when seed falls by the road, on stony ground, among thorns and in fertile soil, he humours the request for an explanation by contrasting

---

[15]   Contra Weedon (1968).

[16]   See further Van der Horst (1972).

[17]   See further Kermode (1979), 23–47.

the disciples, to whom the secrets of the kingdom will be disclosed, with the outsiders to whom he delivers all things in parables, so that 'seeing they may see and not perceive, and hearing they may hear and not understand, lest at any time they turn and it be forgiven them' (4.12). The words are those of Isaiah after his vision in the Temple (Isaiah 6.9–10), and in his mouth they convey no doctrine of predestination, but only an ironic sense that even the Word of God cannot prosper where it is not received. Jesus repeats the scriptural adage with the same inflexion:[18] here, too, there is no predestination, except insofar as what is foretold cannot fail to come to pass and what was true of the prophets must come true again in the Son of Man. The disciples would appear to be a privileged exception to his strictures; yet the mystery divulged to them has less to do with the nature of the kingdom than with the qualities required of the few who will enter it. Each soil represents a species of hearer, and only those who correspond to the rich soil will bear fruits in abundance worthy of the kingdom; what practical observances will enable those fruits to sprout and ripen within us, we are not told.

As it is true that all revelation involves concealment, so it is true – and not so often observed– that something of Christ's identity is revealed in every imposition of silence. He stops the mouths of demons lest they should make him known (3.12), yet in doing so he exhibits power beyond precedent and is forced into controversy with those who accuse him of using Satan to cast out Satan (3.23). His argument – that if Satan casts out Satan his house must fall – is (as many have seen) an adumbration of his own mission; it is a greater attestation of his power to silence demons than it would have been to walk by and let them babble. More formidable still is the submission of the elements at 4.39, after Jesus, reproaching the tempest as he reproached both disciples and demons on other occasions, has spoken merely two words connoting silence; two new locutions ('the wind abated' and 'there was a great peace') complete the miracle, leaving the disciples to ask 'Who is this man, that the wind and the waves obey him? (4.41). This quiescence of demons and natural forces on demand is to be contrasted with the impertinent speech of humans: the word of Christ never fails in efficacy, except where he leaves us free to speak our own.

What, then, is to draw us out of disobedience and incomprehension? The parable of the sower is immediately succeeded by the precept not to hide one's light under a bushel (4.21–22), while the epilogue to the saying about the leaven of the Pharisees is the opening, not without labour, of a blind man's eyes (8.22–26). This is one of two miracles peculiar to the Gospel: the other, which precedes it, is the healing of a deaf-mute (7.32–37). The cognate in the Fourth Gospel (also peculiar to that text) is the gift of sight to a man born blind, expressly vindicating the claim of Jesus to be the light of the world (John 9.5). Thus it becomes apparent that, in Mark as in John and Paul, the medium of revelation is the word but the climax is vision, which gives manifest form to the truths that words communicate under a veil. It will be noted that no distinction is observed in the Gospel of Mark

---

[18]   Moule (1965), 35.

between the blindness of the Gentiles and the deafness of the Israelites; Jesus is the Messiah to the world, and not only to Israel, as he indicates by his excursion to the Decapolis (where he cures the demoniac) and by his appropriation of the phrase 'Son of Man'.[19] This, as we have seen, may signify any human being in the Old Testament, but acquires symbolic import as a collective representation of the saints in the Book of Daniel. On its first two occurrences in the Gospel of Mark, it may be understood to mean simply 'a man', or (as some think) 'this man' in particular (Mark 2.10, 2.27); in either case, the assertion that the Son of Man has power to forgive sins on earth and is lord of the Sabbath need awaken no speculation as to the character of the speaker. Prophecies of the imminent death of the Son of Man form a centrepiece to the Gospel (8.33, 9.31, 10.33), and here, as at Psalm 8. 5 and Ezekiel 37.1, it is the weakness of all the sons of men, and of this man in particular, that is brought home to us. But at 14.62 – where Jesus declares that his priestly antagonist 'will see the Son of Man at the right hand of power, and coming in the clouds' – he says, without openly saying as much, that it is in this man whom Caiaphas despises that the saints will find their redeemer, and that Caiaphas himself, as a captain of Israel, will be among the judged. The high priest's vision will not be beatific but retributive, as he learns that the appellation Son of Man identified Jesus not as one man among a multitude, but as the one who could stand for all. Insofar as the meaning of the term 'Son of Man' is already known from the biblical deposit, it had served as an interpretant to Christ's ministry; at the culmination of the ministry, however, it is Christ who becomes the interpreter, subsuming all previous usages and intimating that only through the one who is pre-eminently Son of Man can the kingdom be opened to all the sons of men.

Forms of Mediation

We have seen that, in the scriptures known to Paul and John, it is not the Word of God that is personified but his Wisdom, and that even in early commentaries it seldom acquires a discrete existence as anything more than an instrument or function of the Creator. We have also seen that the image of God, bestowed upon humankind in general rather than any upon particular specimen of humanity, can be understood as a seal of ownership or a token of delegated sovereignty, and need not express a peculiar unveiling of the Godhead in the foremost of its creatures. It is in his angelic vicars or surrogates, indistinctly distinct from him, that God encounters the patriarchs; and since neither they nor their heirs were present to contemplate the creative acts of Wisdom, the text of the scriptures is now the only dress in which this celestial plenipotentiary becomes visible, though, like the ordinances of the Law itself, she is enthroned at all times within the upright heart. At the heart of the Christian proclamation, on the other hand, is Christ the unrepeatable image of God, who is both Creator and revealer, at once the fullness

---

[19]   I am indebted to Hooker (1967).

of divinity made palpable and the exalted Lord in whom all creatures reverence the name above every name. The corollary of his elevation is that the role of angels is diminished and the Law resigns its dominion: the Christ of the Fourth Evangelist does not share with either the 'glory that was his before the foundation of the world' (John 17.5).

It is not that angels are absent from the Gospels. In Mark the resurrection is announced by a man in a white robe (16.5), and the two beings who take his place in John are expressly described as angels (20.20). Gabriel announces the nativity to Mary at Luke 1.26–35, an angel dissipates the suspicions of Joseph in Matthew's narrative (1.20), and the news is brought to the shepherds by an angelic choir (Luke 2.9–14). Christ is succoured by angels in the wilderness (Matthew 4.11; cf. Luke 4.10) and comforted by an angel in Gethsemane (Luke 22.43 *textus receptus*). That he was seen of angels is an article in the deposit of faith at 1 Timothy 3.16. An angel delivers Peter from prison (Acts 12.7–11), and the seer of Revelation has an angel to thank for his vision (Revelation 1.1, for example). He is rebuked, however, when his thanks take the form of worship (22.8–9), and the veneration of angels is forbidden at Colossians 2.18, in conjunction with other residual practices of the old covenant. In the idiom of the New Testament, there can be no oscillation, as in the Old, between the Lord himself and the angel of the Lord; there is no occasion on which an angel is taken for God, though the voice of God may be speculatively taken for that of an angel (John 12.29). The highest praise that can be accorded to angels is that they were the emissaries from whom Israel received the Law (Acts 7.53).

Yet even this, which is said by Stephen in honour of the Law, serves Paul as an argument against continuing bondage to its exactions. If the Law was 430 years after the covenant with Abraham, it cannot be the foundation of the covenant (Galatians 4.17); if it came by the hand of a mediator, it cannot be of equal force to a compact which was made by God himself. Paul's reasoning – 'a mediator is not of one, but God is one' (Galatians 4.19) – is often misunderstood, because it is assumed that the role of the *mesitês* or mediator here is to stand between two contracting parties. If that is so, the fact that God is one does not appear to preclude mediation between him and one or more beneficiaries, and, since that is precisely the office performed by Christ, it is hard to see why any pejorative sense should attach to the notion of mediation. Paul is here invoking a rarer definition of the mediator, not as one who acts as broker *between* two parties but as one who acts as the single representative of many *on one side only* of a transaction.[20] Moses was a mediator because he received his statutes not directly from the one God, but from a plurality of angels; Abraham, by contrast, made his covenant with God alone, and hence no mediator was required. The premise that the Law was

---

[20]　　Cf. Philo, *Life of Moses* 2.166, where Moses acts as a mediator on behalf of the people to God, though God himself has charged him with a different mission. Also *On the Cherubim* 27, where the Word, as *meson*, is the joint executor of God's power and benevolence, not a medium or mediator between them.

given by angels is accepted, as we have seen, in another apostolic writing and is sanctioned by Jewish tradition, but it is Paul who makes new capital of it to prove that the Law is no teacher for the Gentiles but a temporary guardian to the carnal children of Abraham, for whom it has been a true, though beguiling, shadow of things to come (Colossians 2.17).

To go on observing the letter of the Law is to ape the folly of the Gentiles, who worship the 'weak and beggarly elements' (Galations 4.9). The simile rests on a pun, since the term *stoikheia* can signify either the four material elements (earth, air, fire and water) or the letters of the alphabet. To be under the Law, and therefore subject to its chastisement after every sin, is to bear the curse which Christ took upon himself (3.13). In this sacrifice he blots out the 'writing which was against us' (Colossians 2.13), and those who are willing to die and rise with him will find themselves to be the 'true epistle of Christ, written not with ink but with the Spirit of the living God; not in tables of stone, but in the fleshly tables of the heart' (2 Corinthians 3.3). Paul goes on to argue that, as Moses was obliged to wear a veil which concealed the radiance of his countenance after his vision of God, so the descendants of the Israelites continue to read the truth under a veil (2 Corinthians 3.13–15), which cannot be removed without faith in Christ. The darkness from which the knowledge of God's glory shines forth at 2 Corinthians 4.6 is not so much the night which preceded the first day as the obscurity of the Law before Christ's advent; whereas Jeremiah promised hearts of flesh for hearts of stone, Paul hints that the very stones on which the Law was engraved must yield to the coming of the man in whom the fullness of God dwelt bodily (Colossians 2.9).

A higher view of the Law – a higher view of its graphic repository – can perhaps be ascribed to the Jesus of Matthew's Gospel, who proclaims that not one jot or tittle of it will pass away and that a righteousness superior to that of the scribes and Pharisees is the condition for entry to the kingdom of heaven. He accords an exceptional value to the written Law by contrasting it with the traditions of men, which he takes it upon himself to overrule. It is, however, apparent in his teaching on divorce (19.9) and in his repeal of the Law of retaliation (5.38) that even the written code is of less authority in his sight than his own pronouncements. If the plan of Matthew is based on that of the Pentateuch, as has been maintained, his purpose is not so much to reconsecrate the Law as to announce its supersession in Christ, which, even for this evangelist, entails the abrogation of certain passages and the supersession of stony obedience by cordial love of God and one's neighbour. If the teaching of Jesus in the middle portions of Luke is patterned on that of Deuteronomy, the same exegesis holds. The Jesus of these authors is not so unlike the Jesus of the Fourth Gospel, who approaches the Law with a spirit of divination that allows him to be indifferent to the letter. In Hebrews, Christ is the mediator of a new covenant (9.15), not insofar as he acts on behalf of beings other than God, as Moses did, but in his office as the one high priest who intercedes for humanity before the throne of God.

At the same time, Hebrews is the one work of the first century that compares Christ to a written or graven cipher. 'He is the effulgence of the glory and the *kharaktêr* of his *hypostasis*', says the author of Christ's relation to the Father (Hebrews 1.3). The vocabulary in the first clause is redolent of Wisdom 7.25–26 and there is perhaps no other passage of the New Testament which so clearly assimilates Christ to God's coadjutor in creation. The novel term, however, is *kharaktêr*, which in common Greek can denote a seal affixed to a letter. This would bear the image of the sender, so that if this meaning were applied to Hebrews 1.3, the hypostasis will be construed as the reality or substance of the original, in contrast to the impression. This is not to say, of course, that the incarnation is illusory. It is by virtue of being a man, the author contends in the opening chapters, that he is superior to the angels. God never said to an angel, 'thou art my Son; this day I have begotten thee' (Hebrews 1.5, citing Psalm 2.7), and it was of all humankind, as represented in this one paragon, that the psalmist declared 'thou hast made him a little lower than the angels, and crowned him with glory and honour' (Hebrews 2.5–9, citing Psalm 8.4–5). The author takes this as a prophecy, in which the subjection of 'man' and the 'Son of Man' to the angels (understood here to be 'for a short period' rather than 'only a little') is succeeded by one of glory. Psalm 8 goes on to affirm that all things are under the feet of humanity; evidently, the author of the Epistle to the Hebrews continues (2.9), this is not yet true of all humankind, but already 'we see Jesus crowned in glory'. In his own person, therefore, Jesus anticipates and makes possible the realization of an august destiny for every 'son of man'.[21]

But what does it mean to say that we see Jesus? Not that we know him after the flesh, for the author pretends to no ocular acquaintance even with the resurrected Christ, let alone with his earthly ministry. Nor that we have any written gospel, for there is no evidence that he had such a text before him. The question is nowhere answered in this document, but centuries of doctrinal lucubration and exegetic legerdemain are foreshadowed in a complex trope, which reveals the inadequacy of all narratives encompassing only the mundane works of Jesus and of any faith based solely upon such narratives. We have seen that, for Paul, a veil stood between the Jews and the true intention of the Law; at Hebrews 10.20, adapting the Pauline metaphor as Paul adapts those of the prophets, the author describes the flesh of Christ as the veil which must be parted in order to open a 'new and living way' to God.

It may be said that three of the Gospels terminate with scenes of recognition. But what is seen, for example, when two former intimates, meeting Jesus on the road to Emmaus after the crucifixion, take him for a stranger who is ignorant of Christ's death or any subsequent testimony to his return? As an angel is known by his manner of going in the Old Testament, so it is in the wake of his departure – after meeting, conversation and breaking of bread – that Christ is recognized by his hosts. Even then the proof is in his speaking, or the effect of it – 'did not our hearts burn within us?' (Luke 24.32) – and there is nothing to suggest that they were conscious of any physiognomic likeness to the man whom they knew before the

---

[21]   Sanday (1911), 126–129.

crucifixion.[22] In the Gospel of Matthew Jesus receives the instantaneous homage of his disciples, 'though some doubted' (Matthew 28.17): what they doubted we are not told, but we can be more sure that the faithful devotees honoured him as Lord than that they verified his identity as a man. More striking still is the error of Mary Magdalen, who, on emerging from the empty tomb, accosts a man whom she takes to be the gardener and asks whether he has abducted the body of Jesus (John 20.15). It is only when he calls her by name (20.16) that she knows him, and, although she endeavours to touch him, we do not hear that she learns, or hopes to learn, anything from the perusal of his features. Neither in her case nor in that of Thomas, whose doubts are allayed in the following episode, do we hear that the desire to touch the body of the risen Christ was consummated; the motives of Thomas are less obscure – he wishes to verify the marks of the nails – but it may be that the mere sight of the wounds was enough to produce conviction (20.26–28). Nathanael, at the beginning of the narrative, is half rebuked because he saluted Jesus as Son of God and King of Israel after a trivial demonstration of clairvoyance (1.50); Thomas is admonished that, if he has 'believed because he has seen' (20.29), he is not so blessed as those who, like the beloved disciple, believe without having seen. This same beloved disciple – who appears to be either the author or his informant, though at the same time he is symbolically the one whom every reader must hope to be – is said to have reclined in the bosom of Jesus at the Last Supper (John 13.23), just as the latter dwelt at all times in the bosom of the Father; it is by virtue of this indwelling that Jesus Christ, the incarnate Word and Son of God, is able to make known that God and Father whom 'no one hath seen at any time' (John 1.18).

Conclusion

It might seem that the disciples could have said, with Job, 'I have heard of thee by the hearing of mine ear, but now mine eye seeth thee' (Job 42.5). If the Father is the author of light (Genesis 1.3), the Son is the light of the world (John 9.4). The evangelist who declares that the Son revealed the God whom no one has seen at any time (John 1.18) puts into his mouth the words 'He who hath seen me hath seen the Father' (14.9). Others affirm that he was seen of angels (1 Timothy 3.16) and accredited by miracles (Acts 2.22); those whose eyes he has opened see what prophets and kings have desired to see in vain (Luke 10.24), and the apostle who can boast of having seen the word of life with his eyes (1 John 1.1) assures his correspondents that 'when Christ appears, we shall see him as he is' (3.3). But therein lies the doubt: if even his intimates have not seen him as he is, can we be certain that their eyes have not played them false? Paul's companions were dazzled by the same light that blinded him, but he was the only one to hear an articulate voice; the man of his acquaintance who had been rapt up to the

---

[22]   Fitzmeyer (1987), 420–422.

third heaven received no vision, but only words that it was not lawful to utter (2 Corinthians 12.4). The Christ who proclaimed himself the light of the world says of unbelievers that they have failed to hear his word (John 8.43); his sheep, who know their shepherd by his voice (10.4b), confess that he alone possesses 'the words of eternal life' (6.68). The risen Christ was known by his voice (John 20.16) or the kindling of the heart that his words occasioned (Luke 24.22). The primacy of hearing over sight is illustrated by the fact that it was the word of life that John professed to have seen, and that it was this term – rather than light or any visual metaphor – that became the Church's customary appellative for Christ as the Second Person of the Godhead.

As the generations passed, there were few who claimed to have heard or seen so much as Paul. Knowledge of Christ was communicated only in texts, which were believed because they purported to contain the recollections of a witness or (in Luke's case) to have been verified by the interrogation of numerous witnesses. In the following chapters we shall not discover that this high regard for the Word gave rise to any worship of the written characters. As we have seen, there remained an element of inscrutability in the Gospels, which could be obviated only by the answer of the spirit within to the swing of the Word. The possibility of this response implies that God and his human creation are no longer strangers as they were before the Word became flesh. It is in his second character as image of God that the Word effects this reconciliation; if the expression 'image of God' is more salient in the New Testament than in the Old, the reason seems to be not so much that it carries an intimation of visibility as that this is a characteristic appellative of the second Adam which, unlike 'Word', is equally predicable of all who can trace their lineage to the first. Whether the image pertains to us by virtue of his divinity or accrues to him by virtue of his manhood was a question still to be answered, since the idiom of the New Testament barely permits it to be phrased.

Chapter 3
Word and Image in
Classical Greek Philosophy

From the first, Greek philosophers were engaged in the agnostic use of language, with frequent and self-flattering reflections on the success of their own manoeuvres, but scarcely a pause to demonstrate the inferiority of other media. The folly of speaking to images is more often derided than the making of them,[1] and there is no abiding war between the sculpted idol and the written text. The text itself may be an object of idolatry or of iconoclasm; the writings of Plato inculcate the second, but at length inspired the first, though not in his own time or in the Hellenistic schools that descended from him. His strictures on pictorial and dramatic imitation sit uneasily with his adoption of the dialogue, the most mimetic of literary forms; as we shall see, both Aristotle's defence of tragic mimicry and the Stoic cultivation of allegory as a tool of exegesis find some warrant in his own practice, and especially in those passages where an 'iconic' or mythical idiom supersedes the 'elenctic' method which is personified in his own Socrates as a cure for weakness of memory and the witchcraft of the tongue.

Before Plato

The Homeric poems exhibit a repetitive and formulaic style that is seldom imitated in literary prose. As similar techniques have been observed in the extemporary productions of illiterate bards,[2] it is reasonable to assume that the practice of oral composition and recitation has shaped the diction of the poems, although it may be that oral tradition alone could not account for the evolution of two voluminous and well-knit epics of such uniform sublimity. Even if, however, the final redaction was performed with the aid of writing, it remains true that no knowledge of the art is shown by the heroes or narrators of either poem. Palamedes, the legendary inventor of the alphabet, is not mentioned, and Bellerophon unwittingly delivers the 'pernicious signs' that contain the mandate for his own execution (*Iliad* 6.168). If events are commemorated, it is in song, and it is on hearing the rehearsal of his own victories that Odysseus is moved to speak (or rather, as Homer is his

---

[1]   For ridicule of popular literalism, see Heraclitus (Fr. 115 DK at Graham (2010), 177–178); Diogenes the Cynic at Clement of Alexandria, *Stromateis* 7.4.25.5; Chrysippus at Diogenes Laertius, *Lives* 7.187.

[2]   See, for example, Kirk (1976).

mouthpiece, to sing) of his subsequent peregrinations (*Odyssey* 8.62–68). In the *Iliad* Helen weaves a tapestry in remembrance of the deeds performed at Troy (3.125), and in the forging of a new shield for Achilles, we see the first extended representation in poetry of a visual artefact, depicting episodes both from battle and from common life (*Iliad* 18.478–608). Because the shield is in fact a tissue of words, we are conscious of the poet's dexterity in unfolding a view of scenes remote from Troy which could never have been transfused into any real work of bronze or iron. The same is true of the Hesiodic *Shield of Heracles*, which decorates the hero's buckler with scenes of all his previous battles. Even if it were in the power of any smith to produce such a visual inventory, no picture can convey a linear narrative with the precision and lucidity that can be achieved in words.

Hesiod, like Homer, cannot sing without inspiration. But, whereas in Homer the office of the Muse is to supply the defect of memory, Hesiod owes to the Muses his vocation as a poet. In boasting that they know how to speak the truth but are equally capable of falsehood, they claim for themselves the whole of the poet's craft, and neither ancient nor modern readers have been sure how credulously Hesiod wishes us to receive his genealogy of the gods.[3] The seductive power of verse became a commonplace of Greek poetry in the archaic period; even when a speaker purports to have been ensnared by the tongue or the outward beauty of another, the very words of the enchantment have to be furnished by the plaintiff. A poem could serve its author as a means of solicitation; it could also, as Homer and Hesiod had shown, produce artefacts weightier and more durable than the creations of the forge. As metallurgy and magic were sibling crafts, at least in myth, it was possible for a singer to claim the spoils of both, as Pindar does repeatedly in celebration of his own workmanship.

The lyric poets were not admitted to Aristotle's catalogue of philosophers, but a number of his philosophers were poets. Xenophanes of Colophon[4] has acquired some reputation as an empiricist because he declared that 'the gods have not revealed all things to humanity in the beginning, but by searching they find out more' (Fr. 38). It appears to be an axiom for him that gods exist and that they excel over us in power and virtue. Consequently, Homer and Hesiod are to be reprimanded because they teach that the gods are guilty of theft, adultery and deceit (Frs 17, 18). It does not, however, follow that Xenophanes wished to deny the poets any role in the education of the populace. In the age between Homer and Plato it was a convention, whenever a poet spoke of the gods, for him to take up an eristic relation to his predecessors,[5] and especially to those whom he thought most worthy of emulation. Nor should a contempt for the pictorial arts, or even for the pictorial representation of the gods, be inferred from his celebrated apophthegms

---

[3]   See West (1966), 158–63, for a survey of views on the epiphany at *Theogony* 22–28. On the poet's responsibility for the words of the Muses, see Calame (1995), 45.

[4]   Graham (2010), vol. 1, 95–134. With Graham, I follow the Diels-Krantz (1951) numeration of fragments from the Presocratics.

[5]   See Graziosi (2001).

that each nation has sculpted its deities in its own image and that if horses and oxen had hands they would do the same (Frs 20–21). To say that the gods have been falsely represented is not to say that they admit of no representation. The most famous of all his sayings, which acclaims 'one god, the greatest of gods and men, resembling mortals neither in shape nor in form' (Fr. 23), does not state in plain terms that this divinity has no form at all, and, if anything, implies that we share some traits with the lesser gods. These fragments, if they are genuine,[6] are more trenchant than any writings of their time in their criticism of the prevailing use of images; they do not, however, intimate that the image is less faithful than the word as a medium of religious truth.

Of Heraclitus of Ephesus[7] it was said that he listened to no one but sought all truth within himself. It was also said that he purposely couched his thoughts in an obscure and gnomic style in order to hide them from the multitude; for his part, he declares that he is incomprehensible only to those who choose not to comprehend him.[8] There is, he avers, one *logos* common to all, yet many live as though they possessed a private *logos*. He exhorts them not to listen to the obtuse Pythagoras, the dissembling Hesiod, the ignorant Homer or any of the mere polymaths who receive the plaudits of ill-governed cities (Frs 10–14); if they are wise, they will listen not even to him, but to the *logos* (Fr. 28), and confess that all things are one (or that there is one who knows all things: Fr. 27). This disclaimer indicates that the *logos* is not simply Heraclitus' own discourse, but the rationale from which it derives its cogency; whether we ought to look for this rationale in the anatomy of his own reasoning or in that of the world the evidence does not help us to determine, and it may be that he identified the two. Although he speaks of listening to the *logos,* he pronounces sight the most accurate of the senses (Frs 20, 21); so far as we can recover it, the burden of his argument seems to be that his words represent a truth that cannot be vouchsafed in words alone. Like the common *logos* of the world, his own *logos* becomes perspicuous only to an inquirer who has made himself the first subject of inquiry. 'I searched into myself' is one of his sayings (Fr. 25); on the other hand, even eyes and ears will be treacherous witnesses to men of barbarous souls (Fr. 22).

Parmenides of Elea also delivers in verse the philosophy which he purports to have heard from a goddess. Her tone, however, is only intermittently hieratic, and the longest surviving fragments of her speech are those which purport to reveal the logical inanity of such tenets as 'it is not' or 'it is and is not' (Frs 2, 7). The senses are dormant here as there is no appeal to phenomena, the speech with its mythological concomitants being no more than a picturesque stimulus to the mind's powers of abstract reasoning. And yet, just as the Muses in Hesiod speak both truth and falsehood, so the goddess proceeds to expound a way of *doxa* or

6   Edwards (1991a).

7   Graham (2010), vol. 1, 135–200.

8   On the purposeful ambiguity of Fragments 1 and 2, see Kahn (1987), 96–102.

seeming, of which it appears to be true after all that it is and is not.[9] So far as the meagre remains allow us to judge, this is a description of the physical world, to be accepted on divine authority, but not (one presumes) with absolute conviction. Persuasion, in the nomenclature of Parmenides, is the acolyte of Truth.

Empedocles of Acragas[10] represents himself as the pupil of the Muses and the recipient of divine truths which could not have been discovered by the exercise of purely human wisdom (Fr. 120). That the sage is capable both of receiving knowledge and of meditating upon it is a consequence of his being not merely a mortal but a daemon, who has endured some 30,000 years of exile and dispersion after indulging a fratricidal taste for meat (Fr. 137). He has fallen from a state in which all daemons lived at one under the beatific rule of love; in the cosmos it is love that binds the elements, strife that sunders them, and the daemon is tossed from element to element until he learns to renounce strife and allows love to restore in him the harmony of the lost kingdom (Frs 20–23). This cycle of dispersion and concentration, which the daemon suffers in miniature,[11] exemplifies a law to which the whole cosmos and God himself appear to be subject; Empedocles' description of his own craft as a poet, reproducing at times his account of the work of love, suggests that he saw his own verse as an instrument of reintegration, both for himself and for his disciple.[12] Although this is ostensibly a work to be recited rather than read, it does not subordinate vision to hearing; on the contrary, the painter's skilful combination of pigments affords a simile for the uniting action of love (Fr. 24) and perhaps, once again, for the poet's kneading of his own verse.

The word may deceive when it represents the world, but when it takes itself for its subject it can be sure of exemplifying what it denotes. Gorgias of Leontini was the foremost of a class of versatile teachers, known as sophists, who earned their livelihood as tutors to the sons of the rich, in Athens and elsewhere.[13] As rhetoric was the art in which he excelled, it is not surprising that his most famous work, an apology for Helen of Troy, should be ostentatiously mannered in its diction and self-conscious in its orchestration of forensic tropes. It is indeed the *logos* that should be on trial rather than his client, for if she did not sin willingly or under physical coercion, she must have succumbed to enchantment of the ear or of the eye. There is no resisting the minstrelsy of speech when it fills the mind with soft delusions; nor, if the mind can be unmanned by spectacles of horror, can we ask that it should be immune to beauty. Pleasure is excited by a painting and religious awe by a statue; the reader is, however, more aware of the cajolery of words, since it is only those who find the incantations of the sophist irresistible who will pardon Helen's failure to resist the eloquence of a handsome suitor. Sight is the more

---

[9]   See Palmer (2009), 106–136, for interpretation and bibliography of Frs 8–12, which appear at Graham (2010), vol. 1, 219–223.

[10]   Graham (2010), vol. 1, 326–433.

[11]   Darcus (1977).

[12]   Edwards (1991b).

[13]   Graham (2010) vol. 2, 725–787.

imperious of the senses, hearing the more seductive; the politician will cultivate the latter, since he knows that it is easier to beguile than to overpower a multitude.

That we ought to judge by deeds, not words, is the plea by which the defendant hopes to exonerate himself in the *Palamedes*. Yet Palamedes never addresses the substance of the charge against him, urging instead that, whatever acts of perfidy might be laid at his door, he had neither the means nor the motive to commit them. This reasoning, if valid, would entail that no one could ever be guilty of treason; the fallacy is all the more palpable because he counts the invention of writing, a notorious tool of covert negotiation, among the proofs of his intellectual fertility. A more philosophic exercise by Gorgias, purporting to demonstrate that nothing exists or can be known to exist, proves rather, against Parmenides, that language can refer with equal facility to 'what is' and to 'what is not'. His arguments are not inconsequential and are handled seriously in Plato's *Sophist*. But Socrates and the other hegemonic speakers in the Platonic dialogues are playing Xenophanes to the sophist's Homer, using words to unveil the truth that has been camouflaged by the false rhetoric or bad faith of other speakers. As we shall find, the success of the enterprise, and even its probity, may be doubted: Plato proves himself a skilful painter in words, employs a mimetic form that may be thought to belie his own teachings (if he has teachings) and can be equally captious on both sides of a question. His works, in short, reveal that the inadequacy of speech lies not so much in the mendacity of the speakers as in the fact that words are mere signs, not to be understood without some knowledge of the signifier. This is the origin of Plato's theory of love as well as his theory of Forms; it also justifies his use of sight as a metaphor for the knowledge of things transcending vision. And thus he is led into an intractable paradox, for language is the philosopher's one resource even when he is warning us not to confide in it: the word, assuming the visual form of a book, is asked to point beyond itself to that which cannot be communicated in words.

False Representation in Speech

In Plato's dialogues, Socrates confesses more than once, though not in any case without irony, that he has temporarily lost his wits to another speaker's eloquence. Thus in the *Symposium* he protests that aureate diction of Agathon's speech in praise of Love has struck him as dumb as though he had seen the Gorgon's head (198c). The pun on the name of Gorgias is unconcealed, and scholars have found no difficulty in counting the tropes that Agathon has borrowed from the great sophist. Gorgias celebrated the irresistible power of speech when the lover employs it as an instrument of persuasion; Agathon, in making love the subject of an imitative discourse (195a–197e), becomes not only love's encomiast but his exemplar, as though to intimate that one cannot speak rightly of love unless one simulates the rhetoric of the lover. As the model for this rhetoric was furnished by a preceptor who was patently not in love, it could hardly be shown more clearly that the art of the sophists consists not in being or feeling, but in feigning to be and in causing others to feel. Socrates says as much to Gorgias, in the dialogue named after him,[14] where he complains that, if the sole object of the orator is persuasion, he does not require that a thing be so in order to make it appear so, and can inculcate two contrary beliefs without knowing which of them is true (455a). More famous even than Gorgias for his dexterity in 'making the worse appear to be the better' was Protagoras.[15] The dialogue which bears his name begins with a facetious profession of love on the part of Socrates (309c–e), who pretends to have been stupefied after hearing an orotund sermon on the foundations of society and the principles of moral education (328d). On inquiry, however, it becomes evident that the sophist chose to concoct a parable rather than attempt a definition because he was ignorant of the true nature of his subject, ignorant even of his own ignorance.[16] Only the elenctic method, the adversarial play of question and answer, will enable the teacher to see what virtue is in itself,[17] and thus not only to speak the truth but to communicate the unshakeable conviction that it is true.

In the first book of the *Republic*, Socrates is thrown into confusion by a paradoxical eulogy of the tyrant as the one just man because he embodies the 'right of the stronger' without dissimulation (344c–d). No doubt he is daunted more by the belligerence of Thrasymachus than by the euphony of his diction; nevertheless, this comic episode illustrates the fact – a tragic fact, as we shall soon have reason to call it – that the ordinary Athenian, who formed his opinion according to what he heard, was as apt to be moved by specious trappings which seemed to lend dignity or authority to a speaker as by that speaker's choice of words or the rigour of his logic. It is for this reason that poetry, or the poetic confabulations of the sophist, so often furnish the matter of disputation in a Socratic dialogue. The thesis that the poet is the teacher of the city was taken seriously by Plato[18] – perhaps more seriously than by the first man known to have propagated it, the comedian Aristophanes, whose caricature of Socrates in the *Clouds* could be read as a strict indictment once the real Socrates had been put on trial.[19] The marrow of his defence, or of the posthumous defence that Plato wrote for him, was that, since the unexamined life was no life for a man (*Apology* 38a), he was bound to go on asking questions until he had something to add to the knowledge that he knew nothing (*Apology* 21a–23b). Even such knowledge as this was denied to those – the great majority in Athens – who simply acted as the rules of their trade or art prescribed without seeking to understand the principles of their discipline, let alone the ultimate goals of life. Somnambulists of the unexamined life can only perpetuate the habits instilled in them by education; where poetry is the medium

---

[14]   On the supersession of this 'counter-rhetoric' by voluntary ostracism in the *Phaedo*, see Rosenstock (1997).

[15]   Graham (2010), vol. 2, 706–707, citing Diogenes Laertius, *Lives* 9.31.

[16]   See Edwards (1992) with Kurke (2010), 285.

[17]   See Robinson (1984), Vlastos (1983) and the responses in Scott (2002).

[18]   See Havelock (1963; Asmis (1992).

[19]   See Brown (2007).

of instruction, a mere reciter like Ion, the rhapsode, may imagine that he knows everything because he has memorized everything, though in fact he has become a Proteus (*Ion* 541e), shedding one deceitful physiognomy for another and leaving no residual character to which he could apply the Delphic maxim 'Know thyself' (cf. *Phaedrus* 229e).[20]

Most delusive, because he is most deluded, is the theatrical performer. Wearing another person's mask and speaking only the lines that have been composed for him, he does not understand that if a man's character is good already he will not affect another, since this would entail a diminution of his goodness (394d–397b; cf. 381c). What is worse is that the practice of *mimêsis* on stage encourages the habit of *mimêsis* in the audience, so that sentiments which should never have been enunciated become vernacular proverbs, and the malefactor can justify his crimes by citing actions falsely imputed to the gods (377b–398b). The noun *mimêsis* is not easily translated, since it cannot signify in every instance what we would ordinarily mean by 'imitation'.[21] The English word suggests likeness to an original, but there can be no original of the protagonist in a fictitious narrative. On the other hand, it is often the case that the act performed on the stage and the act that it represents are identical: whenever the actor recites a speech, for example, we cannot say that he merely appears to speak, as we might say in another case that he merely appears to stab himself. If the acts of sitting or speaking on stage remain mimetic and are not of a piece with those that the actors perform when they doff their costumes, this is not because of a failure in execution, but simply because the histrionic act is not performed with the same intention as its quotidian counterpart, and because the sequence of events to which it belongs is a contrived one, which the dramaturge may suspend or change at will.

It might seem that on this account a real breach of the moral or civic law could not be a mimetic action, even if committed in imitation of some deed witnessed on the stage; it remains mimetic, however, insofar as the perpetrator is not acquainted with the true nature of his crime. It must be understood that Plato does not denounce *mimêsis* only when it holds up subjects, real or imaginary, that ought not to be imitated; there is a forfeiture of integrity in every occlusion of the proper self, in the mere assumption of a voice that is not one's own (395c–397b). Hence the Socratic criticism of Homer is that too often he plays ventriloquist to his own characters, simulating what he ought to have described. The true historian never abandons his office as narrator; the ideal city, taking leave of Homer, will be content with hymns to the gods and panegyrics on the achievements of just men (398b; 595b–600e).

---

[20]   Cf. Moravcsik (1982), 28–29.

[21]   See further Verdenius (1971); Keuls (1978), 9–32.

The Visual Counterfeit

We have seen above that Xenophanes may have been the first to urge that statues cannot reveal the true likeness of the gods and that the most exalted among the gods has neither a body nor an external form.[22] Plato offers no critique of sacred art and appears to have been less troubled by the absurdities of popular religion than by the scurrility of the poets. His disparagement of the poets in the tenth book of the *Republic* is prefaced, however, by a satire on the painter,[23] whom he takes as a paradigmatic and obvious specimen of those who reproduce without understanding. A painting of a bed, for example, is nothing but a facsimile of the shape already produced in three dimensions by the craftsman. Neither the carpenter nor his copyist understands the true nature of a bed, which is visible only to God (or the god) who perceives its archetypal form (597a–d). To have only specious knowledge without a *logos* or account is to be unconscious of one's own ignorance, as Socrates urges in dialogue after dialogue. A bed or a saddle is understood not by the one who can replicate it, but by the one who is able to use it for its purpose (601c); by the same principle, no one can explain the constitution of the world without some notion of final causes, and moral principles cannot be taught by one who is ignorant of the ends of life.

The factotum among the journeymen, the virtuoso in ignorance, is the sophist. If the painter is introduced only to illustrate the less manifest frailties of the poet, the impotence of the sophist is exposed by a still more ludicrous comparison. He is like a man who declares that he can recreate everything in heaven and earth and who proceeds to make good his boast by producing a mirror in which he catches the reflections of these objects (*Republic* 596c–d). If his pretensions were true he would be a great enchanter; in fact, of course, by using a receptacle as a means of reproduction he has failed to exercise even the perspicacity of the artist. Here, then, we are offered a different image of the sophist, not as a man whose seductive tongue can persuade us of anything but as the charlatan self-deceived. This is not deny that (as we discover in Plato's *Sophist*) he is still a mighty hunter and an ensnarer of the young (222a); it means, however, that he makes use of weapons which are at once more feeble and more pernicious than those of the imitator, since the painter replicates only what he sees, whereas the tongue of the sophist moulds 'phantastic' images that correspond to no object in the world (236a–d).[24]

Practitioners of rhetoric in Plato's time disagreed regarding the use of books in the preparation of species. Some held that an extemporized speech will always be more persuasive, others that greater cogency can be attained if every word is prepared with care and art. Isocrates, though his treatise *On the Sophists* upheld

---

[22]   See also Edwards (1991a).

[23]   On pictorial illusion as an 'allegory' of sensory perception, see Keuls (1978), 33–42.

[24]   See further Owen (1971).

the first position,[25] laboured for years in the composition of speeches that do not appear to have been delivered. In the *Phaedrus* he is praised by Socrates at the expense of Lysias, who also wrote down his speeches, but for delivery in court by himself or a client (279a–b). Some of his lost works must have been designed only for perusal or for recitation as showpieces, for Socrates' friend, the eponymous interlocutor in this dialogue of two persons, is a besotted admirer of Lysias and precipitates the argument by producing a text from his tunic which, as Socrates says archly, is as good a companion as the man himself (228e). The speech is in fact an overture from an older man to a boy (as it might be from Lysias to Phaedrus[26]) soliciting favours without the pretence of love. It has all the seductive artifice of Agathon's declamation in praise of love and of Gorgias' testimony to the irresistible power of words in the service of courtship; in this case, however, *logos* carries off the palm at the expense of *eros*. The rejoinder of Socrates is, first, to show that he can improvise a better overture than that of Lysias (237b) and then, with the help of the Muses, to offer a palinode in the manner of Stesichorus, a poet who, on being struck blind by Helen, had proclaimed that both his own and Homer's account of her elopement has been untrue (243b–c). The discussion returns to rhetoric and the utility of books. Socrates tells a parable, according to which the art of writing was first devised in Egypt as an antidote to forgetfulness, but was seen by a wise king to be quite the opposite, a narcotic to reflection and the interrogation of our claims to knowledge (274e–275b). Truths cannot be imparted by the dead cipher which captures the seeds of knowledge but forbids them to grow; it burgeons only in dialogue between the professor of knowledge and his disciple, forcing each of them to examine and refine his own beliefs. Where Jews and Christians celebrate the permanence of their scriptures, Plato sets the thinker against his monument, the living word against the petrifaction of the letter.

Parables and Personifications

But is this the whole of Plato's semiology – that words are duplicitous, pictures fraudulent and books inert? There is evidence in his works that he studied the choice and arrangement of words with unusual diligence: he was reckoned among the masters of Greek prose in the Hellenistic era, and one ancient scholar professes to have seen a copy of the opening sentence of the *Republic* corrected eight times in his own hand.[27] Moreover, the pastoral setting of the *Phaedrus*, his account of the harlequinade that Protagoras set up in Athens under the guise of teaching (*Protagoras* 314e–316a), and the coruscating visions, in several dialogues, of the world that awaits the soul after death suggest that his eye could dwell keenly and

---

[25]   Isocrates, *On the Sophists* 9–13; but cf. *Antidosis* 7.

[26]   On Lysias as coercive lover of Phaedrus, who then plays the same role to Socrates, see Svenbro (1988), 198–216.

[27]   Adam (1938), 1, citing Dionysius of Halicarnassus, *On Verbal Composition*.

pleasurably on the surface of things; his Socrates, though ugly, is not indifferent to beauty in others. As for his criticisms of the book, his own fecundity belies them, and those who have tasted his lively and saline manner will scarcely agree with his pronouncement that the written word cannot speak for itself.[28] Where Socrates is the principal speaker, he can rehearse a myth or pursue the design of an ideal city without anticipating any of those objections to prolixity which the sophists hear from him throughout the dialogues; where he is absent, the principal speaker makes no pretence of a fondness for brevity and is seldom interrupted. Might it be said (as some said in antiquity) that Plato the man of letters is as much a sophist as those whom he exposed to the Socratic catechism – that, having failed in youth as a tragedian,[29] he poured out all the wormwood of his able pen on the meretricious practices by which he still hoped to thrive?

His answer, in the *Republic* and the *Phaedrus*, is that beauty in outward show is dangerous only to those who take it for a destination rather than a sign.[30] The philosopher can allow himself to be touched by the bloom of youth in his disciplines because the yearning that it kindles is the fruit of recollection, and he knows this for a memory of the supernal beauty unveiled to our souls in the 'supercelestial place' where they fought and jostled to reach the plain of Truth (248b–c). It is because they fell in the course of this endeavour that souls must make use of earthly phenomena as a ladder to the invisible (250d–251c). The philosopher will venerate his beloved like the statue of a hero, but at the same time will be conscious that his own task is to fashion this statue into a form more worthy of his garlands (252d–e). The beloved, for his part, will perceive the lover as a mirror in which the image of his better self is shown to him; as his soul, under the guidance of the lover, comes to resemble the loftier vision, so the lover's remembrance of that heavenly spectacle becomes more perfect. A Hebrew prophet would see in this ideal a Greek refinement of idolatry; nevertheless, although the conceits are visual, the words of the lover are his only incense, and he is not attempting to browbeat wood or marble but to bring forth the latent pulchritude in the soul of his beloved. Reversing this iconography in the *Symposium*, Alcibiades – a former pupil of Socrates and, as some would say, a deformed piece of his handiwork– compares him to a statue of Silenus, unprepossessing without but filled inside with *agalmata* or statues of the gods (216c–217a). The permutation of symbols reminds us that no true education can be imparted by the autocratic

---

[28]   On the mimetic character of the dialogues, see Kosman (1992). Halperin (1992), 125, suggests that they stimulate *mimêsis* in the reader.

[29]   Diogenes Laertius, *Lives* 3.5; cf. Nussbaum (1986), 124–126, and Charalabopoulos (2001).

[30]   See further Nehamas (1975), 105–117. Whether or not the Forms are assumed to constitute a transcendent universe, they are certainly responsible for the beauty and intelligibility of the present world: see Crombie (1963), 247–325, with Fine (1984) and (1986). Vlastos (1965) maintains that, while the Forms are more real than sensible particulars, it does not follow that they possess 'existence' in a superior degree.

display of 'truths' already known to the master: the truth lies hidden in master and pupil alike, and the duel of intellects brings more to light than has hitherto been visible to either.

We find another tropological use of statuary in a celebrated myth or parable of the *Republic*, though translated from the individual to the collective sphere. Socrates asks his hearers to imagine men in a cave, so tightly fettered that they can neither turn their heads nor move their limbs, and have no matter for vision or conversation other than the shadows which are cast on a screen before them by the *agalmata* which are carried back and forth in front of the fire behind their heads (515a–d). 'Imagine' is an apt word, since, as Glaucon exclaims (515a), this is a curious *eikôn*.[31] Socrates now supposes that one man is released from his chains and led to the upper world, where at first he can rest his eyes only on shadows like those that he has abandoned. At length, he comes to discern the outlines of real objects, and a gradual habituation to objects of increasing luminosity and magnitude enables him at last to look on the sun, which is at once the brightest thing that he sees and the means by which all other things are seen (516b–c). That the sun represents the form of the Good is evident,[32] and those who believe that Plato despised the body should note that, in this allegory of philosophical education, it is after long discipline in the state of embodiment that the soul at last achieves that consummation for which she strove in vain before her descent to earth.

The other elements in the allegory are not easily parsed, but Socrates has already distinguished four degrees of cognition, allotting each to one section of a divided line (509e–511e). The first section represents *eikasia*, or divination from shadows, plainly corresponding to the benighted understanding of the prisoners in the cave. Then follows the state of *pistis*, or belief, which is the perception of mundane objects and might be likened to the inchoate knowledge which the prisoner acquires either when he turns to the *agalmata* or when he leaves the cave. The third section represents the abstraction of the universal from the particular, but the fourth section is the one that betokens true knowledge (*epistêmê*). This is occupied only by the philosopher, who has escaped from the merely hypothetical knowledge of universals that the mathematician cherishes in his diagrams.[33] The mathematician is still, in a sense, in his cave; conversely, the man delivered from his cave is in the 'eikastic' state of the mathematician until he is able to contemplate the sun. As *pistis* stands to *eikasia*, so *epistêmê* stands to *dianoia*; as the fire casts shadows in the cave, so the sun casts shadows of things above.[34] The *agalmata* of the cave should perhaps correspond to true forms of being, though it may also

---

[31] See Tecusan (1992) on the lubricity of this term in Plato.

[32] For the view that the Good in Plato is not absolute but implicit in the totality of Forms, see Charrue (1978), 256; Gadamer (1986), 29–31; Sedley (1999).

[33] See further Mueller (1992).

[34] On the difficulties of the analysis see, for example, Austin (1979) and Cross and Woozley (1964), Robinson (1984), 180–201, denies that the line and the cave correspond.

be that they represent the counterfeits of these forms in sophistical teaching.[35] Perhaps we ought to say that they are forms of being tenebrously conceived, as there is nothing in the cave that is as real as the contents of the upper world, just as there is nothing in the realm of *pistis* as true as the contents of the noetic realm. *Eikasia* is not the contemplation of real shadows, any more than *mimêsis* in drama is necessarily the imitation of anything that has existed; both signify, rather, the apprehension of things under a false garb.

There is no dramatic mimesis in the similes of the line and the cave; not an articulate word is ascribed to the prisoner or his subterranean neighbours, and the growth of knowledge is limned – we might say, veiled – entirely in pictorial images. If there is no clear explanation of the fire and the *agalmata*, it is equally true that nothing is said to explain what in the real world might enable the soul to turn from shadow to light. In many of Plato's dialogues, however, we encounter a theory of incipient knowledge, which is often at the same time a theory of inherited knowledge. In the *Meno*, Socrates contends that an object cannot be found unless we know where to seek it (80d–e), and he demonstrates by experiment that we attain new knowledge by reasoning on principles which were not communicated to us in the present life and which therefore appear to have been imbibed in a previous existence (81c–86c). In the *Phaedrus*, these foundations are understood to be of a different order from the anecdotal knowledge that we acquire on earth and are said to have been brought down by the soul from its supramundane condition. The instinct that rekindles the soul's perception and inspires her to renew her quest for the higher vision is *eros* or love, and, as the *Lysis* intimates, what we love is necessary to the completion of our being and so, in one sense, already ours (221c–222a). Since, however, *eros* almost always connotes desire, we must set against this reasoning the platitude that one cannot desire what one already has. Hence we arrive at the teaching of the *Symposium* – more properly, the lesson of Diotima to Socrates in the *Symposium* – that Love is neither god nor man, neither beautiful nor ugly, but, according to an improvised myth, the child that was strangely mothered on Plenty by Penury, in inheriting both the emptiness of his mother and her craving for the plenitude of Beauty (202c–203c). Love is, as we have seen, the most accomplished of all artificers in speech, and Diotima styles him a cunning sophist (*deinos sophists*: 203d). Yet, unlike the common sophist, he is frugal, single-hearted and submissive to all privations in the service of his beloved. Barefooted though itinerant, he is, as has often been perceived, a caricature of Socrates.[36] As the real Socrates is said to have stood up so that his face might be compared with the impersonator's mask at a performance of the *Clouds* (Aelian, *Miscellaneous Knowledge* 2.13), so the dramatic character who is called Socrates in the *Symposium* portrays his true self under the mask of love.[37]

---

[35]   For discussion and bibliography, see Wilberding (2004).

[36]   Robin (1964), 161–163.

[37]   On Socrates as the true subject of Plato's philosophy, see Friedländer (1958), 136. One cannot argue that this is true for all the dialogues: Long (1998).

In the light of this argument, Socrates' flirtations with his pupils can be seen to admit of an honourable reading, for it is the stimulation of intelligence by carnal beauty that enables the intellect to transcend the carnal. Again, we can acquit him of hypocrisy when others accuse him of numbing them like a stingray, just as he himself complains that the sophists are taking advantage of him by their long speeches. Their stratagem (as Plato represents it) is to put the mind to sleep by engorging it with false impressions; his is to strike off the manacles that bind it to the cave. He is, for all that, not a teacher but a lover – or, as he says in the *Theaetetus*, the son of a midwife, carrying on his mother's trade by educing knowledge from the pregnant souls of his interlocutors (149a). If the book can be defended, it will be on the grounds that its form puts the reader himself to the question and draws him into the lists; if myth is to be defended, it will be on the grounds that certain truths cannot be conveyed by a magisterial dictum[38] and that the eye of the soul will shed its cataracts only when it becomes aware that all that it sees is an obstacle to vision. As the myths devised by Socrates are figurative accounts of the soul's constitution or its origin, they escape the criticism which he passes on the interpreters of more vulgar tales – that they teach us nothing because they cannot teach us to know ourselves.

It may seem nonetheless that there is too much which requires excuse. Those dialogues which are purely aporetic – coming, that is, to no conclusion or withdrawing such conclusions as have been proposed – may appear to be nothing more than essays in verbal legerdemain; others, like the *Laws*, *Sophist* or *Parmenides*, are so didactic as almost to forget that they are dialogues. The myth of the *Timaeus*, though it pretends to be no more than an *eikos logos*, or likely account (29c), invites no rejoinder and seems to transgress the canons of Socrates by putting a speech into the mouth of the Creator which could not have been overheard by a human scribe. We may fear that this cosmogony is merely a superior exercise in the 'phantastic' art, a 'way of seeming' no more faithful to the truth than its antecedent in *Parmenides*.[39] This is also the dialogue in which Plato speaks with an unequivocal praise of an artisan's copying of the forms, for he makes his god, the Demiurge, create the sensible world with no other motive than the communication of goodness. The universe of coming to be and passing away is inevitably subject to the turbulence and lability of the 'receptacle' which supports it, and we cannot hope that evil will ever be banished from it.[40] Nevertheless, the Demiurge has implanted a divinity in each of us in the form of the 'sovereign part

---

[38] On the incommensurability of myth and *logos*, see Friedländer (1958), 201–207, and Szlezák (1993), 136. McCabe (1992), 59–61, argues for a calculated dissonance between Plato's myths and the arguments to which they are appended.

[39] Against the view that the myth is an approximation to truths that could have been expressed in a more 'scientific' or 'logical' manner see Cornford (1997), 29–32.

[40] On Aristotle's view that this is matter, see Cherniss (1962), 116–129. See also Cherniss (1962), 423–431 on the question as to whether Plato imagined a temporal or an eternal creation.

of the soul' (*Timaeus* 90a), and we are therefore able to strive to 'become like God so far as is possible' in the present life, with the hope of emancipation in the next (*Theaetetus* 176a–c).[41]

At last – though not perhaps within four centuries of his death – admirers of Plato found an expedient to repel both the charge of having too much of a system and the suspicion of having none. Not all his works, they argued, are of a piece.[42] Some are gymnastic, some obstetric, some experimental; some teach by induction, others by disclosure. They must be studied in such an order as to guide us, like the prisoner in the cave, to successive planes of understanding; they embody not so much one system as a common goal. We hear nothing in the Hellenistic and Roman periods of an unwritten doctrine delivered only in the form of lectures;[43] at the same time an apocryphal text declares that Plato himself had written nothing and that the works attributed to him were those of 'Socrates, growing young and fair' (Plato, Letter 2, 314c). What remained was to be perused with a gradual maturation of understanding, to which each text in its turn contributed. In this scheme, no less than in the works of Plato himself, it is clear that sight connotes more than hearing in the metaphorical idiom of philosophy because this is the sense that we exercise or suspend at will. A turn of the head will change our field of vision but not the radius of our hearing; conversely we can shut our eyes more readily, and with greater effect, than we can stop our ears.

Aristotle

Plato's *Republic* speaks of an ancient quarrel between philosophers and poets. In his case it could be said to be a quarrel about the nature and use of memory. The subjects of the poet are impermanent, anecdotal, often trifling and too apt to slip away from memory even when they are worthy of remembrance. So it is with the vulgar objects of perception: they never fully instantiate and never possess for long the qualities that we predicate of them, and are not even perfect representatives of their own natural kinds. Only that which is fully comprehended can be perfectly remembered, and only that which is logically identical with itself and could not be otherwise can be fully comprehended. This is the Form or Idea, which, as the archetype of that which is just or straight or beautiful in the present world, is just or straight or beautiful without blemish, change or ambiguity. It was his unwavering and unmediated vision of the paradigm that enabled the Demiurge to create the physical universe and thus perform the one act of *mimêsis* that cannot be traced to ignorance or bad faith; it is when beauty in this world awakens a recollection of supercelestial beauty that we turn from phantasms to the pursuit of truth. For all that it has come to be regarded as Plato's salient doctrine, however, the

---

[41]   See further Sedley (1999).

[42]   See Albinus, *Isagoge*, with Tarrant (1993), 31–57.

[43]   See Vlastos (1963); Reale (1997).

theory of Forms has never been subjected to such exacting criticism as in his own *Parmenides*. In the hearing of an otherwise obscure philosopher named Aristotle,[44] Socrates is reduced to tongue-tied imbecility by objections that were later to be raised against Platonism, if not against Plato, by the more famous Aristotle. Can a universal be wholly present in each of its particulars? Can it instead be divided among the particulars like a sailcloth? Does the particular resemble the archetype by virtue of something else, of which both are copies? Such arguments, if valid, are timelessly so, and we may suspect that, in coy defiance of his own strictures, this able dramatist has imagined an ancient setting for disputations which were far from imaginary.

Aristotle is no empiricist in the modern sense.[45] The quiddity or essence is, according to him, the true object of perception, and it is only through the mind's union with the essence that we can apprehend the material thing as this particular instance of its species. At the same time, the essence itself cannot be apprehended as a particular: there is no autonomous realm of Forms which we see, as it were, by a parallel mode of vision and without recourse to their instantiations in this world. 'Prime being' (*prôtê ousia*) belongs to the concrete individual, not the species; just as we cannot perceive this without sensory organs, so we cannot think it in absence without an exercise of our image-making capacity, *phantasia*.[46] In philosophic contemplation, the mind discovers its likeness to the gods – we might even say that it reveals its godlike origin[47] – but Aristotle cannot promise the mind an apotheosis that will enable it to put away the phantasm as Socrates bids the mathematicians put away their diagrams. Representation is not a betrayal of knowledge, but the indispensable key to it; on such a view it is possible to agree with Plato in characterizing tragedy as a form of *mimêsis* without subscribing to his disparagement of the mimetic arts.

When Aristotle employs the term he adds that a deed, or *praxis*, is the object of *mimêsis*, and might therefore appear to mean what we should mean by 'imitation' (*Poetics* 1448a1). Yet the action represented, as he well knows, is not simply given to the dramatist, since the latter is free to vary the particulars, and even to change the sequence of events. Moreover, it is unlikely that Aristotle or his Athenian contemporaries believed that a play was always a re-enactment of a historical event. The relation between the *praxis* and the *mimêsis* is not simply that of archetype and image;[48] at times it would be better understood as the relation between the given and the constructed. Aristotle does not share Plato's abhorrence of *mimêsis*, though he does not regard all illusion as deceit, and, if he is looking

---

[44]   As Fine (1995), 39, observes, he is one of the Thirty Tyrants at *Parmenides* 127d, and hence cannot be the more celebrated Aristotle.

[45]   Owen (1965).

[46]   Frede (1992).

[47]   See *On the Soul* 430a22–24 with Robinson (1991). Note the comparison to a blank writing tablet at 430a1.

[48]   Ricoeur (1977), 37–43.

for truth in drama, this consists in something other than a sincere expression of the actor's sentiments. It is not even what we call truth to the facts, and another of his aphorisms – that poetry is superior to history because it represents the universal, not the particular (*Poetics* 1451b4–7) – suggests that the poet's task is not to be limited, as Homer and Plato both contend, to the faithful republication of past events.

The poet Simonides of Ceos is credited with the dictum that 'a poem is a speaking picture, a picture a silent poem'.[49] Plato admits this symmetry insofar as he considers both arts equally meretricious. Aristotle sometimes prepares the reader for a comparison of poets by citing analogous differences among the painters: in both spheres there are some who excel in the representation of character and some who neglect it, some who make their subjects better and some who make them worse than their living prototypes. In his *Rhetoric* – which avowedly takes as the object of inquiry not the true, but that which is *pithanon*, or worthy to persuade (1355b15–27) – he regards it as a virtue in the orator to bring his topics before the imagination with the immediacy of vision. His term for this desirable property is *enargeia*,[50] which in English we render as 'clarity' or brilliance' (1410b33–35), though in Aristotle its sense appears to be tinged at times by that of *energeia*, a cardinal term in his ontology, which signifies either the exercise of a characteristic power by an agent or the proper form that is realized in the agent by the conversion of power into actuality.

Stoics and Epicureans

There was no franchise for incorporeal being in the economy of the great Hellenistic schools.[51] The Epicureans believed that all our sensory impressions are veridical, that the earth is as flat as it seems and the sun no greater in diameter than the eye guesses.[52] We believe that the gods exist because they are seen in dreams and their lineaments are preserved in statues; this would not be possible if they were not composed of atoms as we are or if they did not throw off a tenuous simulacrum which, like those of the other bodies, stimulates our receptive organs by infusion. Poetry, which counterfeits things that never were or dresses real events in a fanciful motley, was despised by Epicurus as an abuse of the philosopher's patrimony; turning Homer against himself, he urged his disciples to shun it 'like the sirens'.[53] Epicureans of a more liberal temper were prepared to countenance it insofar as it offered pleasure to its readers and disarmed them of false objectives. The epigrams of Philodemus achieve at least the first of these

---

[49]   Plutarch, *Glory of Athens* 346f. Cf. Aristotle, *Poetics* 1450b1.

[50]   See further Zanker (1981).

[51]   Watson (1966), 38–42.

[52]   Taylor (1980).

[53]   See Plutarch, *On Hearing the Poets* 15b, with Kaiser (1964).

two goals and both were underwritten by genius in the six books of Lucretius' *On the Nature of Things*.[54] The emollients of verse allowed Lucretius to administer philosophy by stealth, and his prayer that the goddess Venus will interpose – in defiance of Epicurean principles – to save Rome from intestine discord suggests that his real Muse was the Venus or beguiling artistry of his own composition (*Nature of Things* 1.1–20). Nevertheless, the Epicureans offered no philosophical rejoinder to Plato's assault on the arts, preferring instead to tax him with a betrayal of his professed convictions in his use of myth.

The Stoics, while they agreed that our everyday senses are the only ports of knowledge, did not hold that they can always be trusted without interpretation. It is the hermeneutic faculty that makes a significant image of the visual phenomenon; and this is true *par excellence* when the mind is required to decode the symbolic figures that are devised for the communication of knowledge and thought by other human beings.[55] The Stoics reckoned speech as one of the senses, together with the procreative and hegemonic faculties. The last is the one that humans alone possess, and it is by virtue of this immanent rationality (*endiathetos logos*) that we are able to give a name to what we perceive and to enunciate that name in a form that is more distinct than the mere *prophorikos logos*, or vocalic utterance, that is vouchsafed to animals. *Katalêpsis*, or comprehension, as distinct from mere sensation, is, in common life, the perception of the phenomenon as an instance of a particular type; in the understanding of human speech, *katalêpsis* is the recognition of a particular vocable as a 'signifier' (*sêmainôn*). Its logical counterpart, the *sêmainomenon*, is one of those 'somethings' to which one cannot deny reality, though it does not possess existence in the proper sense, which is predicable only of corporeal entities.

Since existence can be ascribed to the *endiathetos logos*, it is not a strictly incorporeal subject, but a portion of that divine *logos* which, in the form a tenuous fire, pervades and regulates the physical universe. This is the god to whom mythology gives the name of Zeus; the very positing of this cosmic *logos* is thus an act of *allegorêsis* – that is, the discernment of a more edifying sense behind the apparent meaning of linguistic signs.[56] It is by the divine within that we know the gods; the *endiathetos logos* is the torch that illuminates their arcane disclosures. One example of its exercise is divination; another is decipherment of sacred images, as Chrysippus showed in his decorous reading of an icon which depicted Zeus and Hera in the act of sexual congress.[57] Here we observe an extension of the principle that the mind has the power to improve upon sensation by *katalêpsis*, which was to serve the Stoics as a palliative to the immoralities and absurdities of hallowed texts. When we read in the *Iliad* that Athena restrained Achilles by the hair, explains a certain Heraclitus, the episode will not seem so grotesque if

---

[54]   Asmis (1991); Clay (1983), 202–266.

[55]   Long and Sedley (1987), 238–253.

[56]   Long (1996), 58–84; Imbert (1980).

[57]   Diogenes Laertius, *Lives* 7.187–188, with Imbert (1980), 202–203.

we understand it as an allegory of the curbing of passion by reason (*Homeric Allegories* 17–20); Proteus, the Old Man of the Sea, who can change his form at will, is not a monster idly imagined but a symbol of the ductility of matter (65). When Hermes gives Odysseus a plant that will shield him from the enchantments of his hostess Circe, our *endiathetos logos* sees in this a parabolic illustration of its own work in the quickening of the senses. The process of decipherment is hidden in the cipher, for it is only by its own act that the activity of reason is construed.

We see an anticipation of Stoic practice in a fragmentary papyrus, which was discovered in 1962 at Derveni in Macedonia.[58] The greater part of what remains is a commentary on an Orphic poem which, in praising Zeus, also attributes to him a number of temerities. The commentator equates Zeus with the mind that contains all things and from which they issue; by marrying the procreative and hegemonic faculties of this mind, he can give an anodyne interpretation to every sexual act described in the poem, not excluding the rape of Demeter. Whatever his philosophy, his chief tool is etymology – not a new device, as the mystagogue Euthyphro had already employed it in the fifth century BC, and the notion that some natural bond between word and world is revealed by the inspection of the 'legislator's' purpose had been treated with some levity in the *Cratylus* of Plato (for example, 399a). Nevertheless, etymology had not hitherto been such a fertile instrument as it became in the hands of the Stoics who, in the absence of any scientific method, found a synonym in any term that shared a few characters with the name of a deity. In the *Handbook* of Cornutus,[59] allegory is not merely a polysemic operation but a transitive one, in which the object which, under one interpretation, is denoted by the appellative becomes in its turn a symbol with a loftier and less tangible denotation. Apollo, for example, may personify the sun because one cognate of his name is *apollumi* ('I destroy') and the heat of the sun brings drought and pestilence; again, however, his name may connote the state of being 'strange to the many' (*a-pollôn*), which permits an identification with the sun only insofar as this is an emblem of transcendence (*Handbook* 32). Although the Stoic successors of Cornutus and the Derveni commentator are unknown to us, we shall find their epigoni among both Platonists and Christians. It was not under Plato's guidance – not at least according to any explicit precept in his writings – that they learned to regard the Greek language as a mine of truth, to engage in polysemic and incremental exegeses of a single text or to look in that text for a mirror to the operation of the reader's mind.

Afterword

In a classical city like Athens every thoroughfare was populated by images of the gods. It may be that their very ubiquity rendered them inconspicuous – less

---

[58]   Funghi (1997); Jourdain (2003).
[59]   See further Most (1989).

conspicuous in all surviving literature than the text itself, which as a written artefact was useful only to those who could read and had the means of obtaining it either by purchase or by favour of the author. All classical writers prize the word more highly than the image, though, with the exception of Plato, they do not set the word against the image as often as they set it above the image as an authoritative repository of meaning. At the same time, they were conscious, as heirs to Hesiod and Homer, that speech can be used not only to inform but to deceive, and it was not to be expected that in their polycephalic culture any one *logos* – any one argument, discourse or narrative, written or oral – would turn the scale against all the rest. Plato feared the mimetic power of words, as he despised that of the image; to counteract the fusion of verbal and visual imposture in civic drama, he fashioned Socrates as a living image of truth, whose tongue is a solvent to the illusions cherished or propagated by his interlocutors. He could not persuade Aristotle to shun the theatre or the Stoics to forgo the interpretation of statues; to Christians, too, he was only the greatest of the philosophers, not the only one. There is evidence that some Christians availed themselves of Stoic logic and semantics;[60] they were not to be cowed by Plato's fulminations against the book, or against the application of hermeneutic casuistry to dead authors, when he himself owed his survival in the Roman age to those alphabetic characters whose invention he affected to deplore.

---

[60]   Robertson (2008), 41–43; Rist (1981).

Chapter 4

Philosophers and Sophists of the Early Roman Era

We have seen that when he has to speak of that which truly is, of the reality that stands behind the phenomenon, Plato uses optical metaphors, notwithstanding his contempt for the trumpery of the visual arts. The quest for truth is a turning of the eye of the soul, the release of the mind from its cave to an upper region, where it passes from conjecture to opinion, from opinion to knowledge, and at last to the contemplation of the Good, whose rays have secretly illumined every stage of the ascent. The way lies open only to those who are willing to submit their beliefs to the cross-examination of a teacher who has already reached the end of it; those who prefer the shorter route to ignorance will lend their ears to the minstrelsy of the sophist or embrace the book as a proxy for the author. In the present chapter we shall consider one apologist for the book and a series of tributes to the representative power of the plastic arts, but we shall not discover that either of these positions is held in wanton defiance of Platonic teaching. Philo ascribes unqualified authority only to one book, which he reads, or rather hears, as a continuing exhortation to turn away from the phenomenon to its suprasensible origin, to look within for that which lies above. On the other hand, the defenders of cultic images maintain with all the vehemence of Plato that the human mind is no more capable than the human hand of framing a true facsimile of the divine. According to Dio, Maximus and Philostratus, we accept the imperfect sketches of both painter and poet because we are all too conscious that there is no such thing as an adequate portrait of the archetype.

Philo on Divine and Human Images

Philo is counted among the middle Platonists[1] – he is indeed the author of more than half the extant writings which fall under this description – but he was also a Jew and a sedulously observant one, the legatee of a wisdom centuries older than the oldest traditions of Greece. Commentaries on the first five books of the Septuagint make up the greater part of his work, and the few surviving texts that are not exegetic are celebrations of peculiarly austere modes of discipleship or vindications of the

---

[1]   See Runia (1995) on ancient nomenclature.

Jewish people in the teeth of oppression and mockery.[2] 'Platonist' is therefore not the best term for him if a Platonist is one who professes to navigate by reason alone with Plato as his lodestar. On the other hand, it seems to the modern scholar that he is not properly an interpreter, since he does not attempt to ascertain what the text may have meant for its author or its first audience, but knows already what he hopes to elicit from it and achieves his end by the application of hermeneutic principles derived from other sources. He himself would have answered that the application is its own apology, because the sense that he finds in the text is frequently an endorsement or illustration of his hermeneutic method. The text, that is, will teach us how it ought to be read so long as we know how to read it – that is, so long as our exposition has been conducted according to precepts which we know in advance to be latent in the text.[3]

Can we redeem this method from the all too obvious charge of circularity? This may not be impossible, so long as we grant at the outset (as most contemporaries of Philo would) that antiquity is a sovereign test of authority in matters of religion. It was a commonplace among Romans that the *mos maiorum*, the way of the fathers, offers us a likelier route to knowledge about the gods than could be opened by the exertions of any latter-day philosophy;[4] Plato and Epicurus might demur, but their own conjectures had become immutable dogmas to their followers, so that, to many, the interpretation of a canonical text had become synonymous with the discovery of truth. The antiquity of Moses, and of the nation that he was said to have led out of Egypt, were not universally admitted, but persuasive calculations could be employed so long as no one could refute the veracity or the authenticity of the narratives that Jewish tradition ascribed to Moses himself.[5]

According to this narrative, moreover, it is not only the date of Moses that gives him a claim to belief: he is said to have performed miracles that no sorcerer could imitate, to have received the Law directly from God, to have contemplated the tabernacle in heaven before he framed it on earth, to have witnessed a manifestation of divine glory that was not vouchsafed to any other prophet, and to have been translated after his death to a place of which we hear only that no one knows it to this day. Such a man could not fail to know whatever we ourselves have found to be true by deliberation and experience: since, therefore, we know by introspection and not only by authority that the mind is a loftier faculty than the senses, we may be equally sure that even in scriptural passages which appear to be exclusively concerned with the outward and palpable there will always be a lesson addressed to the intellect. The intellect fathoms this lesson by the exercise of the same faculty that enables it to discern the immutable form behind the transient particular and thus to embrace in one act of understanding the disparate bulletins

---

[2]   See especially *Against Flaccus, Embassy to Caligula* and *On the Contemplative Life*.

[3]   On Philo's scholarship see Kamesar (2009).

[4]   See Cicero, *On the Nature of the Gods*, Book 3; Minucius Felix, *Octavius*.

[5]   See further Droge (1989), 12–48.

that it receives from the outer world. By permitting the idiomatic substitution of *ti*, or 'what' for *dia ti* or 'wherefore', the Greek tongue shows us that to comprehend the essence of a thing we must know why it is as it is (*Allegory* 2.16): the same maxim, when we bring it to a text in which no word can be used in vain, will forbid us to suppose that any choice between cognate terms is arbitrary, any pleonasm redundant, any etymologizing in Greek or Hebrew inconsequential. Since intellect is the organ of moral discernment and not only of conceptual refinement, the deep sense of the scriptures will be invisible even to those who dissect them with the best tools of scholarship if they have not also cultivated the holiness that the Law enjoins. Holiness is achieved by the contemplation of the holy in obedience; the scripture is both an instrument and an object of contemplation, but it points beyond itself to a higher blessing, which enlarges our understanding of the text and gives authority to all that has been correctly understood. The reward that awaits the saint is nothing less than the vision of God himself, not perhaps as he disclosed himself to Moses but in a measure and manner proportioned to the capacities of the soul.

Our twofold nature is symbolized in the opening verses of Genesis by the creation of heaven and earth (Genesis 1.2). Heaven in Philo's glossary stands for mind and earth for sensation (*Allegory* 1.9.21). This key will explain why the narrative records two successive creations of humanity; the efficacy of the key is proved, conversely, by its success in unlocking the narrative. At Genesis 1.26–28 God proposes to create humanity in his image and likeness; since, however, reason informs us that God has neither body nor parts, even this most godlike of his creatures cannot resemble him in any corporeal property, and his image must reside only in intellect (*Creation of the World* 23.69). The body is merely a statue which the soul carries about the world like an indefatigable athlete (*Allegory* 3.22.70); the wings of love, however, give the intellect power to rise from the contemplation of the heavens and the symphonic counterplay of the natural elements to the models and ideas of which things here are the merest shadows (*Creation* 23.70). Thence we may ascend, by a sort of Corybantic ecstasy,[6] beyond the bounds of mind itself until our highest faculties are dazzled by the pure and unmingled radiance of the King (*Creation* 23.72). This evocation of the pagan mysteries (or, to be more precise, of Plato's reading of them) is soon followed by Greek testimonies to the mystical properties of the number seven (*Creation* 30.9–137.110).[7] At the same time, we are warned that the seventh day which crowns the labours of the first six is not to be measured in hours, as God does nothing by stages and the bodies by whose revolutions time is measured had not yet been created (*Allegory* 1.8.20). Philo completes his salvo against the anthropomorphic reading of Genesis 1 by appealing to a peculiarity of Hebrew accidence: the Greek words that mean 'God rested' represent a causative verb in the original, which implied not that he suspended his timeless activity, but that he grants rest to his creatures at intervals marked out by the planets (*Allegory* 1.3.5–10).

---

6   Also a 'sober drunkenness': Lewy (1929), 73–107.

7   See further Staehle (1931).

The man who is fashioned from earth at Genesis 2.4 is inferior to the sexless and incorporeal man created by divine fiat. Endowed with every virtue that pertains to his condition, he remains inert until he is quickened by the breath of God, which we are not to mistake for the Spirit that moved upon the primordial waters. Eden is a map of the soul, the four rivers symbolizing the cardinal virtues, while the statement that it had not yet rained implies that mind had not yet animated the lower faculties (*Allegorical Interpretation* 1.63–73). Because the male in the human pair is rational and active, the female sensuous and passive, the shaping of Eve from Adam's rib betokens the creation of a carnal sphere to be governed by the intellect (*Allegory* 2.19; cf. *Creation of World* 151). The surrender of intellect to the undisciplined appetites and dispersed perceptions of this lower self is the eating from the tree of knowledge, which must have stood outside the garden (that is, outside the domain of soul) because the first humans were permitted to eat of every tree within it. Adam's attempt to hide from God in the middle of the garden is the subterfuge of a guilty mind which imagines that it can act as its own foundation and forgets that it owes its origin to God (*Allegory* 3.48). Adam's apostasy is to be contrasted with the unwavering servitude of the mind to God in the life of Moses and with Jacob's flight from Esau, which exemplifies the judicious retreat of mind from vices that it cannot subdue (*Allegory* 3.18*)

The Fall entails an opening of the bodily eyes, which occludes the light of the intellectual world. Thus a deep sleep must fall upon Adam before the creation of Eve, who, as we have seen, personifies the seductive contiguity of the physical realm (*Allegory* 2.26–29). Quite a different cause is assigned, however, to the 'horror of great darkness' (Genesis 15.12) in which Abraham sees the Lord passing between the elements of his sacrifice in order to seal an everlasting covenant with his seed (*Heir of Divine Things* 249–259). In the oblation the birds remain undivided by divine command, as witnesses to the indivisibility of intellect (*Heir* 230); yet the God who surpasses all that words can express or thought conceive cannot be known until the familiar workings of the intellect give way to subtler and less discursive motions. God himself initiates the sacrifice by calling Abraham out of his tent or, as the Greek text has it, 'out-led him out' – no careless dittography in Philo's view, but an emphatic rebuke to those who believe that the mind's quotidian powers will suffice for the knowledge of God (*Heir* 81–85 on Genesis 15.5). Among these Philo may, for all we know, have reckoned the Platonists, for no member of this school had yet thrown such a penumbra of negatives round the deity, denying him every predicable attribute and proclaiming that we cannot say anything true about Him Who Is except by rehearsing what he is not.[8]

The intellect or *nous* is our organ of intercourse with God, being, as it were, a fragment of the Deity housed in flesh (*Dreams* 1.6.34). And as the emancipation of *nous* is the bondage of the senses, it is no surprise that God should speak most

---

[8]   None of the parallels adduced by Dillon (1990) would appear to be indubitably older than Philo: see further Runia (2010). On rabbinic parallels to Philo's exegesis of Exodus 3.14, see Starobinski-Safran (1978).

plainly to us in dreams. Of these there are three varieties, the clear, the enigmatic and an intermediate class which is not entirely clear but lends itself readily to interpretation (*Dreams* 2.1). Into the first and most perspicuous class fall the direct annunciations that are received by Abraham more as words than as visions, and occasionally in darkness. Typical of the enigmatic class are the dreams that Joseph enjoys or expounds for others, lucid enough to the senses but, for that very reason, dark to the soul that is conscious of no other medium than the senses. Such communications proceed from earth (*Dreams* 2.16.110) and show a man nothing but his own fortunes (2.23.158); the interpretation of them is vouchsafed to Joseph because, as his coat of many colours foretells, he is a man of craft and policy, not without virtue but too rich in guile to prosper in contemplation (*Dreams* 1.39.224; 2.6.42–47). His father Jacob, by contrast, though he is not a perfect sage, is the exemplar of practical virtue, and his vision of angels ascending and descending on a ladder from earth to heaven is a specimen of the intermediate class, in which the presence of the divine is unmistakable, though there is no direct encounter with God himself.

When he comes to a place named Charran – the name of which signifies, according to Philo, the porosity of the sensory envelope that acts as a citadel to the mind – the sun is setting, as though to intimate that God has withdrawn his own beams and is enlightening the soul through the instrumentality of his *logoi* and his angels (*Dreams* 1.8.41; 1.11.69; 1.13.72–87). Even when poaching a simile from Plato, the Jewish philosopher is at pains to remind his readers that the scripture is better acquainted with these angels than the Greeks, who style them daemons (1.22.141). He is more Jew than Greek when he argues 'place' functions not only toponymically, but also as an allegorical designation for God himself, as the one who encompasses the whole creation, or for that Logos,[9] replete with his incorporeal powers, which God prepares as a place of access for his worshippers (1.11.62). This Logos – Philo prefers to employ the singular, like the rabbis when they spoke of the *dabar* or *memra* of God – is the image that God has impressed upon the entire creation (*Dreams* 1.7.46); it is also the archetype of this creation, not, as in Plato, an extrinsic model which the Creator is bound to imitate, but the offspring of his own wisdom.[10] It can also be personified as a being distinct from God himself, a Son of God, or even a second deity – though, as Philo insists, there is properly only one God and the divinity that we encounter in emanations and hypostases of this One is *theos* only in a 'catachrestic' or abusive sense (*Dreams* 1.39.229); the locution 'second god' is not an accommodation to polytheism but a prophylactic against false notions of the true God as a being of finite properties who can inhabit his own creation (cf. *Dreams* 1.50.233–236). It is as a representative of God that the Logos is styled a high priest – a title denoting one who is more than man because he stands for us in the place of holiness (1.29.188–189). This is the language used of Christ in Christian scriptures written perhaps a generation after

---

[9]   Discussed as an element of his Platonism by Dillon (1977), 155–164.

[10]   See further Runia (1999); Radice (2009).

Philo's death; there is, however, no incarnation in Philo, though the same Wisdom that mothers the Logos (2.35.240–241) is also the parent of the 'self-taught' lovers of God who are typified in Isaac (*Change of Names* 24.137). No human is identical with the Logos, but it is the garment given by God to all rational creatures as a defence against shame and as a medicine to the passions of the soul (*Dreams* 1.17.106–18.11).

Philo is perhaps the first Greek writer who, instead of contrasting the *logos endiathetos* or intellect in humans with the *logos prophorikos* or mere clamour of brutes,[11] maintains that both are present in rational utterance, one as the source and one as the stream (*Moses* 2.25.127; *On Drunkenness* 16.70). Mind is personified by Moses, speech by his brother Aaron (*Migration of Abraham* 14.77–15.81). It is Moses who studies the archetype according to which the tabernacle is fashioned, but it is Aaron who acts as hierophant to Israel (*Drunkenness* 32.128). As the author of the infallible scriptures, in which God proclaims his own ubiquity and immutability (*Dreams* 2.32.221–222), Moses rightly compares the Logos of God to a book in which all that comes to pass is chronicled already (*Allegory* 1.8.20). Allegory is the architect who enables us to raise our own edifice of interpretation (*Dreams* 2.2.8), and those who understand her laws will perceive in Hagar, the bondwoman of Abraham, an emblem of Gentile learning, which is serviceable only to those who remain content with common or encyclopaedic knowledge; the knowledge of God is represented by Sarah, the legitimate spouse of Abraham, who is literally the mother of the chosen people and figuratively the wisdom to which all righteousness and godliness in humans owes its birth. It is by virtue of the mind's capacity for the knowledge of eternal forms that we can be said to be in the image and likeness of God (*Creation of the World* 23.69–72); the flight that ends in Corybantic ecstasy (*Creation* 1.71) commences with our choosing to live according to the word which teaches everything in season (*Dreams* 1.11.68). The disfigurement of the image, the betrayal of reason within and of the word without, is idolatry, the devotion to lifeless effigies of non-existent beings. The commandment forbidding such worship is, of course, to be taken literally, though the fact that pagan statues are often sculpted from precious metals authorizes a second reading of this ordinance as a prohibition of avarice and the pursuit of those worldly phantoms which the sage perceives to be nothing but images in a vapid mirror (*Special Laws* 1.4.21–24). Idolatry is at the root of polytheism (*On Drunkenness* 28.110), and its vanity is proved by the fact that image-worshipping nations do not deify the sculptors but allow them to die in obscurity and want (*Decalogue* 14.70).

If the human being, as the image of God, is his surrogate in the exercise of sovereignty, there was never a man in whom this image was realized more consummately than in Moses (*Moses* 2.12.65). Philo, who believed in the pre-existence of souls (*Giants* 2.6–3.12), is not afraid to surmise that he acquired the liberal arts by *anamnesis* or recollection, rather than by the offices of his tutors,

---

[11]   Sextus Empiricus, *Against the Mathematicians* 8.275.

to whom he nonetheless grants proficiency in the use of hieroglyphic symbolism (*Moses* 1.5.21–23). Temperance and courage, too, were indigenous virtues to him (1.6.25), and such was his mastery of the passions that others saw him as a shrine within which mind was set up as a godlike image (1.5.27). Here Philo adapts a simile from the *Phaedrus*, anticipating Plotinus and Gregory of Nyssa; his Moses, however, does not share the reluctance to serve his inferiors which Plato thinks so natural in the man who has been delivered from the Cave. Instead, when forced into exile for the justifiable killing of an oppressor, he becomes a shepherd, a life which Philo commends to all earthly monarchs in a tacit animadversion on Plato's dictum that society will never thrive until kings become philosophers (1.11.60). When he takes up this apophthegm in Book 2 of the *Life of Moses*, Philo declares that Moses was the one man who combined the role of king with those of legislator and prophet (2.1.2–7). As a direct recipient of the divine command, he was able to propound a system of law so comprehensive and harmonious that it exhibits the 'image and likeness' of the whole cosmos (2.9.51). Under the divine ordinance again he caused a tent or tabernacle to be constructed after the pattern of a heavenly archetype (2.15.75), in which the holy of holies rested within five pillars as an emblem of the invisible mind ensconced within the five senses (2.16.81) and the seven planets were represented by the seven lights of the candelabrum (2.21.103). The two cherubs which support the tabernacle stand respectively for the goodness and the sovereignty of God (2.20.99) – a forking of powers that Philo professes to have been shown by inspiration (*Cherubim* 9.27–30). The stones on the high priest's breastplate stand for the 12 signs of the zodiac, the two pomegranates at the hem of his robe for earth and water, the emeralds on his shoulder-blades for the sun and moon, the inscribed Tetragrammaton for the progression from point to line, from line to plane and from plane to solid (*Moses* 2.23.115).

Moses receives his mandate as a prophet in his encounter with the burning bush, which Philo, as his scholiast, interprets as a parable of the tribulation of Israel (*Moses* 1.12.67). In the midst of it, says Philo, stood a brilliant form, an image of the living God, which is described as an angel (or messenger of God) because the silence in which Moses beheld this vision was more distinct than any utterance (1.12.66). When speech succeeds this epiphany, God's commission is perfectly intelligible to Moses, as is his disclosure that he is the God who spoke to Abraham, Isaac and Moses (1.14.72–76). Light is thus the harbinger of a revelation that remains incomplete without the word that perfects understanding and compels obedience. When God addresses Moses on Sinai at Exodus 20.18 the difficult text implies to Philo that the voice was so clear to the populace that they were said not so much to hear as to behold it (*Decalogue* 11.46). What is certainly seen, according to the Hebrew, is a fire enshrouded in smoke: Philo deduces that, as it is the property of fire both to illumine and to burn, there are certain hearers of the Law to whom it shines as a perpetual light and others feel it as a devouring flame (11.49). Philo adds a third branch to this dichotomy at *Giants* 13.60–61, where the sons of God in Genesis 6.1 are equated with priests and prophets, the sons of heaven with adepts of encyclopaedic learning and the giants with votaries of carnal pleasure. It is in the sons of God that *logos* or reason plays the role of high-priest, honouring God at all times and occasionally 'entering into the darkness' where it performs the most sacred mysteries (*Giants* 12.55). While, therefore, there is a darkness that occludes the dazzling beams of God in vicious and ignorant souls, there is darkness of another kind (as we saw in the case of Abraham) which is a medium of transcendent knowledge to the eye within.

This eye, according to Philo, should never be closed (*Migration of Abraham* 39.222). It is true that even a Moses cannot gaze upon the unveiled majesty of God, in the way in which Plato expected his philosopher to become inured to the radiance of the intellectual sun (*Flight and Finding* 29.165); for this reason it is true again that the Word of God in scripture holds a place in Philo's pedagogic scheme that Plato could never have accorded to a book, and that every vision or occultation of vision that the scriptures record is crowned by some divine utterance. For all that, Philo cannot be said to evince a simple preference for hearing; on the contrary, he exhorts us not to confuse God's Word with a 'beating of the air' (*Immutability of God* 18.83). To hear wrongly is to see wrongly: only the ignorant will dwell on the tenebrous surface of the scriptures, making no attempt to disinter the true sense from the picturesque figure (*Migration of Abraham* 2.12; *Immutability* 13.60). In his own experience of inspiration, an invisible shower of ideas is succeeded by an 'enjoyment of light' which accompanies 'richness of interpretation' (*Migration* 7.35). This is not to say that speech is lost in sight, but that, in order to distinguish the voice of God from the dense vibrations of the air that pass for speech among us, we must liken our inward perception of it to the exercise of our most discerning sense, as though the Word, though strictly invisible, were not so much heard as seen (*Migration* 9.48–52).

The Second Sophistic

Plato presents the sophist as a caricature of philosophy, a siren whose artful cadences purvey no more truth than the moribund compositions of the painter. The sophists of the Roman era readily accepted that, whatever rhetoric is, it is not philosophy. If some were also occasional philosophers – as Plato had been more than an occasional rhetorician – they did not disavow the comparison with the artist, and the description of pictures, real or imaginary,[12] became a recognized text of eloquence. So, too, did the apology for the depiction of gods in sculpture, which enabled Dio, Maximus and Philostratus to flaunt the superiority of the pen while ostensibly putting it at the service of the chisel. Whether or not they knew anything of Christian jeremiads against idolatry, they followed the contemporary rule of avoiding reference to contemporaries, and took for their whetstone the most illustrious of ancient essays in the representation of Zeus.

---

[12]   See Beall (1993).

Dio Chrysostom

Dio Chrysostom's twelfth oration, purportedly delivered at Olympia, begins with an eloquent protestation of his own incapacities as a speaker before electing as his theme the praise of 'the god in whose presence we are' – that is, of Zeus, whose statue had been the boast of the city since Phidias sculpted it in the fifth century BC. Poetic depictions of Zeus are adduced from Hesiod and Homer (*Oration* 12.24–26), though, as Dio goes on to urge, the universal *epinoia* or impression of the divine (27) is implanted in us (39) not by the poets, but by the harmonious revolution of the heavens (28) and the maternal prodigality of the earth, which is so delicately tempered to our needs by the passage of seasons and the interplay of the elements that barbarians and Greeks alike have extolled it in their mysteries (28–33). What we know of the gods by nature is reinforced among the Greeks by the exhortations of the poets and the injunctions of the law (42–43), and we may add to these three the 'plastic and demiurgic' imitation of divine workmanship in images and statues of the gods. Concerning the last, however, a doubt arises: if all who came before Phidias were nameless and inconsequential figures (53), was it that cities like Sparta and Elis lacked artisans of his talent or rather that they found no use for them (54)? The answer is entrusted to the sculptor, who is credited by Dio with a facility in speech that he does not claim for himself (55).

In his apology Phidias confesses that the sculptor makes use of intransigent materials, whereas those of the poet are infinitely ductile and can be enlarged at any time by neologism and variation of metre (71–72). The hyperboles which come easily to verse cannot be translated into stone; the barbarian sculptor, who has no model in poetry, may hope to excel his peers in the solemnity and magnificence of his creations, but the gods communicate a loftier notion of their powers in the fashioning of the sun and moon than he can emulate in his zoomorphic figures (58–60). In Homer the Greeks have a wizard whose enchantments produce *ekplexis* or stupefaction in the audience (67), pouring out a multitude of words in a single act of imagination (*epinoia*) to deposit in us the *phantasma* of impression of his own conceit (70). His countrymen, who have come to the art of sculpture in his footsteps, can assume the poet's liberty of conferring visible features on the invisible. Iconographic conventions will enable him to represent the gravity, the benevolence and the munificence which are betokened by various epithets of Zeus (77–78); the refulgence of his lightning and the might with which he shakes the earth, on the other hand, are prerogatives which the human demiurge cannot steal from the father and king of the gods (75), although the former is allowed to make use of the *hulê* or substrate from which the latter has fashioned the visible cosmos (81). So the speech ends, and Phidias is crowned with the laurel commonly awarded (as Dio's readers knew) to poets and victors in athletic contests. In his own person Dio now takes leave of the reader by praising his putative audience, the citizens of Olympia, for their pious celebration of the games and other ceremonies which have made them peculiar favourites of the gods.

In this oration we hear two speakers, each of whom could be said to have fashioned the other by his rhetoric. Dio, who provides the frame, admits to eloquence only when he assumes the voice of Phidias; the latter's declamation, however, has no existence outside the text created by the sophist, and even as he claims the honours due to his own profession, he concedes the superiority of the poet. In the fictitious vindication Phidias contrasts himself, in his more familiar role as the prince of sculptors, with the recognized exemplar of sublimity in verse; no vivid impression of either is conveyed, perhaps because it was Dio's intention to expose the inability of rhetoric to illustrate, let alone to emulate, the highest effects of poetry and the plastic arts. To excel in any discipline is to know its limitations: the more perceptive a critic is, the more conscious he will be that he is clipping the wings of Homer by his quotations and that no eye can grasp what he paints in words as vividly as it perceives the work of the sculptor or artist. It was, after all, to the craftsmanship of Phidias, not the compliments of a passing sophist, that the statue owed its celebrity; if those who came to admire it were also able to attend the games, they witnessed a succession of mobile images, a fusion of the sensuous and the linear, that could not be achieved by brush or pen alone.

Other works by Dio play off the muteness of the artefact against its durability. He chides the people of Rhodes for their custom of superimposing new names on the statues of past dignitaries (*Oration* 31.152–157) – a practice that indirectly glorifies his own profession, as it reminds us that we owe our fame to words and not to the stuff on which we inscribe them. On the other hand, when he undertakes to correct the lies of Homer in his *Troicus*, he appeals to an older narrative, inscribed at the behest of Menelaus on steles, some of which survive while local memory compensates for the loss of others (*Oration* 11.37). We are to understand, no doubt, that this account retains its pristine form precisely because it was not as ductile to the fancy as the spoken word or a text preserved in a perishable medium. The mendacity of Homer was, as Dio notes, already a familiar theme in poetry, and was later to be spun into entire books by Philostratus, Dictys Cretensis and Dares Phrygius. Of all these authors, Dio is the one who admits most freely that he has usurped the poet's freedom to invent his own subject-matter, though he urges that his fictions are more becoming to the dignity of a heroic age than are those of his predecessor (11.150–154). Thus, the immutable archetype proves after all to be the creation of its supposed amanuensis: the chisel is at the service of the tongue – or, if you will, of the pen which simulates the cadence of the tongue.

Maximus of Tyre

An essay by a younger sophist, Maximus of Tyre, has the title *Whether it is right to fashion images of the Gods*.[13] Maximus is not so much a Platonist as a rhetorician with a fondness for Platonic tropes. His question is not expressly raised in the dialogues of Plato, though it follows inescapably from his strictures on the futility

---

[13]   For commentary see Trapp (1997), 15–24.

of *mimêsis*, since the sculptor of gods cannot even hope, like the painter of beds, to produce a deceptive copy of the original. How can the marble likeness of a man convey the majesty of God, who, as Maximus writes with trite conviction, is 'father and demiurge of all, Older than the sun, older than the firmament, superior to time and age and all labile nature' (*Oration* 2.10)? His answer is also commonplace: images may be useless to the few who are able to contemplate the gods with the eye of the mind alone, but the imagination of the untutored majority must be assisted by some palpable representation (2.2). And what could this be but the image of that body which is most suited to the operations of the noblest soul, erect in bearing, stately but mobile in proportions, august but not intimidating (2.3)? He concludes with the observation that it is not only in the plastic arts that the truth about the invisible God is accommodated to our mortal senses, but in all that we write and even in the natural creation:

> God, who is the father and demiurge of that which is, older than the sun, older than the heaven, superior to time and eternity and to the flux of nature, cannot be named by a lawgiver, expressed in sounds or perceived with the eyes. Unable as we are, then, to apprehend him as he is, we rely on sounds and names and living creatures, on figments of gold and ivory and silver, on plants and rivers, peaks and streams. We yearn for knowledge of him, but in our weakness we give the name that befits his nature to the beautiful things with which we are acquainted. (*Oration* 2.10a)

'God' here is a synonym for the Demiurge, whom Maximus seems to regard as the highest divinity. The writer's advantage is not that he can produce a more faithful counterfeit, but that he can provide a rationale for the use of either medium while confessing the inadequacy of both. In another dissertation, *Whether the Poets or the Philosophers speak better about the Gods*,[14] he argues that the two disciplines teach the same matter with equal profit, though they are tempered to different ages of society. The philosopher, coming later and addressing riper ears, can say in unvarnished words what the poet imparted in nursery-tales and ciphers to a simple generation (4.3c). The use of verse, like the decoration of altars in precious metals, lends solemnity to truths that might be despised if they were communicated plainly (4.5c–d); it is also an emollient to hard reasonings, which are as odious to the vulgar as a rich man in a crowd of paupers (4.6c). The philosopher himself, when he comes to speak of the divine, has no resource but myth: if Plato did not dream idly of the birth of love in the garden of Aphrodite, or of winged chariots which carry souls to the heaven above the heavens (4.4c–d), we cannot pronounce it frivolous in the poet to imagine the nod of Zeus, the bow of Apollo or the hand of Athena upon the locks of Achilles (4.8b–c). It is the frivolous Epicurus,[15] who, while mocking the absurdities of others, has propounded the most absurd of all

---

[14] Trapp (1997), 31–40.

[15] Cf. Heraclitus, *Homeric Allegories.*

myths by teaching that the gods spend all their days in remote carousal, recking nothing of our affairs (4.9e). That being said, philosophers and poets alike are bound to speak in riddles, and the man who translates these riddles into specious myths, if he does so without understanding, resembles the celebrant who adds robes and precious metals to a statue which hitherto had been prized simply for the sake of the god to whom it was dedicated (4.5a).

The superior distinction of one philosopher is acknowledged, however, in *Who is the God of Plato?*[16] A philosopher may smile at the 'insolvency of vision' in Homer's depiction of Zeus as a giant who contracts his azure brows as he shakes the welkin (*Oration* 11.3a), yet his god is as much the fruit of his own *phantasia* as the painted or sculpted image (11.3c). It is equally manifest that, while the rudest nations are bound to confess the existence of a deity (11.5e), no two would agree with regard to his attributes (11.4a). Yet it seems that they ought to agree, because in Plato we find such a luminous conception of God that those who find it obscure would be blind to the setting of the sun or the descent of the evening star (11.1e). There is an intimation here that Plato acts upon his readers as he himself imagined the form of the Good to act upon the philosopher, supplying the light by which we understand him; a similar conceit enables Maximus to characterize the maturing of our theology on earth in words that Plato had used of the soul's ascent to the plain of truth (11.10e; Plato, *Phaedrus* 248c). We must learn, as Plato teaches us, to subdue the fickle clamour of the senses, freeing the mind to apprehend that which is visible to the mind alone. 'Visible' is the word, because God himself apprehends the objects of his knowledge by a single act, as we do in seeing, not in stages, as we do in speaking (11.9a). So long as we are engaged in discursive reasoning, we are pedestrians; as we rise, our course will terminate in vision (11.10c). The knowledge that we seek is thus attained not by the parsing of the text, but by the cultivation of the intuitive faculty that it awakens in the soul.

Maximus employs a different analogy between literature and the visual arts to answer the inescapable question *Whether Plato was right to banish Homer from his City*.[17] Imagine, he says, that a sculptor were create a statue not by copying any one original, but by a combination of all the most beautiful models afforded by the natural world. Such a figure – being, after all a statue, free from the deformations and infirmities that afflict a living organism – would not be in need of physicians, and it would be idle to complain that no correctives had been provided for evils to which it would never succumb (*Oration* 17.3). In the same way, the offices of a poet would be of no use to a city in which the populace was perfectly docile to an incorruptible caste of guardians; in the cities that we know, however, it is the poets who, by the exercise of *phantasia*, produce the *ekplêxis* or stupefaction that imprints moral truths, summarily but indelibly, upon the juvenile intellect (17.4.117). Since Plato himself has admitted that his city could not be founded until philosophers became kings, this is no heresy, but a lawful sophistry which

---

[16]   Trapp (1997), 84–92.
[17]   Trapp (1997), 149–156.

permits Maximus to retain his veneer of Platonism while reuniting elements of the Greek patrimony that Plato (like Epicurus) had done his best to put asunder.

Philostratus

This coupling of *phantasia* with *ekplêxis*, endorsed by Dio, is deprecated by Philostratus, the historian of the second sophistic movement, in his *Life of Apollonius of Tyana*. In this, as in other respects, the work could almost be read as the author's valediction to the movement which he anatomized in his *Lives of the Sophists*. There he distinguished sharply between the sophist and the philosopher, allowing the two to coalesce only in Dio: the protagonist of the *Life of Apollonius*, on the other hand, is undoubtedly a philosopher in his gallant inflexibility, the austerity of his diet and his single-minded zeal for the reformation of false religion.[18] When occasion demands, he can speak as long and as daintily as a sophist, yet he often prefers to cajole a thought from his interlocutor by Socratic questioning, and the oration that he composes for his defence before the Emperor Domitian is never delivered, since he chooses instead to translate himself miraculously to another place at the opening of his trial (*Apollonius* 8.7). Thaumaturgic episodes are common enough to suggest that the *Life* is conceived in emulation of the Gospels,[19] yet Philostratus tells us openly what the Gospels say only in the imagination of modern scholars – that the miracles are not proofs of his divine character, but sops for those too vulgar or too obtuse to perceive the source of his inspiration.[20] Every sage is a *theios anêr* (divine man) insofar as human and superhuman intellects are partakers of the same wisdom. For the same reason, Apollonius argues, it is possible for the artist to impress on marble the form that has been vouchsafed to him through a privileged exercise of the imagination:

> Imagination (*phantasia*) produces these effects, and imagination is a more cunning artificer than mimicry (*mimêsis*). Imitation can portray in art what it has seen; imagination even what it has not seen, for it will suppose the unseen by the analogy of the seen. Mimicry is often disconcerted by wonder and awe, but nothing disconcerts imagination, which moves with imperturbable advance towards its ideal goal. The man who meditates on a design for Zeus must see him with heavens and seasons and stars, as Phidias did in that eager sally of ambition. (Philostratus, *Life of Apollonius* 6.19, trans. Phillimore)

---

[18]   On his sources see Bowie (1978).

[19]   Baur (1932).

[20]   See *Apollonius* 1.3, with the repudiation at 1.2 of Moiragenes' depiction of Apollonius as a magician. On the Greek conception of the divine man see Bieler (1935–36); against the abuse of the term in biblical scholarship see Edwards (2006). As Plato intimates at *Meno* 99d–e, the *theios anêr* is a man imbued with the wisdom of the gods, not a worker of miracles.

At an earlier stage in the narrative, Damis, the satellite of Apollonius, is teased into an admission that God himself is a painter because he mixes pigments from the sun to dye the clouds in a medley of colours. The simile resembles one that Empedocles had applied to the craft of a poet and perhaps also to the work of Love in the miscegenation of elements; here, as Apollonius is quick to point out, it flatters the human artisan without slighting his Creator, who accomplishes his designs without clay or manual exertion. The dispute to which the passages alludes was a living one, for, while Galen contrasts the doctrine of creation by divine fiat with his own, more rational notion of a demiurge who works by natural laws upon a substrate, it was also possible to urge, with Aristotle, that demiurgic action is not consistent with the dignity or the immateriality of God.

Epilogue: Myth and Imagery in Plutarch

The authors whom we have learned to call Middle Platonists have only Plato in common, and often little in common with Plato. Philo, as we have seen, set out to reconcile philosophy to the book, or rather to enthrone one Book above all philosophies.[21] A dogmatist without humour or rhetorical vivacity, who believed that his dogmas were not his own but God's, he was even less of a Platonist in spirit than the sophists of the next century, who used Plato's tropes as stepping-stones to ends that he never foresaw. The one author of this period whose works survive in bulk, and who read Plato's works to understand them rather than to play off his own thoughts against them, is Plutarch of Chaeronea. It is fitting that this chapter should end with him, as he strikes many notes that are heard again in Plotinus, Porphyry and Iamblichus. Although one of these notes is a profession (in certain treatises) of absolute fidelity to Plato, he never fell into the secular bibliolatry of which Plato's devotees in late antiquity can be accused. His own dialogues resemble those of the master less in content than in freedom of speculation and elasticity of form. His more scholastic pieces, *On the Generation of Soul in the Timaeus* and *Platonic Questions,* testify to a faith in the transmission of truth by words, which also informs his treatises *On the E at Delphi* and *On Isis and Osiris*. In these works he threshed the wisdom from the ancient husk with tools that Plato had ridiculed; it was not, however, likely that Plato himself would be treated as scripture except in a milieu where a like reverence was accorded to the authorities that he had hoped to supersede.

Philo, as we have seen, believed that if a realm of forms is to be posited, it must reside eternally in the mind of an omniscient Creator, first prefiguring and then informing the visible harmony that he has brought into being by a determinate exercise of wisdom. Plutarch agrees with Philo, against some of his predecessors,

---

[21]   See Dawson (1992), 73–126, with Dillon (1990) on his 'creative adaptation' of Plato.

in ascribing to Plato the tenet that the material cosmos has a temporal origin;[22] having no other scripture as a corrective, he also gives the most literal sense to Plato's representation of the paradigm as a model independent of the Demiurge, which he cannot choose but to follow. Since, however, the Demiurge is good, he himself is a model to his creation; in imitating the paradigm, his object is to make the creation as like himself as possible. He finds an impediment to perfect likeness in the presence of a refractory motion in matter (1014b); his instrument for the imposition of form upon this hitherto unconditioned chaos is Soul, a composite of the Same and the Other which mirrors the concord of the four elements. It is also the source of the concord and of the elements themselves, insofar as they represent the first stage in the subjection of matter to form. Sameness in soul is the unifying power of intellect; difference the capacity to grasp distinct particulars by perception (1024a–1025a). According to Plato, the architecture of the sensible universe is governed by mathematical proportions corresponding to the ratios that define the notes of the octave; it is for this reason, Plutarch opines, that a god always carries an instrument in ancient statuary (1030a–b).

Thus, one must unlock an acoustic metaphor in order to decipher the heraldry of the visual artefact. Statues punctuate the lives of Plutarch's noble Greeks and Romans;[23] if tradition vouches for the outward likeness, the text will tell us whether the physiognomy reveals or belies the true character of the statesman. The fidelity of a sacred image to its invisible prototype, on the other hand, will be apparent only to those who have mastered the grammar of analogical representation. In his treatise *On Isis and Osiris,* Plutarch notes with approval that a statue of Zeus in Crete has no ears, to indicate that 'the ruler ought to listen to no one', while the trident of Poseidon signifies the third part of the cosmos which has fallen to his lot (381d). The Egyptians portray Harpocrates with his finger to his lips as an emblem of the reserve and silence that ought to accompany our immature discourse about the gods (378c); in Thebes there are handless statues of judges, betokening the incorruptibility of justice (355a). At times the knowable peeps from the unknown in an inscription, like the one which announces that Isis is all that is or will be and that no mortal being has ever lifted her robe (354c). Etymology, too, may carry understanding to its limits: glosses on Amun,[24] the Egyptian name of the supreme being, indicate both that he is concealed and that he is an object of unceasing salutation (354d). The appellative Min, by contrast, is given to Horus to imply that his works are visible in the cosmos, while the titles of Isis may connote motherhood, goodness or receptivity to form (374f). Vesture, too, may be more than decorative, as when the priests of Isis show by wearing linen clothes on their hairless bodies that one ought to be cleansed of all superfluous matter when

---

[22]   *Generation of the Soul* 1013e, though the authors of this false doctrine are unnamed by Plutarch and unknown to us. On the casuistry of Plato's readers in this period see Dillon (1989), esp. 57–58.

[23]   Mossman (1991).

[24]   Cf. Griffiths (1970), 285, with 101–120.

approaching the divine (353e). In Egypt the word is inseparable from the image, as writing itself is pictographic, the name Osiris (for instance) being represented by an eye because *os* means 'many' and *iri* means 'eye' (355a). Greece, too, can furnish analogues to the hieroglyph in the cryptic sayings attributed to Pythagoras (354e), and speakers in another of Plutarch's dialogues suggest that the E inscribed above the shrine at Delphi encodes a number of truths. As the fifth letter of the alphabet, it may symbolize the concerted operation of the senses; or, in search of a higher meaning, we may sound it like the verb *ei*, 'thou art', thus making it the indicative counterpart to the imperative 'know thyself'.[25]

Should we say, then, that mysteries accessible only to intellect are conveyed to us allegorically through the senses? Plutarch inherits from Plato a distaste for both naive and allegorical interpretations of Homer,[26] who, according to his treatise The Right Way of *Hearing Poetry*, should be read as an exemplar of vice and virtue. This may be called a synecdochic reading, in which the moral sense is elicited by a shift, not from like to like, but from part to whole or from universal to particular. The trappings of myth and metre enable the poet to work on less philosophical intellects through *ekplêxis* or stupefaction, just as the colour of life in a painting arrests the eye more than a mere outline.[27] In *Isis and Osiris* Plutarch deprecates the subtle abuse of allegory which makes Hades merely a cipher for the body (362b). There are wise men who construe the death of Osiris at the hands of Typhon as an allegory of the shrinking of the Nile in an arid season (364b); if, however, one were to suppose that these figures are *nothing but* personifications of the natural elements – if one were to hold that Dionysus is wine and Hephaestus flame (377d) or that the partial resuscitation of Osiris is merely a parable for the return of spring (377b) – one would quickly become a disciple of the atheist Euhemerus (360a), who argued that belief in the gods arose from the practice of glorifying mortals after their deaths.[28] This precipice of atheism awaits those who are afraid of the superstition which accrues from the vulgar and literal interpretation of hallowed rites and symbols (378a); we avoid it, once again, by adopting the synecdochic method, by acknowledging that, while the gods of myth are personages in their own right belonging to the daemonic order, each of them also instantiates one of the two opposing powers that inform the cosmos. Thus Typhon is not desiccation, wind or darkness but 'all that is noxious and deleterious in the natural realm' (369a), and each of the gods, insofar as he exemplifies the good or the evil force, may be identified, either partially or entirely, with its other representatives. Apis, a god who takes the living form of a bull, is an animated image of Osiris (368c); it is lawful to equate him with Serapis, the factitious god of Ptolemaic Egypt, and also with Hades, the lord of the dead, so long as we remember that all myths contain an

---

[25]   For commentary see Whittaker (1969). Flacelière (1965), 193, detects Pythagorean antecedents.

[26]   See Hunter and Russell (2011), 110–111, *On Hearing the Poets* 19e.

[27]   See 16b, with parallels at Hunter and Russell (2011), 86.

[28]   See De Angelis and Garstad (2006).

element of the fabulous. No interpretation which forgets that divine power works invisibly and omnipresently can be veridical, and we should therefore understand that when the dead are assigned to the underworld, this is merely an intimation that they are unseen (382e).

Since a divine being, even of the daemonic caste, is wholly or preponderantly an intellect, we are not guilty of an atheistic reduction if we identify Osiris with Logos, the unmixed and passionless intellect which governs the revolutions of the cosmos (373b). In the Egyptian myth, the sponsor of Horus, the son of the dead Osiris, is Thoth or Hermes, because, if Horus stands for nature and Hermes for *logos*, it is the work of Logos to testify that the cosmos is modelled upon a celestial paradigm.[29] The procreative functions of Osiris (373c) attest the fecundity of reason, which is able to bring forth a world from inert and formless matter. Logos, being simply the work of mind in the lower plane, cannot be characterized as an intermediate deity, and the translation 'speech' or 'word' could never be apposite, since, as the use of the tongueless crocodile as an emblem for Osiris proves, divine *logos* needs no voice (381b). It can be argued that the synecdochic principle is at work throughout the treatise, for it is our own participation in this *logos* that enables us to represent the mysteries of the upper realm in icons, words and ceremonies. The ubiquitous diffusion of such knowledge permits the exegete to call on Zoroaster as a witness to the rivalry of good and evil powers throughout the cosmos (369c–370c); it also equips the Greeks with tools for the etymology of Egyptian names, as when Osiris is derived from *hosios* (holy) and *hieros* (sacred), or when Plato's remarks on the 'friendliness' of Hades are adduced to corroborate the derivation of the name Serapis from an Egyptian term connoting 'joy' (375d–e; 362d).[30] All humans possess the same faculty of reason, though it is expressed in countless tongues; Plutarch hints that the wordless communication of iconography and ritual may enable us to overcome this cacophony. At the same time, we should not suppose that when the gods speak they will easily adopt a riddling and bombastic tone; as a speaker explains in another of Plutarch's dialogues, the seeress at Delphi no longer speaks in verse because her suppliants are no longer of that puerile generation which could not be instructed until it had been astonished. The business of the philosopher in a more enlightened age is to ensure that speech and reason coincide.

---

[29]   See Griffiths (1970), 505 and 555–557, with Dillon (1986a), 214, on the difficulty of ascertaining the 'genuine beliefs' of a second-century polymath.

[30]   Dillon (1996), 130, opines that in Philo's time one would have looked to the Stoics and the scriptures, not the Platonists, as exemplars of this.

Chapter 5

Image, Text and Incarnation in the Second Century

In the previous chapter, two epistemologies were contrasted. On the one hand, Philo held, as a Jew, that any plastic representation of God is sacrilegious and that even his self-disclosures through his angels or his Word are perceptible only to the elevated or enraptured faculties of his prophets. By the exercise of a kindred faculty, lovers of God can penetrate the meaning of his written word, the Torah, which is at once the record and the interpretant of the prophetic visions. On the other hand, a cultivated polytheist could hold that the daemonic was the visible integument of the divine, and that even statuary, though inferior to the literary arts, was able at times to reproduce an impression of more potent forms that had been revealed to the sculptor's imagination. The authors who furnish matter for the present chapter all agreed with Philo in rejecting the graven idol; they also held, with equal unanimity, that an image of the unseen power to which the world owes its origin still abides in the world, though whether the world was its prison, its paradise or both there was no consensus. Again, they all believed that an image of this unseen power had lately assumed a more visible guise, though there was no one view as to whether he had taken on palpable flesh in this epiphany, and there were some who ascribed more efficacy to his teaching, some to his life and some to the spectacle of his death. All concurred in granting both prescriptive and prophetic authority to at least some portion of the Torah, while believing that they now possessed a more tangible key to its hidden sense in the advent of the Saviour who, to some, was nothing less than the Word made flesh. If this was not exactly true of the earliest theologians, whom we call Gnostics, it will be evident that – no less than the apologists who succeeded them and the bishop who immortalized their doctrines by reviling them – they believed they were disinterring the image from the shadow and expounding an ancient cryptogram in the light of a new revelation, which the text at once foreshadowed and belied.

Gnostic

The term 'Gnostic' is used more sparingly in ancient than in modern heresiologies[1] and generally signifies one who (to borrow Porphyry's definition) holds that the maker of this universe is deficient or malign (Plotinus, *Enneads* 2.9, title). Early

---

[1]   Brakke (2011), 29–51.

reports and recent discoveries indicate that the cardinal text for the Gnostics strictly so called – their book of Genesis, as it were – was the *Apocryphon of John*, which survives in three Coptic redactions. The present chapter examines the relation between the true and the fraudulent image of divinity in the longest of these versions. The word *gnôsis* may also denote – and almost certainly does denote in the usage of those whom their Christian censors knew as Naassenes – a knowledge of the deep lore at the root of the diverse creeds inherited by the nations (Hippolytus, *Refutation* 5.6.6). The rarity of allusions to the Naassenes in Christian texts, however, suggests that their influence was small, and our exemplars of this hermeneutic *gnôsis* will be two masters of the notorious Valentinian school, in which esoteric readings of the Torah and the Gospel furnished proof-texts for more anodyne variation on the narrative of the *Apocryphon of John*.[2]

The revealer in the *Apocryphon of John* is an iridescent figure, appearing to John, son of Zebedee, first as a youth, then as an aged man and finally as a servant (NHC 2.1.2.1–19). Love in some Greek texts exhibits a similar versatility, and Christ undergoes rapid changes of appearance in an early Christian novel, the *Acts of John* (29). We may add that he escapes recognition or capture more than once in the Gospel ascribed to the same apostle (John 1.10, 7.30, 10.39, 20.15, 21.4), while the theory that he passed through every phase of human life to effect a universal redemption was espoused by Irenaeus, the father of Catholic theology. We find the closest analogue, however, in the epiphany of Poimandres, the mind of the sovereignty, in the opening treatise of the Hermetic corpus;[3] the resemblance is enhanced by the fact that in both texts the thing revealed is already manifest in the person of the revealer. Like Paul on the road to Damascus, the seers in both texts understand what is shown to them only when it is explained in words: Poimandres recounts the origin and the creative acts of the mind that he personifies, while the visitant in the *Apocryphon of John* implies that his threefold likeness ought to have been decipherable as an image of that being – Father, Mother and Son in one – who 'is always with you' (NHC 2.1.2.10–14). The identities of Father, Mother and Son are to be disclosed in the ensuing discourse on the history of creation and the Fall.

First in the order of being, says John's informant, is the virginal Spirit, illimitable in perfection, inaccessible to speech or understanding, unconfined by temporal or linear quantities, greater than anything that we know as God (NHC 2.1.2.33–4.10). In eternal repose he contemplated himself in the light that surrounds him (NHC 4.20–21; cf. 1 Timothy 3.16); as the Creator beheld his own image in Wisdom at Wisdom 7.24–5, so he looks on his own reflected majesty in Spirit, which is not yet a separate being but his own essence objectified. For this effulgence, however, there issues a new power, the aeon Barbelo, who is his image and the

---

[2]   All references are to the internal pagination of the texts as edited by Robinson (1990); hereafter NHC.

[3]   For an attempt to reconstruct the original Gnostic myth from the Hermetica and the Naassene sermon, see Reitzenstein (1904), 1–100.

expression of his foreknowledge (NHC 2.1.4.32–35). At once Mother-Father and Holy Spirit, she glorifies her progenitor and becomes the womb of all that proceeds from him (NHC 2.1.5.5–10). At her request, he confers upon her thought, foreknowledge, indestructibility, eternity and truth (NHC 2.1.5.12–6.2). Once this pentad is formed, his radiance fills her, and she becomes pregnant with the pure light who is the firstborn and only-begotten of the Father (NHC 2.1.6.15–18). This new emanation, anointed by the goodness of the Spirit, is Christ the Autogenes, or self-begotten; having glorified the Father in turn, he requests a fellow-worker, as all creation in Gnostic thought is vicious when it is not the work of a pair or syzygy (NHC 2.1.6.20–34; cf. 1 Corinthians 3.9, Philippians 4.3). The mind desires a deed, and the text goes on to relate that when this deed was accomplished by will, the will was followed by word, on account of which the Autogenes created everything (NHC 2.1.7.9.11). From the sequel the meaning of this appears to be that the Autogenes, in conjunction with life, will and mind, became the vessel of the Word that brought into being the angels, the virtues and the spiritual lights (NHC 2.1.8.1ff). The gift of the Word can also be conceived as the Father's honouring of the Christ by a mighty voice, which bestows on him the name above every name (NHC 2.1.7.28; cf. Philippians 2.9).

In combination, the will of the Father, the will of the Autogenes and the foreknowledge of Barbelo bring forth the first man, Adamas, who is imbued with the invincible power of the Father and set over the first of the aeons to glorify his three progenitors (NHC 2.1.8.29–9.12). His son Seth is set over the second aeon, while the third, in which the souls of the saints abide, is governed by the seed of Seth. A fourth aeon is also created as a habitation for souls who are obdurate at first, but then repent (NHC 2.1.10.13–24). Further acts of procreation, however, disturb the harmony of the aeons, for one emanation of divine thought, Sophia or Wisdom, conceives a desire to engender a likeness of Spirit without the approbation of the Father or the assistance of her male consort. The offspring of parthenogenesis in ancient myth is always deformed, and when she beholds the lion-headed monster which has emerged from her womb, she conceals it in a luminous cloud (NHC 2.1.9.25–10.19). Here, the monster gathers strength and, with the light that he has imbibed from his mother, sets about fashioning his own world of chequered luminaries and myopic archons (NHC 2.1.10.20–12.33). Like the divine revealer, this false creator possesses a multitude of faces, all of them bestial (NHC 11.25–12.2; cf. Ezekiel 1.10);[4] he announces that he is God and that beside him there is no other – the boast of God himself at Isaiah 4.5.5, though here it is treated as a false pretension, comparable to the usurpation of the divine prerogative by the prince of Tyre at Ezekiel 28.9.

Thus, the true image is now contrasted with the material counterfeit; the Father who was glorified by his progeny has become the envy of his simulacrum. Sophia in the meantime wanders to and fro, bewailing the diminution of her own light, until a place of repentance is appointed for her (NHC 2.1.13.13–14.11). The voice

---

[4]   See also Quispel (1980).

that endowed the Autogenes with the power of creation thunders forth again to condemn Yaltabaoth, the artificer of the lower world, and the likeness of the invisible divinity is unveiled in the image of primal man (NHC 2.1.14.24). In their dismay, Yaltabaoth and his lackeys conspire to make an effigy of the luminous image, in the hope of appropriating light from above. This copy of the archetypal Adamas, created in God's image but according to their likeness (NHC 2.1.15.1), receives the name of Adam and is placed in an earthly paradise, where he is not permitted to eat from the tree of knowledge (NHC 2.1.21.16–22.15). This tree, however, is the abode of the Epinoia or thought of God, and Adam is drawn to it because the same Epinoia has been implanted in him surreptitiously by the Father (NHC 2.1.20.15–27). Yaltabaoth, who is capable of no act of reproduction except the replication of bodies from bodies (NHC 2.1.24.30), casts a sleep of forgetfulness upon Adam in order to create a woman (NHC 2.1.22.31–23.3). This carnal Eve is, however, merely a copy of the luminous Epinoia (NHC 2.1.22.35), and when the latter wakes Adam, he recognizes the counterpart to his own supernal image and is able to beget Seth in imitation of his spiritual prototype (NHC 2.1.23.9 and 25.2). The indignant creator achieves his own purpose only by seducing the carnal Eve and fathering on her the bear-faced Eloim and the cat-faced Yave, whose names are disfigured forms of those that translators of the Old Testament commonly render as 'God' and 'Lord'.

There are two forms of imaging in the Gnostic universe – one auspicious, one malign. The first we may call pleromatic or archetypal, a promulgation of the Father's hidden godhead in the pleroma or totality of the powers which radiate from him as living mirrors to his glory. We may say that these powers, or aeons, are inferior insofar as they depend on him as the cause of their existence, but not in the sense that they reproduce anything less than the plenitude of his divinity: the aeon on whom the Father confers his glory and the Father who is glorified in the aeon are equipollent, differing only in that what is manifest in the one remains inscrutable in the other. The beauty and fecundity of the image are marred, however, when the aeon becomes rebellious or the male and female issue of the Godhead are untwinned. These are the errors of Wisdom, and the corollary is a second form of imaging – the cosmic or ectypal. This is a presumptuous adumbration of the divine world in a dusky and shifting medium, too unstable to serve as a canvas to the eternal, yet so viscous that it seems more real to our benighted eyes than its heavenly pattern.

As the spurious creator of the lower realm is the God from whom the Jews received their law, their sacred histories and their faith in their own election, Gnostic thought could neither affirm the plenary inspiration of the Old Testament nor deny its occasional truth. Moses mistook the wanderings of the penitent Sophia for a divinely-ordered motion of the Spirit (NHC 2.1.13.20), he did not understand that the sleep which fell upon Adam was a calculated occlusion of the intellect (NHC 2.1.22.23), and he wrongly believed that Eve originated from Adam's rib (NHC 2.1.23.3). But even when he is most profoundly in error – as when he fails to perceive that the jealousy of the Demiurge is a vice and that it was Epinoia, rather than the serpent, who incited Adam's revolt (NHC 2.1.22.3–15), there is a superficial veracity in his narrative, a shadow of the true history corresponding to the shadowy relation in which this world stands to its paradigm above.

This theory of partial inspiration ripened into a hermeneutic system for Ptolemy the Valentinian, who of all second-century Christians is most patently indebted to the *Apocryphon*, though he makes more liberal use of terms from Paul and John and tempers the dualism of Gnostic thought by deriving matter from the tears of fallen Wisdom. In a letter to his 'sister' Flora, Ptolemy distinguishes three elements in the Law which the Jews purport to have received from Moses:[5] the ordinances of God, the complementary or corrective legislation of Moses himself and the interpolations of the Jewish elders (Epiphanius, *Panarion* 33.4.). We find the evidence for this taxonomy in the text, where Christ condemns the oral teaching as an adulteration of the written Torah and points out that Moses, yielding to the weakness of his contemporaries, sanctioned the divorce which had been forbidden in the divine institution of marriage (33.4.4). By 'God' he means the Demiurge, who is not to be equated with the devil, as some malcontents imagine, nor with the merciful father of Jesus. His laws, too, are of three kinds, as the Gospel intimates (4.3.2–8). Those that are truly good – such as the precepts against adultery, theft and murder – are fulfilled to the letter by Jesus; those that are imperfect, like the injunction to take an eye for an eye and a life for a life, are rescinded; thirdly, the acts of Jesus reveal the significance of the figurative commandments, as for example when he undergoes the death foreshadowed in the sacrifice of the paschal lamb (33.5.4). Valentinians were alleged to have drawn an analogous distinction between three orders of humanity: the spiritual who are saved by nature, the psychic who are not yet saved but redeemable, and the earthy or hylic who are beyond deliverance. It has been surmised that this predestinarian scheme is a parable in which the three tribes personify the three choices that are open to every agent;[6] if that is so, the spiritual agent is also the expert reader, as capable of filtering the provisional and incorrigible sayings from the text because he has already strained the psychic and hylic dregs from his own composition.

In the untitled tract from Nag Hammadi whose opening words are 'the gospel of truth', the work of Christ is recounted in a series of enigmas, the decipherment of which calls forth the spiritual capacities of the reader, so that the cryptic text is at once a parable and an instrument of emancipation from error and ignorance. The Son, we are told, is the name of the Father,[7] the one through whom all that is knowable of the Father is made known (NHC 1.3.38.3–40.29). As the Word or proclamation of the Father, he is the living book, whose letters are not quotidian vowels or consonants, since each by itself conveys truth in its unity and fullness to the aeons (NHC 1.3. 23.1–19; cf. Revelation 1.8). He is called the Word

---

[5]   For analysis see Markschies (2000), though I do not share his reluctance to apply the term 'Valentinian' to this author.

[6]   Löhr (1992).

[7]   See further Mortley (1992).

because the thought of the Father is disclosed in him (NHC 1.3.14–15); if we divide his meditation into words, each is the expression of an undivided will (NHC 1.3.37.1–7). Through his mouth comes the light which communicates thought and understanding to the elect (NHC 1.3.31.15–17), and through this naming of the ineffable each of the saints receives the name that was already known to the Father before the ages (NHC 1.3.21.5–22.21; cf. Romans 8.30, Ephesians 1.4, Revelation 2.117). It is he who reveals the purpose of the Father to the totality of the ages, thus dispelling the consternation which arose from ignorance (NHC 1.3.17.5–14). Error nonetheless continues to thrive in the material world, and those who remained enthralled by matter failed to comprehend his likeness (NHC 1.3.30.1–3) and were blind to the presence of the Father's image (NHC 1.3.23.27). Putting on the book in which the Father inscribed his eternal plan, the Saviour allowed these carnal oppressors to nail him to the Cross (NHC 1.3.19.36–21.1). But through this death he became the fruit of the knowledge of the Father (NHC 1.3.18.21–19.28), confounding the jealousy of his benighted captors who mistake their own folly for wisdom (cf. 1 Corinthians 1.21–24) and the Creator of the aeons for one of themselves (cf. 1 Corinthians 2.8)

To such oppressors the Word is a sword of judgment (NHC 1.3.26.1–25; cf. Revelation 1.16, Hebrews 4.12). It could also be said of this tract that it puts a sword between the false and the true understanding of the Christian proclamation. While it does not refer by name to any writing of our New Testament, its narrative is a tissue of concealed citations from the evangelists, Paul and Revelation; it is also a commentary on these citations, though the gloss is not infrequently more arcane than the allusion. Sometimes it will interweave two senses of the same term, as when words denoting fullness are applied both to the plenitude of God and to the sum of the elect. Sometimes a parable is expounded through another parable, as when the lost sheep is said to pass from the left hand to the right hand when it is added to the other ninety-nine, this being an ancient method of counting to a hundred on one's fingers (NHC 1.3.31.35–32.17).[8] Sometimes a conceit becomes more pregnant, as when the Cross is not merely contrasted as tree of life with tree of knowledge, as at Revelation 22.2, but declared to be itself the tree of knowledge (NHC 1.3.18.25). Sometimes an ambiguity proves to be fertile: thus, John 1.18 is construed to mean not that the Son who is in the bosom of the Father reveals the Father, but that through the Son the Father reveals his bosom, which this author identifies with the Holy Spirit ((NHC 1.3.24.10). It has often been remarked that, while the so-called *Gospel of Truth* is allegorical, it is not mythopoeic: Wisdom is not personified as a fallen goddess, and jealousy, though a vice in unbelievers, is not imputed to their Creator. The deficit in matter which Christ came to fill (NHC 1.3.35.9) is not so much in the cosmos as in the cosmologies of those who lack the spiritual eyes to hear the true import of the Word.

---

8   Van Unnik (1973), 179–182, comparing Irenaeus, *Against Heresies* 1.16.2.

Justin Martyr

In his *Apologies*[9] Justin maintains a counterplay between the common usage of the term *logos* and its titular application to Christ as the instrument or surrogate of God. Where *logos* designates the human faculty of reason the Greeks possessed it in a pre-eminent degree: it was 'by true logos and investigation' that Socrates exposed the *eros* of poets and the subterfuge of demons (1 *Apology* 10.3). It is to his credit that, like the Christian martyrs, he incurred death for his pains (1 *Apology* 10.4; 2 *Apology* 10.5); since, however, he failed to grasp the 'whole Logos, who is Christ', he was unable to persuade anyone else to die for his convictions (2 *Apology* 10.8). The Word achieved by his own power what the laws of human societies could not do: he exhibited perfect rectitude in himself and inspired it in others (1 *Apology* 10.6; 2 *Apology* 10.7). It was only among the barbarians, however – that is to say, among the Jews whom Socrates' countrymen despised – that he took flesh and was called Jesus Christ (1 *Apology* 5.4). It is because God is ineffable and has no name that can circumscribe his essence that we require the mediation of the Logos (1 *Apology* 10.1), though it must be added that the Logos, too, adopted on earth one title, 'Christ', whose meaning still eludes our comprehension (2 *Apology* 5.3). His other appellation, 'Jesus', is a proper name, but with the connotation 'Saviour', and is potent enough to be employed against demons who have defied the incantations of pagan sorcerers (2 *Apology* 5.4–6). Before his advent as man, the Logos – or rather the Holy Spirit in the character of the Logos – delivered prophecies of his own coming under the veil of a psalm or prophecy (1 *Apology* 36.2, 38.1–8). It is difficult to ascertain whether Justin believed that he spoke directly to the Greek philosophers. Although he is often credited with the view that the Word sowed knowledge of himself in minds attuned to the divine, as a Stoic or Platonist might have held, he was bound as a Christian to deny that the soul and God have any natural affinity (*Dialogue with Trypho* 4). When he speaks of a distribution of 'seeds of truth to all' at 1 *Apology* 44.10, he is not alluding to any act of direct insufflation, but to a custom of plagiarism from the Hebrew prophets, so widespread that 'whatever has been said by the philosophers and poets about the soul's immortality, punishments after death, the contemplation of the heavens and like doctrines, they have been able to know and expound because they received the elements from the prophets' (1 *Apology* 44.9).[10] Examples of Plato's borrowings from Moses are amassed in 1 *Apology* 60, though none will seem persuasive to a disinterested reader. Nowhere does Justin attribute to the philosophers a spontaneous apprehension of the truths disclosed in scripture, unless he means to suggest this at 2 *Apology* 13.3, where he states that each saw 'that which was akin' (*to suggenes*) through a part of the spermatic *logos*. The translation is, however, far from certain, and it may be that any kinship

---

[9]   Conventionally deemed to be two: see Minns and Parvis (2009), 1–73.
[10]   See Edwards (1995).

between the intellect and the truths that it discerns has been established only by the incarnation of the Truth in Jesus Christ.

As the Word is not only a doctrine but the teacher, so he is not only a function of deity but an object of devotion in his own right. 'The Word from the ingenerate and ineffable God we worship and love, inasmuch as he also became a man on our account, in order that, having become a confederate in our sufferings, he might also effect the cure' (2 *Apology* 13.4). Reason prescribes that the God who made the world and all its denizens should be worshipped with prayers of thanksgiving and adoration, not with holocausts and the slaughter of fellow-creatures (1 *Apology* 13.1–2); and likewise it is 'with reason' that Jesus Christ, the Son of the true God, is given the second place in the liturgy, while the third is assigned to the Spirit (1 *Apology* 13.3–4). The story of his birth as a man from a virgin is no stranger than those which are told of many gods (1 *Apology* 21.1); to proclaim a crucified man the Son of God cannot offend anyone who accepts the Homeric designation of Zeus as father of gods and men (1 *Apology* 22.1); what the Church says of Christ as the Word, or speaking plenipotentiary, of God is no more than pagans say of Hermes (1 *Apology* 22.2). Christ differs from his analogues in the pagan world, however, in that they are fictitious whereas he was real, and he is Son of God, not merely in the sense that he was a righteous man and worthy of his creation but in the sense that before his second birth his was the first *dunamis* or power of God (1 *Apology* 32.10), and that his name on earth is Emmanuel, 'God with us' (1 *Apology* 33.1, citing Matthew 1.23).

In order to die for us, he assumed a body, which enabled him to give precepts of salvation with his own tongue: the majority of these appear to be drawn from the Gospel of Matthew (1 *Apology* 15–16), though we cannot be sure that Justin would have known the text under this name, since he alludes only to the reading of *apomnêmoneumata* or memorials of the apostles (1 *Apology* 66.3, 67.3). There is nothing to suggest that he would have countenanced any visual representation of Christ, any more than he would have tolerated an idol of his father. Images are at best redundant effigies of the dead and at worst facsimiles of demonic apparitions (1 *Apology* 9.1); it was the crowning infamy of Simon Magus, the arch-deceiver and sometime rival of Christ, that after his death a statue was erected in his memory with the inscription *Semoni Sanco* (1 *Apology* 26.2). Justin would not have been perturbed by the modern scholar's discovery that Semo was a deity of the Samnites. All cults, being equally false, are superseded by the orisons of the Church to the Father, Son and Holy Spirit; any truths that had glimmered faintly in myths or in man-made systems of philosophy are made clear by the toil and teaching of the Word made flesh.

In Justin's other surviving work, his dialogue with Trypho the Jew,[11] the supremacy of the text is not in question. Both interlocutors hold that if the claims made on behalf of Christ are true they can be verified by a study of the Law and the prophets as these were vouchsafed to Israel. Both agree that *logos theou* or

---

[11]   Perhaps not an entirely unilateral conversation: Horner (2001).

'Word of God' is one acceptable designation for this common patrimony. They are not entirely at one regarding the content of the scriptures, since Justin holds that the Septuagint, or amplified Greek rendering of the Hebrew, is in fact the more pristine form of a text that the Jews have mutilated in order to hide its most perspicuous testimonies to the work of Christ. More profoundly, they differ as to the meaning of the text, for the burden of Justin's argument is that the Jews mistake the figurative for the literal, the provisional for the absolute, and thus derive timeless ordinances from precepts that were given only as types of things to come. To prove that this is no arbitrary judgment, he appeals to texts of recognized authority which accuse the Jews of deafness to their own law and foretell that the covenant which was given to their fathers will be supplanted by a law that goes forth to the nations (*Trypho* 11–12, citing Isaiah 51.4–5, Jeremiah 31.31–32, Isaiah 55.3). The Jews, as Isaiah foresaw, have failed to heed his admonition (55.3ff.) that righteousness consists not in outward ceremonies, but in the disposition of the heart; as a result, they misconstrue the marks of separation which the Law imposed upon Israel as phylacteries of holiness, when in fact they are omens of their estrangement from God. The bloody rite of circumcision sets them apart by prefiguring the punishments that they alone will suffer on account of the murder of Christ (*Trypho* 16); sabbaths and sacrifices were enjoined not to sanctify Israel, but to atone for her transgressions (21–22); it is merely a proof of the spiritual hardening of the Jews that they could hope to be saved by abstinence from certain meats, yet set up a golden calf in place of God – and this at the very time when the Law of which they boast was being communicated to Moses (20). All these arguments presuppose a distinction between the self-interpreting character of the Law, which gives it permanent authority, and the malleability of the physical sign which, when the Law has been forgotten, is apt to be cherished with no understanding of its true signification.

Nevertheless, the full import of the Law did not become evident until prophecy and performance coincided in the ministry of Christ. His birth from a virgin was prophesied at Isaiah 7.14 as the prelude to his enthronement as king of the nations and an age of affliction for Israel (*Trypho* 43); his death, prefigured in Isaiah's lament for the suffering servant of God, effected at last that expiation of sin which was merely adumbrated in sacrifice and burnt-offerings (*Trypho* 13, citing Isaiah 53). The Jews will strive in vain to show that any other miraculous birth was the one foretold by Isaiah (*Trypho* 84); if they urge that crucifixion is too ignominious a death for God's anointed, they can do so only because they have suppressed a text declaring that the Lord will reign from a tree (*Trypho* 73).[12] In undisputed scriptures a Christian eye detects auguries of the crucifixion (*Trypho* 86–91), and in the course of his passion Christ disclosed his sonship by repeatedly addressing God as Father (*Trypho* 103–105). His very abasement is thus the surest token of his sovereignty; if, however, the Jews demand that their Messiah should come in visible glory, that, too, is expected by his followers (*Trypho* 32), and it was

---

[12]   On antecedents and interpretation, see Derrett (1989).

Jacob, in his benediction on those who gave their names to the tribes of Israel, who foretold that a ruler of Judah would appear first in humility, riding the foal of an ass, and then in garments stained with the blood of the vine (*Trypho* 52, citing Genesis 49.11). The exegesis is fortified by a citation of Zechariah 9.9, the text quoted at Matthew 21.5 to account for the manner of Christ's triumphal entry into Jerusalem. The returning Christ will be a more worthy recipient of empire than the weak and idolatrous Solomon, to whom the Jews perversely apply the promises of the seventy-second Psalm (*Trypho* 34). In the interim his people observe the Eucharist, which gives meaning to the oblation of fine flour which follows the healing of a leper at Leviticus 14.10 (*Trypho* 41), just as the death of Christ explains and consummates the release of the scapegoat and immolation of the paschal lamb (*Trypho* 40, alluding to Exodus 12 and Leviticus 16).

Justin avails himself of two assumptions, one of which all Jews would grant him – that no prophecy of the Old Testament can be idle – and the other of which he grants himself without argument – that the Gospels, or at least some form of the Gospel of Matthew, offer a veridical account of the life of Jesus. Even when both assumptions are conceded, a further act of legerdemain is required to persuade the sceptical Jew that Christ had the power not merely to perform symbolic or miraculous acts that had been predicted in plain terms, but to make prophecies of texts which had hitherto seemed merely descriptive or imperative, or to impose a typological sense upon acknowledged prophecies which, if literally construed, could not be said to have been fulfilled in his own career. In other words, one must accord to him the prerogative not merely of interpreting the text, but of infusing himself as subject into texts where no other subject than the literal one had hitherto been looked for, which he exercised in the Fourth Gospel as the incarnate speech of God. Justin's knowledge of this Gospel may be doubted, but there is no doubt that in his *Dialogue with Trypho*, as in the *Apologies*, he regarded Christ as the Logos, who, although he owes this title to his function as an ambassador to the Father and must therefore be numerically distinct from him (*Trypho* 129), remains so 'indivisibly and inseparably' united to him that the unity of the Godhead is not impaired (*Trypho* 128). Justin appears to be alluding in these passages to Jewish conceptions of a power of God, distinct from God himself, which is exercised in creation; however, whereas Jews believe this power to be the creator of the angels, Justin professes to demonstrate, from the story in which three angels appear to Abraham and two then depart for Sodom, that the third of these angels has a peculiar dignity (*Trypho* 56). If the Lord himself proposed to go down to Sodom at Genesis 18.21, he must have been present at its destruction, and we can hardly fail to identify him as the third of the angels when we hear at Genesis 18.33 that 'the Lord left Abraham' in the wake of the other two. There is consequently one angel who has the character of God: so much can also be divined from the text which states that the Lord rained fire from the Lord on Sodom (Genesis 19.23), and from the apparition to Moses of an 'angel of the Lord' who declares himself to be nothing less than 'the God of his fathers Abraham, Isaac and Jacob' (*Trypho* 59–60, citing Exodus 3.16). If we ask why this angel should be Jesus Christ, we need only turn to Isaiah 9.6, where the child who is destined to rule is called the angel of great counsel (*Trypho* 76); if the mere name of Joshua had the power to arrest the sun for 36 hours, we need not hesitate to say of the second Joshua, whose divine paternity is revealed by the virgin birth, that he is the very name of God (*Trypho* 75).[13]

A Valentinian, as we have seen, would have said that the name of the Father is not Jesus, but the Son. This is an echo of John 1.18 and is thus no evidence of their contempt for the incarnation, but only of their indifference to the typological reading of Israel's history. The inspiration of Moses they acknowledged where his laws were not palpably mischievous; Joshua, on the other hand, could be nothing to them, as his was a ministry of flesh and blood. The incarnate Saviour was indeed the image of the Father and his living book; but to turn from this to the vowels and consonants of the written Torah was to substitute an effigy for an icon, to mistake the world apart from Christ as a true iteration, rather than a meretricious copy, of the divine.

Tatian

Justin's pupil Tatian, though he acquired a reputation for heterodoxy,[14] agreed with Justin himself in holding that there is one God who created all things well. A Syrian by birth, and writing Greek more barbarously than he knew, he begins his *Oration to the Greeks* with a lampoon on the pretensions of contemporary sophists. One does not know whom to call Greek, he scoffs, when the Doric idiom differs from the Attic and the Aeolic from the Ionic (1.2). If each city claimed a monopoly of its own dialect, this cosmopolitan babbling would be impossible (26.1); yet the rhetorician prides himself on his Attic style, presuming to call the Christian a barbarian (26.4), though he cannot refrain from tricking out his own speech in foreign words (26.1). The grammarian employs his sterile lexicon in the dismemberment of Wisdom (26.2), the rhetorician in fabricating senseless figures of speech (26.3) and in pouring scurrilities on his opponents (27.2). The philosophers multiply their syllogisms without arriving at a common view on anything (27.3); Plato is at odds with Epicurus and both with Aristotle, though all concur in making merchandise of their opinions (25.1–2). The bombast of the stage (24.1) and the mimographer's simulation of one obscene role after another (22.1–2) are the most pernicious depravations of this misprized eloquence. The visible accomplice of verbal imposture is the *stoikheion*, a noun that, as Paul knew, can denote not merely a letter but an 'element' of the cosmos, of a philosophical system or of an intellectual discipline. Tatian may be consciously imitating the apostle when he plays on this variety of senses. Men who can set the characters of the alphabet at war – as Tatian sneers at 22.3, with an eye to such works as Lucian's

---

[13]   See further Hurtado (2007).
[14]   See further Hunt (2003), 20–51.

essay *Consonants at Law*[15] – will not shrink from worshipping the material elements or even from imagining that they can palliate the absurdities of Homer by substituting the elements for his human protagonists (20.3). Many of these perversions can be attributed to demons, fallen angels, for whom the elements of deceit – their *stoikheiôsis*, as Tatian styles it at 9.1 – was to impart counterfeit life to inanimate beings, transforming them into objects of veneration. The demon, who is himself no more than a wraith (*phantasma*) since his revolt against God (7.3), avenges himself upon God's most precious creature by detaching the human soul from the image of God which resides in the spirit (7.3; 12.1). Wrongly believed by the Greeks to be immortal, the soul is as much a product of matter as the heavenly bodies or the corporeal envelope of the demon (12.1–3); the latter, having persuaded the soul to worship his material simulacrum, teaches it also to people the heavens with emblems of fictitious criminals and monsters (10). Hence arises a false belief in the fatal influence of the constellations; hence it is that the deities whom the Greeks adore are subject to birth, vicissitude and passion (8.23), juggling letters as lots to determine their place in the cosmos (9.3); when even the lewdest human acts are admired if an artist creates an agreeable statue of the malefactor (34), we need not be surprised that matter itself should be the one subject to which the Greeks attribute neither an origin nor an end in time (5.3).

Expressions that would have been at home in a Gnostic text recur throughout the diatribe. Soul and spirit are rigidly distinguished (12.1), when soul falls away from spirit it inclines to the matter from which it has been created (15.1), the term 'psychic' is used to characterize the possessor of such a soul (15.3, 16.2) and when a being is wholly lost, not only the soul but the spirit is deemed to be hylic or material (12.3). Erroneous belief about God is represented as *plane* or wandering, as in the *Gospel of Truth*. Where Gnostics known to Plotinus spoke of a nodding or inclination (*neusis*) of Wisdom to the material plane and of the captivity of her members in the world that was born of this tragedy, Tatian describes the cleaving of souls to matter as a *neusis* (13.2) and complains that the grammarians tear apart the members of wisdom (26.2). It is clear in all these passages that the same tongue is being employed to a different purpose: Tatian never held that the material world is the outcome of some schism or aberration in the Godhead, and even when he notoriously fell into the heresy of reading Genesis 1.3 ('Let there be light') as a prayer addressed by the Son to the Father, he was contradicting those who set creation against redemption, attributing them to independent or even hostile deities.

Nowhere is this desire to correct the abuse of speech more evident than in Tatian's application of the term *dêmiourgos* and its cognates to the Logos, or Word of God. Plato and the Gnostics, while they passed opposing judgments on the wisdom of the Demiurge, agreed that he could not work without a substrate: Tatian insists that matter is itself a divine creation (6.1), whose properties are antithetical to those of its author. The procession of the creative Word from God is therefore

---

[15]   Where sigma and tau contend before a jury of vowels; see also Nasrallah (2005).

not to be conceived as an abscission, but as the kindling of a torch from a torch, which does not entail any diminution of the original flame (5.2). When the Word is said to have leapt forth from the Father, we may think of the eruption of Athena from the head of Zeus, but also of Wisdom 18.15, where the Word leaps down from heaven to defend the Israelites as they flee from Egypt. This scriptural text contrasts the omnipotent governance of the Word with the futile cult of hand-made deities; Tatian regards idolatry as one of the stratagems by which the demons, who have no share in the image of God, conceal from us the fact that this image resides not in the body but in the spirit (7.1, 7.3, 12.1). Once it is perceived to be incorporeal and as free as God himself from the cycle of death and generation, the spirit renews its bond with Spirit, sprouting the wings which (as in Plato) carry it back to its heavenly abode (20.1).

When he avers that the sick are released from demons by a *logos* of God (16.3), Tatian would appear to be subsuming under one locution the Word himself and the word by which the exorcist invokes him. The analogy is first broached in chapter 5, where we read that the Word takes nothing from the substance of the Father in coming forth from him, any more than Tatian, the handiwork and offspring of the Word, relinquishes any part of his substance when his own speech communicates form to 'kindred matter' (5.2–3). Nevertheless, the mere possession of speech alone will not suffice to set human beings apart from beasts, let alone to preserve in them the image and likeness of God (15.2–3); so much is evident from their abuse of the written word as a vehicle for the menaces and false precepts of the demons (17.3). Counterfeit oracles may abound in the pagan world (19.3), but the Word himself is the one true source of Law and prophecy (7.2). The written text in which we receive his ordinances and teachings is distinguished from the erudite logomachies of the pagan world by the plainness of its style, its moral acumen and its accurate foreknowledge of things to come (29.2). The books ascribed to Moses are not only older than any Greek text, but antedate the invention of the alphabet (31.1) and are therefore of more authority in their account of the creation and their witness to the unity and omnipotence of God. The Christians who follow the Word (26.3) are guilty of no innovation, but are reclaiming a buried patrimony (30.1). Young and old, the poor and the wealthy alike are taught by God (32.1, 29.2), while Greek philosophers reserve their teachings for a claque of rich admirers. They may scoff at the Christians as barbarians – and Tatian himself is proud not to be a native of Rome or Athens (35.1–2) – but if they wish to know why nation can no longer speak to nation in a common tongue, they must turn to the story of the tower of Babel (30.2). While he makes no reference to a written Gospel or any previous work of Christian literature; recurrent echoes of Paul can be detected in the *Oration*, together with three allusions to the prologue to the Fourth Gospel. He asseverates that the Father was 'in the beginning' (5.1), and that through his Word all things came into being and not a single thing without him (19.4); in a playful inversion of John 1.5, he urges that it is possible for the darkened soul to comprehend the light that God unveils to it in the Word (13.1). The first Johannine axiom to which he appeals is that 'God is spirit' (4.2), though he happily courts the ridicule of sophists by proclaiming that the fleshless God not only dwells in believers through the spirit (15.1) but was born in the form of man (21.1).

Theophilus

Theophilus, Bishop of Antioch, is generally agreed to have been the last of the Greek apologists writing under Marcus Aurelius. He is certainly the most prolix, the least polemical and the only one to address himself to a private citizen rather than the Emperor. He opens the second of his three books *To Autolycus* with a quotation from Paul disclaiming the power of speech (2 Corinthians 11.6), and proceeds at once to a denunciation of idols. In the course of manufacture, they are, as Paul said, 'nothing' (1 Corinthians 8.4); once painted, they serve as pretexts for superstition and thriftless expense (*To Autolycus* 2). The word in the pagan world offers no corrective to the image, for, as the artisan imagines that a god can be fashioned from wood or stone, so the poet sings of gods who have come into being by casual acts of procreation (3). Tossed from error to error by the prompting of demons, the poets say now that the world is eternal and now that it is created; they affirm that providence governs all things and that all goes by caprice, they acclaim the monarchy of God yet make the world a cockpit of conflicting powers (8). Homer and Hesiod profess to have learned more from the Muses than the Muses themselves could know, since they are younger than the cosmos (5–6); if the agents whom the poet's informants celebrate existed at all, they were never more than men (7). Some understanding of God can be conceded to the poets when they escape the seduction of demons (8); the best of the philosophers, too, are aware that the world is the handiwork of an uncreated deity, though, in positing a demiurge who required pre-existent matter as a substrate, Plato has accorded no more power to him than common sense would grant to the maker of idols (4). Just as the delirium of the poets and the cacophony of the schools are silenced by the genuine inspiration of the Sibyl and the Hebrew prophets, so the carved divinities of the pagan world are shown to be mere simulacra when compared with the God who called the world into existence out of nothing. The prophets of Israel could proclaim the truth and foretell the future because, as Theophilus now undertakes to show, the word that they speak is an expression of the Word that served God as an instrument of creation; the Wisdom that informs his works is the animating principle of the scriptures in which those same works are revealed.

These scriptures attest that God, existing alone before the ages (Psalm 54.20), desired to be known by man and therefore prepared the world as his domicile. Nothing distinct from him was coeval with him; his partner in creation is the Logos or Word, disgorged, as the Psalms inform us, from his own bowels (Psalms 109.3 and 44.2), in company with Sophia or Wisdom (*To Autolycus* 2.11). Through their condescension to the world that they themselves have framed, the prophets have been able to speak of events that antedated the birth of any human being – of the primordial creation of all through the Logos (John 1.3), and of Wisdom's presence at the side of God when he set bounds to the earth (Proverbs 8.22). Rumours of this wisdom have reached nations unacquainted with the scriptures, who revere the number seven, though without knowing that it was hallowed by God's respite after his labours on the Sabbath (13). God's own utterance, 'let there be light', has taught us how to name the illumination that the Logos imparts to the world. This same illumination can disclose an allegorical sense behind the historical narrative, so that the notion of a primeval sea is understood to signify the continual infusion of divine goodness into the world through the law and the prophets (14), while the first three days, preceding the creation of the sun and the moon, are types of God, the Word and his Wisdom – a group to which this author is the first Greek to give the name *trias* or 'Trinity' (15). The fourth day represents the human race, since it is we who are in need of the light that God bestows; the stars in their steadfast courses symbolize righteous observers of the law (15). Meek animals, created on the fifth day, are another emblem of the righteous (16); the carnivores of the sixth day show the traits of their oppressors (17). But, whereas these are mere tokens, the human being is the true image and likeness of God, created – as his own words 'let us make' imply – in conjunction with his Word and Wisdom, to rule his place as the one creation worthy of his hands (18).

The planting of the first human being in paradise was not his creation, but a manifestation after the seventh day of the work that had been completed on the sixth (23). Confined now to a single place for the exercise of virtue and the propagation of offspring, humanity maintains its conversation with God though his Word, whom he sends forth from himself without surrendering any of his own substance, just as a human speaker emits his own words without loss of substance. Borrowing from the Stoic lexicon, Theophilus describes the word at rest within God – his reason or intelligence – as the *logos endiathetos*, and the uttered Word, who takes the form of a walking voice in Eden at Genesis 3.8, as his *logos prophorikos* (10.22). Moved by this *logos*, illiterate men and shepherds in Israel rebuked not only the popular cult of idols, but also every species of moral turpitude, with an eloquent unanimity that puts the Greeks to shame (33–35). An exception must be made for the Sibylline oracles, which upbraid the sinner and ridicule the idolater in terms that Theophilus sees to be almost biblical, though he fails to draw the obvious conclusion that they are Jewish or Christian forgeries (36); he does succeed, however, in quoting a number of authentic passages when he argues that the tragedians and Homer had some notion of divine providence and an indistinct presentiment of judgment after death (37–38).

Irenaeus

The first Christian to undertake a systematic theodicy, or account of the relation between divine justice and the world is Irenaeus of Lyons, another bishop and almost an exact coeval of Theophilus. He and Theophilus have in common one tenet which was abandoned by Episcopal theologians of the fourth century – that

Adam and Eve were *nêpioi*, or children, at the time of their creation, apprehending only as much of the glory of God as was consistent with their immature state of knowledge (cf. Ephesians 4.13–14).[16] This premiss enables Theophilus to explain to the Greeks how beings who were not vicious by nature came to abuse their freedom; for Irenaeus, however, since his aim was not so much to entice the Greeks as to disarm the Valentinians, this postulate of an immature creation is the linchpin of his argument that the making of the world and its redemption are the work of the same divinity. Christ came not to undo a tragic error, but to complete a play that was never intended to have been staged without him; the image of God which we bear in our embodied state is not a caricature or death-mask of his glorious countenance, but a pledge and an adumbration of the glory that he bestows on every creature who is willing to be saved.

The Gnostic opponents of Irenaeus held that, while a portion of God's substance is present as spirit in beings of the pneumatic order, the body is a mere idol, created by inferior powers in imitation of a luminous countenance which shone forth from heaven. To Irenaeus, this is a tissue of blasphemies: firstly, because it denies the insurmountable disparity in essence between Creator and creature; secondly, because it attributes human features to the invisible God; and, thirdly, because it denies God's role in the fashioning of a body for the man whom he created as his image. It is, however, one thing to convict the Gnostics of error by appeal to scriptural axioms and another to show that these axioms are consistent. That a visible thing should be the image, or have any part in the image, of the invisible God is surely a paradox; Irenaeus himself perceives it as such and therefore urges that it is only God who can overcome the antinomy by making himself a man. And this he must do without deficit or dissimulation: the Word of God became incarnate not to deceive the archons, but to exhibit the image and likeness of God in its fullness (*Against Heresies* 5.16.1). This would have been a pedagogic necessity even had there been no transgression in paradise: the plan of God demanded first that nature should be revealed, then that the mortal should be swallowed by the immortal and corruption by incorruption, so that at last humanity, having acquired the knowledge of good and evil, might attain the image and likeness of its Maker (4.48.3). In contrast to the majority of Christian readers after him, Irenaeus regards God's interdict on the eating of the fruit from the tree of knowledge as provisional rather than absolute: the knowledge of good and evil is a prerequisite of human perfection, rather than a disfigurement of a perfection already bestowed, but not to be plucked before Adam and Eve had seen the consummate manifestation of human nature in the incarnate Word.

---

[16]   Paul's juxtaposition of the childlike neophyte with the 'perfect' man (*teleios anêr*) that Christ sets before his Church deserves more than the passing mention that it receives in Steenberg (2004), 5n – not least because it was Ephesians 1.10 that gave Irenaeus his notion of 'recapitulation'.

Should we conclude that the image and likeness are still to come, and that neither has yet been imparted to humanity?[17] Irenaeus could not have held this view, since at the core of his argument against the Gnostics is a plain and literal reading of Genesis 1.28, where God creates man and woman after his image in accordance with his previous resolution to create humanity after his image and likeness. At *Against Heresies* 5.6.1, Irenaeus avers that the whole man was created in the likeness of God; as soul and spirit are not the whole but portions of the whole, they evince the likeness only in accordance with the body, which God moulded after his image. The image thus inheres in the body – or rather, as becomes evident, in the body ensouled – while the likeness is a property that this composite acquires when informed by spirit. There is nothing novel in this anthropology, since Paul understands the sonship of the elect as a redemption of the body (Romans 8.23), which will be quickened by the spirit that raised Christ Jesus from the dead (Romans 8.11) and perfectly conformed to the body of glory which Christ already wears in heaven (Philippians 3.21). All human beings, according to Irenaeus, possess a body and a soul; the spirit is not the undeserved bounty of nature to a few, as the Gnostics imagine, but the free gift of God to all who exercise their power to believe in him and serve him in steadfast faith. Consequently, all humans bear the image of God, but the likeness is realized only in the saints. When, therefore, Irenaeus speaks as though both image and likeness were still to be realized, he is treating them as one and is not denying that the image is already in our possession, albeit in an imperfect and debilitated form. When he implies at 3.18.1 that we have forfeited both the image and the likeness, we should not take this to mean that both image and likeness were already mature in Adam or that both have now been wholly obliterated. What is lost is the perfection of the image in the likeness through the union of spirit with soul and body. As Irenaeus explains more lucidly at 5.16.2, it was the likeness alone that Adam relinquished by his disobedience, though if this statement is to remain consistent with others, it must refer only to the promise of the likeness or to the partial enjoyment of it, since neither the image nor the likeness had yet been revealed in its plenitude.

Why should it be the Word who became incarnate? Because the purpose of this event was the revelation of the image and likeness of God, and it is only through his word – that is, through his voluntary speech about himself – that God is known. This speech may take the form of a proclamation, as when he discloses his name to Moses as 'I am that I am' (4.5.1) – or of a prophecy, as when he promises to Abraham that he will become the father of many nations (4.5.3, alluding to Genesis 15.1–6). The angel in these episodes who speaks with the voice of God must be more than a creature, yet cannot be the infinite Father of whom it is said that none can look on his face and live. These apparitions must therefore be theophanies of the Word (4.20.8–11), and this is proof enough that he did not come into existence for the first time as Jesus of Nazareth. It is because this Jesus of Nazareth, when

---

[17]   Note the Gnostic precedent at *Against Heresies* 1.5.5, with Edwards (2009b), 35–56.

preaching to his disciples, is the same figure who spoke to Abraham as an angel that the latter can be said to have 'rejoiced to see his day' (4.5.3, quoting John 8.56). It was this Word who, in company with Wisdom or the Spirit, served as one of the hands of God in the making of Adam (4.20.1); as Psalm 33 informs us that God spoke and all things were made, so we learn from John 1.3 that all things were made through the Word who was with God in the beginning (3.2.4). The Word is no less the author of creation than of the Gospel, and the demons knew him and trembled even before he allowed them to name him because his omnipotence had been revealed to them from the very beginning of the world (4.6.6).

The Old Testament is a treasury of the expectations planted in the hearts of righteous men and prophets by the Word himself (4.11.1). Now that the seal has been broken by his own coming in the flesh, we are able to see, as they had not yet seen, that it was he who led Jacob and instructed Moses, and that when he appointed the 'place in which the name shall be invoked' as the venue for the observance of the Passover festival, he was alluding to his own death (4.10.1). His own discourse, as a man among men, was not free of dark sayings, but we must not allow these to obscure the more luminous passages, as the Valentinians do when they scour the parables for recondite attestations of beliefs that are elsewhere contradicted by the plain words of Jesus and his harbingers (2.17.3). Yet, quoting as he does from every book of our New Testament, and conscious as he is that some quotations are more perspicuous than others, Irenaeus can evade two questions which it was possible to ignore so long as one wrote only for pagans. The first is: who determines which of the texts that claim authority is canonical? The second is: once a text has been admitted to the canon, who is to arbitrate where the meaning is ambiguous or unclear?

That the limits of the canon should be fixed within the canon would be a cogent principle if it did not inevitably rest on circular reasoning. When Irenaeus argues that, in addition to the four winds and the four corners of the earth, the four beasts of Revelation testify that the Gospels are four in number (*Against Heresies* 3.9), he not only assumes the authority of a book that was later reckoned among the dubitable candidates for admission to the New Testament, but also appears to grant himself that faculty of private divination which he denies to his Valentinian adversaries. No doubt this is his prerogative as a bishop, since his answer to the second question is that a rule of faith has been preserved by the episcopate since the time of the apostles; this principle can be reinforced by appeal to a chain of elders who have handed down the true sense of the works and utterances of Christ (4.26–4.27). The Church, as the visible body of the Word, is thus the interpreter of the words that he bequeathed to us, first by inspiration, then in his incarnation. This is a sound enough principle, so long as text and tradition are plainly at one; we shall see, however, in the following chapter that, in an age when the typical exegete was an able scholar and no mean rhetorician, it could not be guaranteed that one man's churchmanship would be congruent with another man's vision of Christ.

Chapter 6
Image, Text and Incarnation in the Third Century

Origen laid the foundations of Christology, hermeneutics, anthropology and the doctrine of the Trinity for all theologians after him. For him, these four were reducible to one discipline, the pursuit of the Word incarnate in the word of scripture, from which it was his task to unweave the Saviour's image and knit that image to the reader's soul. Because of his exceptional powers of synthesis, he deserves to be the protagonist of this chapter. At the same time, a brief review of the work done by his predecessors is necessary, in case we should be tempted to mistake the exception for an aberration, or imagine him as a solipsistic genius, unconstrained by the Catholic teaching of the Church.

Tertullian of Carthage

For Christians of the third century, persecution was the distemper of the age, and forced idolatry its most egregious symptom. Tertullian's *Apology* turns on Rome the witticisms that her own satirists had levelled against the man-made deities of other nations (12.7, 29.2, 50.10). In a tract addressed to Christians, *On Idolatry*, he inveighs against the lewd customs that prevail at the feasts where images are worshipped[1] and pronounces the Christian guilty of complicity if he manufactures idols for the use of his pagan neighbours or allows his slaves to hang garlands on a door that is consecrated to a false god (15.7). To those who object that Moses himself held up a brazen serpent to the Israelites, he replies that this special ordinance, issued for reasons now inscrutable, cannot be permitted to override the plain word of the Decalogue. The serpent is a figure, not in the sense that it is an effigy of Christ, but in the sense invoked by Paul when he wrote at 1 Corinthians 10.6 that the probation of the Israelites was a *tupos* or figure 'for us' (*On Idolatry* 5.3–4). If the serpent represents anything, it is an emblem of Satan, perishing on the scaffold that he had prepared for Christ; to cite it as a precedent for idolatry is to make common cause with the Marcionites, who fall into contradiction in their efforts to set the Creator at odds with himself. In the proem to his five books against this Heretic, Tertullian implies that, as a shipwright, he is no position to mock the divine Artificer; he tosses a similar quip at another enemy, Hermogenes, who, being a painter himself, imagines God as a fellow-artisan, who had no

---

[1]   On the *pompa diaboli* in Tertullian (*On the Shows* 7), see Daniélou (1977), 412–418.

choice but to build his world from the truculent stuff that lay to hand (*Against Hermogenes* 2.1ff.).

Were matter coeval with God we should do well to venerate it (*Against Hermogenes* 7.3); the doctrine of creation out of nothing teaches Christians to esteem it without depriving God of the adoration due to him as its Author. At the same time, Tertullian was too learned in the scriptures to forget that God had at certain times been visible to his saints and that a man of flesh and blood had once said 'he who has seen me has seen the Father' (John 14.9). The assertion of John that 'no one has seen God at any time' (John 1.18) suggests that any such encounter would be an epiphany of the Second Person; since, however, face-to-face knowledge (as Paul implies at 1 Corinthians 13.12) is the perfection of acquaintance, not vouchsafed in the present world to the majority of believers, one might reasonably suspect that *facies* (face) is a peculiar designation of the Father, while the Word, like the Spirit, is apprehended only as an image (*Against Praxeas* 14.9). Yet such a conceit cannot be reconciled with common usage or with the axiom of divine invisibility; Tertullian therefore reasons that, if the Father is the *facies* of the Son, he is so 'by virtue of unity' (*ex unitate*) – that is to say, he is the Son's face when the Son is present to reveal him – and not because any visual apprehension of him is possible without the mediation of the Son.

The Son became visible, first in the angelic guise under which the patriarchs knew him, then in the palpable flesh of the Nazarene. The connotations of the title Logos can be discovered by inspection of the image and likeness of God within, for this reveals that every uttered word has its antecedent in an exercise of *ratio* or reason, perceptible to the mind alone (*Against Praxeas* 5). By analogy we can say that the Second Person, as divine reason, coexists with the Father eternally, but assumed a distinct *persona* as the *sermo* or speech of God when the Father resolved to create a world. In this role he is eminently fitted to express God's will to his creatures, whether by angelophany or by incarnation. Tertullian nonetheless has little to say of the relation between the Word incarnate and the Word in scripture, though he undoubtedly holds that the scripture is God's witness to himself and the one infallible source of knowledge. On matters which are open to speculation, such as the nature of the soul, the dreams of women and the surmises of philosophers are of equal weight (*On the Soul* 9.4, for example); when our task is to winnow the true from the false conception of God, Tertullian's motto is *quid Athenis et Hierosolymis* – what has Athens to do with Jerusalem? (*Prescription against Heresies* 7; cf. Mark 1.24). As the Word is the operation of the Spirit (*Against Praxeas* 26.4), we may be sure that the doctors of the new Jerusalem spoke at his prompting; nevertheless, Tertullian does not go so far as to argue that the scriptures are a continuation of the incarnate ministry. The soil for this conceit was Alexandria, where scholars and librarians wore the laurels that could be reaped in Carthage only in the arena or on stage.

Clement of Alexandria on the Logos

Clement is the polymath among the Christian fathers, the only one of whom we can say with confidence that he read Plato without the help of an excerptor and not always to wrangle with him. Of all his eccentricities, none has offended his critics more than his belief that, since the perfection of knowledge is wisdom, the Christian should aspire to be a master of all the sciences, including those in which the Greeks had excelled the prophets and chroniclers of the Old Testament. His premiss is that every human possesses the image of God in the form of reason, though it is left it to each of us to perfect the likeness by the free cultivation of our higher faculties.[2] Since the Greeks have been the most zealous votaries of reason in the pursuit of astronomy, logic, agriculture and geometry, we are guilty of no impiety if we study them in order to learn these arts. In short, we must be eclectics in philosophy (*Stromateis* 1.5.38); it does not, however, follow that we must be pagans in theology, for the truths dispensed to prophets and apostles by direct inspiration (*Stromateis* 6.42) have reached the philosophers only at second hand, and as a consequence of their surreptitious opening of the scriptures. The Greeks can teach us to think to better purpose, but so long as they think independently of the Logos they remain ignorant of the nature of God and his plane for the consummation of the world.

Photius, the Byzantine scholar and prelate, accuses Clement of bifurcating the Logos, and denying the identity of the incarnate Redeemer with the 'paternal Word' (*Bibliotheca* 109). The majority of scholars are persuaded that he misread his author: he may, for example, on meeting the admonition not to confound the paternal Word with the *logos prophorikos*, have understood the latter term in the Christological sense that was certainly given to it by Theophilus of Antioch. To Clement, however, it means syllabic utterance and would not therefore be predicated of Christ by those who hold him to be a *dunamis* or active power, rather than a mere operation or mode of an undifferentiated Godhead.[3] There are scholars who contend, nonetheless, that Clement went so far with the second-century apologists as to postulate a temporal emergence of the Logos from a timeless phase of latency as the wisdom or reason of God; this was still an orthodox tenet, acceptable (as we have seen) to his contemporary, Tertullian, and his readiness to equate the realm of ideas with the Logos indicates that he would not have thought it untenable. The evidence that he held it must, however, be weighed against the affirmation, in a Latin translation from his *Outlines of Doctrine* (*Hypotyposes*), of an unconfused coexistence of the Father and his Word before the ages.[4] We can say with more assurance that the incarnation marks a new stage in his being, and that is succeeded by a third stage in which he makes his abode in the hearts of all who

---

[2]   *Stromateis* 1.22.131.5; on the incorporeality of the image, see *Strom.* 2.19.182.6; and on the consummation of both in Christ, see *Paedagogus* 1.12.98.

[3]   Edwards (2000), 169, citing *Stromateis* 5.6.3.

[4]   See edition by Stählin, vol. 3, 209–210.

are willing to receive the Gospel.[5] It would not be fair to imagine that the historical Christ evaporates in this universal ministry, for the written word of scripture is still a necessary means to the knowledge of him, and we are not allowed to forget that the Word to whom the nations now look for instruction is the one who was repaid for his teaching with a crown of thorns (*Paedagogus* 2.8).

In his *Protrepticus*, or *Exhortation*, Clement vigorously derides the cult of idols. Against the graven image his *Paedagogus*, or *Educator*, sets the living Jesus Christ as the *prosôpon*, or face, of God (1.57). In a quotation from the Valentinians, which he seems to endorse, the Demiurge is characterized as the image of the invisible God and Sophia as the painter who first fashions this image, then animates it by an infusion of spirit which foreshadows the making and quickening of humanity in God's image.[6] In the nineteenth of his *Excerpts from Theodotus*, the formula 'image of the invisible God' is understood to have the same meaning as its sister-locution, 'firstborn of creation' (Colossians 1.15), and to signify that the Logos, while he makes all things, has a special relation to us as our creator. The Word would thus appear to possess the generative capacity which is ascribed to the Platonic forms as archetypes and patterns of all things sensible; at the same time, Clement's Logos has come into the world as the ideal man, the epitome of the virtues and perfections which have yet to be exhibited in his saints. As Plato defined the goal of the philosopher as 'likeness to god' (*Theaetetus* 176b), so the goal of the Christian life is to be at one with Christ in obedience, in fortitude and at last in immortal glory. He can be shown to the philosophers as a model of courage and probity, but to recognize him as God's own Son and the image of divinity, we must also be acquainted with the prophecies of the old covenant, which were fulfilled in his suffering and his vindication. It is not by chance that Paul is quoted twice as often as Plato in the works of Clement, for Plato had been his own sculptor, guided only by the *logos* within with occasional plagiarisms from the scriptures,[7] whereas Paul, submitting his judgment to the same scriptures, took for his paradigm the image of God as this had been revealed by the fulfilment of the word of prophecy in the Word made flesh.

Origen's Principles of Exegesis

Origen's exegesis always follows the rule of interpreting scripture from scripture, which was authorized not only by the example of Philo, his fellow-Alexandrian, but by the practice of Homeric scholars in the same city since the third century

---

[5]   For full discussion, see now Jourdain (2010).

[6]   *Stromateis* 4.13.902. Stead (1980), 86–87, compares Plato, *Republic* 598b–c, *Excerpts from Theodotus* 47 and *Gospel of Thomas* 84.

[7]   For example, *Stromateis* 5.73.3. On the synergy of Pauline and Platonic thought in Clement, see Ashwin-Siejkowski (2008), 84–93.

BC.[8] Origen himself – though he urged in a famous letter that the spoiling of the Egyptians by the Israelites gave exegetes of the Bible a claim on the treasures of pagan scholarship (*Philokalia* 13) – professes to have received the tools of scriptural exegesis not from the Greeks, but from an Alexandrian 'Hebrew' to whom he owed his elucidation of a number of passages in the Old Testament.[9] This man must have been a convert to Christianity, since he identified the seraphs whom Isaiah saw in the train of God as Christ and the Holy Spirit; it is likely enough, however, that some rabbinic simile lay behind his advice to treat the scriptures as a hallway flanked by numerous doors, by each of which lay a key which was often not the key to that door, but to another (*Philokalia* 5). Origen understood him to mean that, while the scriptures contain the resources necessary to the elucidation of any text, the requisite clue will not always be found in the vicinity of the text and will sometimes be discovered only by long searching. Such divagations are foreign to the principles of modern critical scholarship, but were as natural as 'explaining Homer from Homer' to Jews and Christians who believed that the human authors to whom we attribute the different scriptural books were writing at the dictation of the same spirit. Once every verse is seen to be replete with the same inspiration, it is not so much the student's right as his duty to scour other writings in the canon for licit alternatives to the anthropomorphic reading of a text in which God is called a 'consuming fire'.[10]

A Jewish interpreter might have followed Origen so far, though Philo is seldom so industrious, and rabbinic methods strike the Christian reader as aleatory by comparison. Neither Jew nor pagan could have followed him, of course, in his appeal to the work of Christ – or, more precisely, to the written perpetuation of his ministry in the New Testament – as a mystical key to the histories and prophecies of the New Testament. It is one thing to accord to a word the metaphorical sense that it undeniably carries in another passage from the same corpus; it is quite another to argue that such characters as Joseph, Job or Jeremiah are mere silhouettes of a being who acquired human contours only in the latter days, and even only insofar as he chose to reveal himself to some by the light that he hid from others. Even a modern believer in the plenary inspiration of the scriptures will accuse Origen of reading more out of the text than God breathed into it; in ancient times, he was more apt to be charged with having impoverished the plain sense of the scriptures,[11] since to treat a historical personage as a symbol is to value the narrative only for what it signifies and not for its veracity as a record of God's providential dealings with his creatures. To the second objection Origen would reply that we must not

---

[8] Neuschafer (1987), 276–285. The maxim that Homer ought to be interpreted from Homer was coined by Porphyry, according to Pfeiffer (1968), 226–227, but it encapsulates the practice of Aristarchus and other Alexandrian critics. See also Van der Poll (2001), 188–198, on Clement's deft adaptation of ancient scholarship on Homer.

[9] See *First Principles* 1.3.4, *Philokalia* 5 etc., with De Lange (1976), 43.

[10] *First Principles* 1.1.1, citing Deuteronomy 4.24.

[11] On the strictures of Epiphanius, see Dechow (1988), 315–332.

confound the beginning of things in time with the true Beginning, whose identity became manifest when he took on palpable flesh, proclaiming his divinity by his works and teaching us by his resurrection that, as he made all things of old, he can make them anew. And by this recognition of Christ as God the first objector is also disarmed, for only those who fail to perceive that the flesh is the veil of the Godhead will persist in denying the presence of any subcutaneous meaning in the scriptures. We who must learn diachronically what God knows from eternity must receive our first instruction from the 'literal voice' which addresses us in the scriptures (*Against Celsus* 4.15) until, by passing from truth from truth, we at last discover that the many words of scripture are the same Word (*Philokalia* 5.4), in whom author, sign and signified are one.

This coinherence of saying and being, of text and world, of the typical and the typified, cannot be understood without some fructification of our internal faculties, which accompanies and makes possible the disclosure of hitherto unfathomed meanings in the text. It is not uncommon for Origen to pre-empt a literal reading of some anthropomorphic passage in the scriptures by explaining that we have 'spiritual senses' which enable us 'taste', 'hear', 'touch' or 'see' the God whom we know to be wholly inapprehensible to our physical senses.[12] These powers are discovered not by introspection, but by hermeneutic inference; nevertheless, it would not be illegitimate to see here the germ of Christian mysticism,[13] since the logic of the deduction plainly implies that we cannot unearth the latent meaning of the text in an earthbound state of consciousness. It must be observed, however, that Origen is never enough of a mystic to assume that his own construction of a text is sufficiently ratified by his own powers of divination: the key, as his teacher enjoined, must be sought in the text, although a certain elevation of our perceptions may be required before we perceive it as a key. Thus the digging of three wells by Isaac attests the presence of three senses in the scriptures, but only for one who comes to the text in the expectation of detecting those three senses.[14] In *First Principles* 4.2.4, the threefold reading is supported by an analogy with the threefold constitution of humanity as body, soul and spirit; no such analogy would, however, be readily accepted in the pagan world, where only a complementarity between the soul and body of a text is acknowledged and even then the soul is not so much a hidden meaning in the text as its gist or burden, in contrast to the verbal haberdashery which detains the grammarian or the rhetorician. Origen's conceit will be intelligible only to those who already subscribe to the threefold anthropology which he derives from Paul, and who therefore believe, as he does, that the Word who is present in every word of scripture has taken on body, soul

---

[12]   *Commentary on John* 20.43.405, p. 386.22–27 Preuschen.

[13]   Rahner (1979). Dillon (1986b) expresses surprise that Origen should take literally a conceit that seems to him patently allegorical; but in Origen's view the literal reality of the spiritual senses, like the historical reality of the threefold incarnation, is the indispensable charter for an allegorical reading.

[14]   *Homilies on Genesis* 13.2, pp. 115–116 Baehrens.

and spirit in the world in order to deliver the higher elements from their bondage to the lower. Just as the ascent of the soul after death entails a discarding of the gross body, but not a liberation from all corporeality (which would not be liberation, but extinction), so the excavation of a deeper sense in scripture brings about a refinement, not a suppression of the literal sense.[15]

The differentiation of the soul from the spirit of scripture has exercised modern commentators more, perhaps, than it exercised Origen himself. Mediaeval and modern usage distinguishes typology, the prefigurement in the Old Testament of an event in the New, from allegory, the use of a historical figure or some other concrete particular as an emblem of the generic or invisible. There is, however, no evidence that Origen was familiar with the antithesis, and, while it is often true that he finds the spiritual sense in an adumbration of the work of Christ or the sacramental remembrance of it, there is nothing in his own prose to warrant our speaking of the soul as the allegorical sense in scripture. *First Principles* finds an instance of the psychic application in 1 Corinthians 9.9, where the unmuzzled ox is taken to represent the Christian minister, supported by the alms of his congregation;[16] to circumscribe the psychic sense by the term 'ecclesiastical', however, is to ignore the latitude of Origen's usage; on the other hand, the adjective *moralis*,[17] which commends itself to Rufinus on occasions, seems to have no equivalent in Origen's Greek. Origen speaks freely of the anagogic or tropological import of the scriptures; the noun *allêgoria a*nd its cognates are used most frequently (though not exclusively) in commentary on Galatians 4.24. None of these, in his vocabulary, is coextensive with the psychic sense of scripture, and it is possible that he attached to it no more than a provisional and transient authority, since his doctrine of the last times predicts that soul will be absorbed in the ardour of spirit. In any case, we wrong him if we treat body, soul and spirit as static elements and ignore the two-legged motion of his *Homilies* and *Commentary on the Song of Songs*, where an increment to the wisdom of the reader is always balanced by the emergence of a new meaning in the text.

Origen on the Song of Songs

Origen's *Homilies on the Song of Songs*, preserved now only in Jerome's Latin translation, commence with a lesson in the progressive interpretation of scripture from the scriptures. As Moses spoke of a holy of holies and a Sabbath of Sabbaths, meaning in each case that there is one of its kind which surpasses all the others (p. 27.5–20 Baehrens), so the title of the Song of Songs implies that this is the last and best of the seven songs which adorn the scriptures (28.1–19). The first of these is Moses' hymn to God on the bank of the Red Sea, which, as every

---

[15]   Edwards (2003); Dawson (1997).

[16]   *First Principles* 4.2.12; cf. *Against Celsus* 2.3.

[17]   For example, *Song of Songs Commentary*, p. 75.12 Baehrens.

text in the scriptures is written for us, should be read as a summons to a spiritual exodus. Next, as the living waters begin to flow within, we can chant with Israel 'spring up, O well!' (Numbers 21.17). With the third song (Deuteronomy 32.1) we join Moses in his celebration of the arrival in the promised land; the fourth, a paean of victory sung by Deborah in Judges 5, is for us at once a prophecy and a judgment, characterized as the song of a bee because the name Deborah is also the Hebrew term for this emblem of chastity[18] and priestly separation from the multitude. When we make the fifth song our own, we unite with David in his anthem of thanksgiving for his deliverance from Saul (2 Samuel 22.3); this salvation engenders a fervent love for God, expressed for us in Isaiah's apostrophe to his beloved regarding his vineyard (Isaiah 5.1). And so we come, according to the order of the books in Origen's canon, to the seventh and most sublime of the biblical songs, in which the soul exchanges vows of love with her Bridegroom. It is evident to us – perhaps more evident to us than it was to Origen – that he could not have traced this pattern in the scriptures if he had not made use of assumptions derived from pagan literature; the bee which supplies a hieratic metaphor to Greek poets appears to have no symbolic value in the Old Testament, and, while the appointment of the Sabbath as a day of rest had already been cited as a testimony to the virtues of the number seven by Philo, the Jewish exegete had been forced to seek authority for this inference from the Greeks, since it was not sustained by any explicit pronouncement in the text that he was purporting to construe.[19]

It is Paul who invites us to read this work of Solomon through a Greek prism, for, in speaking at Ephesians 5.27 of Christ's desire to present his bride without spot or wrinkle, he has tacitly identified Christ and the Church as the chief protagonists of the Song. Origen regards it as the first specimen of the literary form which pagans knew as an epithalamium, the conventions of which require that dramatic parts should be allotted in the poem to the friends of the bride and groom (*Homilies* 29.16). Origen decides by fiat, rather than by appeal to any similar or contiguous text, that the friends of the bride are angels and saints in the retinue of Christ, while souls in the process of redemption make up the entourage of the bride (29.7–14). He forbears to explain what is meant by the prayer 'let him kiss me with the kisses of his lips', confessing only that he longs to feel those kisses; the bride's praise of the sweet ointments of the bridegroom, is, however, glossed by reference to the anointing of the king as God's vicegerent (Psalm 44.8), to Paul's description of those who have been consecrated to Christ as a 'sweet aroma' (2 Corinthians 2.15), and to Moses' lamentation over the stench of his sins at Exodus 31.53 (29.10–22). By explaining scripture from scripture, then, we learn that bad odours represent vice and fragrance represents sanctity; since the reader for whom the homilies are intended must align himself with the friends of the bride and not with those of the groom, he is to understand that passages which the expositor

---

[18]   Davies and Kithintamby (1986), 69–70.

[19]   *On the Making of the World* 91–127. On the use of Philo by Clement and Origen, see Runia (1993), 132–183.

declines to interpret carry a scent too heady for his nostrils. The allusion to the *ubera* or breasts of the bridegroom also symbolizes the state of pilgrimage, for the scriptural equivalent of these, in Origen's view, is the *pectusculum separationis*, the portion of a beast's thorax which is removed in sacrifice (*Homilies* 32.7). When the offering is complete, we recline, like John the Apostle, not on the *pectusculum* but on the *pectus* or bosom of the Saviour (52.11–12); the Solomonic text, when properly understood, bears witness to the incompleteness of our understanding. The olfactory metaphors[20] are not yet exhausted, for Origen now goes on to maintain that the prostitute who anoints the feet of Jesus at Luke 7.38 thereby proves herself inferior in holiness to her counterpart in Matthew and John who pours out a casket of nard upon his head (31.13–17). Those who are yet to be sanctified see their own portrait in the bride who is 'black but beautiful' (Song 1.5–6): she is black because of her sins and beautiful because she is forgiven, but her colour remains unchanged even when she is pardoned because so long as we sin we cannot fail to be scorched by the rays of the Sun, though this is the very Sun who communicates his glory to the elect (36.20–22).

The end of the Song implies that the bride is fair at last; in the meantime, black-skinned as she is, she must rove the streets of Jerusalem in search of the one whom she has known and lost. The homilist himself, in a famous passage, calls to mind his own fugitive meetings with the groom, though, as he warns us, those who have not known such encounters cannot hope to understand another's recollection of them:

> Often, the Lord is my witness, I have seen the Groom approach me, and to be with me to the utmost; then suddenly he has receded, and I have not been able to find what I sought. Again I have desired him, and from time to time he has come; and when he has come, and been embraced in my arms, again he has slipped away; and when he has slipped away, again I go seeking him. (39.17–23)

'To be with me to the utmost' is a literal translation of a phrase which might have borne an erotic connotation in the original Greek. But only a desultory reader would take this passage, or any text in the Song of Songs under Origen's guidance, as a charter for profane love, for we have only to turn a few pages to reach the beginning of the next homily, where Origen distinguishes the love that unites the soul to God from the love that immerses it in carnal pleasures. And, just as it was no part of his purpose to encourage common sexual relations, so he had no intention, a hundred years before the foundation of the first monastery, of preparing a detailed chronicle of his inward throes and ecstasies for the sake of other aspirants to communion with God. This is not to deny that his reading of the scriptures was informed by such experiences, but only to remind historians of 'mysticism' that he alludes to such experiences only to promote lucidity of exposition.[21] It is possible

---

[20] On the language of odours in early Christian literature, see Harvey (2006).

[21] Louth (2007), 69.

that he himself regarded this epiphany as a proof of his success as an interpreter, but we should hesitate to conclude that it involved nothing more than a sense of hermeneutic illumination. Indeed, we should beware of a false antithesis between direct cognizance of the Bridegroom and the knowledge obtained from the text, for, as we have seen, it was Origen's premiss that every word in Holy Writ is an expression of the one eternal and prophetic Word.

That all knowledge of God is mediated by Christ,[22] and hence that only a Christ-shaped key will unlock the scriptures, is the burden of Origen's second homily. The unguents of the Song 1.11–12 include the myrrh which perfumes the garments of Christ's kingly representative at Psalm 44.9 (45.18). The bed to which the groom alludes at Song 1.15 is the one from which Christ raised the paralytic at Matthew 9.6 (49.5–6); when we hear that the pair are sleeping in the shade we discern the presence of the Spirit, through whom the power of the Most High overshadows Mary at Luke 1.35 (51.4). The bride's prayer that the groom will give her the ordinances of love (Song 2.4) was answered in Christ's admonition that one who loves his parents more than the Gospel will lose the kingdom (Matthew 10.37) and in Paul's distinction between the 'one flesh' of a carnally married couple and the union of the inner man with God to become 'one spirit' (Ephesians 5.29–31). If the bride feels his love as a wound, we must look for the cause to Isaiah 49.6, where the Servant of God is sent abroad like an arrow (54.4–12); the symptoms are best interpreted by the disciples who, having met the risen Christ on the road without knowing him, perceive that his identity has been secretly revealed to them by the kindling of their hearts (Luke 24.31). 'Lo, he comes, leaping upon the hills and crossing over the hills', exclaims the bride at Song 2.9: it is the office of the preacher to say 'he comes' and of the believer to make himself a mountain rather than a mere hill, lest the Word pass over him (55.25–57.16). If the groom entreats his beloved to come to him 'under the shelter of a rock', he is guiding her to the recess in which Moses hid to protect his eyes from the glory of God, and a reader who has come so far will not require the homilist to assemble the numerous passages from the New Testament which prove that the rock is Christ (60.6–21; cf. 1 Corinthians 10.4, Matthew 21.42, for example).

The principles that inform the *Homilies* are set out with passion and solemnity in the proem to Origen's more ambitious *Commentary* on the Song. At the outset he repeats that the Song is a drama, and that its personae include the friends of the bride and groom. He now intimates, however, that his treatise, like the work to which it is dedicated, is not for those who are infants in the faith, and who (to quote Paul's simile at 1 Corinthians 3.2) have not yet weaned from milk to meat (62.1–9 Baehrens). The New Testament is, as always, the torch by which he reads the Old, but in this case the Jew, the Christian and the Greek combine to justify his exclusion of the neophyte. Solomon's co-religionists, according to Origen, keep in reserve four portions of the scriptures when they pass on the remainder, whether

---

22   He may have been the first to propose, in a variation on *Republic* 509c, that God is higher than intellect. See Whittaker (1969b) with reference to *Against Celsus* 7.38 and 7.45.

canonical or apocryphal, to their juniors (62.24–63.6): these are the Mosaic account of the creation, the epiphany of the cherubim in Ezekiel, the vision of the new Temple in the same prophet and the whole of the Song of Songs. Next to this example, and as a foil to it, we may set the misplaced indulgence of the Greeks. The noblest of their philosophers have extolled the love which lifts the soul to a realm beyond illusion and vicissitude, yet the books that meet with favour are those which gratify the passions and desires of the carnal soul (63.6–24). In such readers the image and likeness of God is eclipsed by the grossness of the physical body, as those who are able to read can glean from the two successive accounts of our creation in the Book of Genesis. But this, as we remember, is an esoteric text among the Jews, and one must read with the understanding of the spiritual man – that is to say, with the eyes of Paul – to perceive that Moses is here contrasting the inner man, the first-created and immortal element in us, with the outer man, who is doomed to perish when the soul takes flight (64.4–5, quoting 2 Corinthians 4.16).

Only those who are able to distinguish the image of God from its garment will be conscious of the presence of two senses in the text, and only those in whom the image has freed itself from the garment will be attuned to the deeper sense. Even to those who lack spiritual organs it will be evident that many terms in scripture are used homonymously (64.13) – that is to say, the ostensible denotation is not in every case the true one, as, for example, when the text speaks of the eyes of the wise, the foot that does not offend or the open sepulchre of the throat (65.19–66.8). The spiritual eye perceives more than this – that love, for example, is in essence the attribute of God alone, and hence that even love of one's neighbour, let alone the love of the world and its worthless booty, is by comparison a mirage. It is generally true that scripture eschews the term *eros*, since in ordinary Greek it was the commonest name for the passion which a carnal mind mistakes for the incandescence of true love; in relation to God, however, the terms for love are interchangeable, and *eros*, with its Latin equivalent *amor* in the translation of Rufinus, signifies not a less chaste but a more intense variety of the *caritas* or *amor* which is enjoined upon all believers.[23] A commentator on the Song of Solomon may speak freely of this inward conflagration – he may even speak of the nuptials of the soul and Christ, and of chastity as their offspring – since the Christian who is admitted to the perusal of this book will already know that a prurient application of its imagery would not be consistent with the notorious wisdom of its author (67.12–14). Some may have been acquainted with a reading that identified the bride as the Church, in accordance with the symbolism of Paul at Ephesians 5.32; while Origen does not contradict this Hebraic interpretation, in which the Church takes the place of Israel, it represents for him the soul, not the spirit, of the Song. The highest level of exegesis – the 'mystical', in his vocabulary – accentuates what is omitted in Paul's simile, the love of the soul for God, and thereby brings puts

---

[23]   Commenting on the structures of Nygren (1953), Rist (1964), 206–209, proposes that Origen was acquainted with a non-acquisitive sense of *eros* in *Enneads* 6.8.

the reader in a relation to the Word within the text that may be called 'mystical' in our sense of that term.

Author, text and the Word who gives life to both coalesce in the figure of Solomon as he is represented in his own writings. The Hebrew canon preserves three of his innumerable books, as his intention was to illustrate the three stages of philosophy, the moral, the natural and the theoric or contemplative.[24] The Book of Proverbs imparts knowledge of right and wrong as a necessary preparation for the higher knowledge that is unfolded to readers of Ecclesiastes. Some precepts are clear, while others take a riddling form to exercise our latent faculties. Under this discipline, readers of Ecclesiastes learn to despise the vanity of the perishable universe and to seek the eternal mysteries which are concealed in the Song of Songs. A Greek template for this division of philosophy has not been found,[25] but if Origen, as some manuscripts indicate, characterized the third as the 'epoptic' stage, he was thinking of the ineffable revelation, the *epopteia*, which followed upon the *dromenon* and the *legomenon*, the 'thing performed' and the 'thing explained', in certain pagan cults. But Origen is speaking here of study, not of participation in a corporate ceremony, and the proficiency expected of the reader corresponds in each book to its mode of naming Solomon (83.20–86.27). In Proverbs he is son of David and king of Israel, a chosen man among the chosen people. In Ecclesiastes, he becomes the preacher, and king no longer in Israel but in Jerusalem, the city which awaits us above when his preaching has detached us from the world. In the Song he is merely Solomon, 'Prince of Peace' because, of all his appellatives, this is the one that presages the eternal reign of Christ.[26]

The rubric 'Song of Songs, which is Solomon's' intimates in Origen's view, that Solomon composed the last and crowning work in a biblical catena. It is, he surmises, the one among many, the canticle in which the Word is one with his human surrogate, whereas the other six were sung by mediators. This is not to deny the wisdom and sagacity of the Hebrew king, who exposed the folly of Greece and refined its wisdom; it must be observed, however, that he himself is not present bodily in the Song, as it is the one text in the canon that does not admit of a literal or historical exegesis (87.7). This caveat must be qualified in its turn, since the comprehension of this bodiless text[27] is possible only when one book of Solomon has taught us how to live and another has shown us our place in the scheme of providence. And even in the Song the text survives as a tenuous vehicle, just as in Origen's apology we retain a vestigial body even after we and the Lord have been made one spirit, and even when the Father becomes our all in all.[28]

---

[24]   *Song Commentary*, p. 75.2– 76.16; against the common reading 'enoptic', to which De Lubac (1959), 205, gave currency, see Tzamalikos (2007), 359. The reading 'epoptic' is also attested, and favoured by the example of Clement: Riedweg (1987), 142–147.

[25]   Cf. Edwards (1997).

[26]   See further King (2005), 255–272.

[27]   King (2005), 74.

[28]   Cf. Edwards (2003).

The *Commentary on John*

To paraphrase the four books of the *Commentary on the Song* would be to ring the changes on themes that have been sufficiently illustrated. Origen's maxim that every word in scripture is a new instance of the one Word could be applied to his own exegesis, and is pre-eminently true of his exegesis of the Song, in which no sense that can be wrung from the text is deemed to be even superficially tenable unless it pertains to the Word or to the reader as his bride. If we are not to make a postmodernist of Origen – if meaning is not to be lost in the perpetual antiphony of reader and text – we must turn to a scriptural book in which the Word is not just the thing written, but the thing written of, the invisible and intangible reality which is made present but not constituted by the words of the author, and by virtue of which those words are not merely significant, but true. The first grammatical subject in the Gospel of John is the *logos*, and the relation of the truth that the text subtends to the text itself is thus the subject of Origen's prologue to his great *Commentary* on this Gospel, which for him, as for many since, is ostentatiously the least legible of the four and which can therefore serve us, when its own seal is broken, as a picklock to the mysteries concealed in the other three.

Origen begins with what is more palpable to us, the text itself. 'Gospel' (*evangellion*) is the title of four texts which can be said to comprise the *stoicheia*, or elements of the scriptural canon (*Commentary* 1.4.21). Origen here imitates Paul's play at Galatians 4.9 on the two meanings of *stoicheion*: the works that bear the title *evangellion* are as fundamental, and in one sense as simple, as the four elements which make up the physical universe, and they are, as it were, the rudimentary letters that we must master before we can hope to peruse the scriptures with understanding. It is the cosmic, not the alphabetic, analogy which explains why there must be four, yet there is a sense in which these texts themselves are not Gospels but deponents to the good news that the apostle, too, invokes when he proclaims the truth 'according to my gospel' (1.4.28). And there is still another sense in which every writing in the canon can be said to contain the Gospel, since the writings of the Old Testament anticipate the coming of the Word and the epistles of the New Testament elucidate the apostolic record of that coming (1.6.32–36). The Word in his palpable incarnation revealed himself as the object of the prophecies which he himself had sown as hieroglyphs in the scriptures of Israel; the four Gospels, read through the lens supplied by Paul and his fellow-exegetes, bear witness to the fulfilment of these prophecies by God's own apparition in human form, surpassing the expectation of those who parsed them according to the letter. It is not, however, equally true of all four that they constitute the *nous*, or mind, of the scriptures, for it is in the fourth that we find the import of the others (1.8.36; cf. 1.31.221). To decipher its cryptic proem is to know why it must be cryptic, and why its decipherment can never be complete – to become aware, in short, of the simultaneous disclosure and occlusion of divinity that is implied by the use of the title Logos or Word.

Origen commences with the observation that, since the Word is said to have been with God 'in the beginning', it was not itself the beginning, and asks which of the many titles that the scriptures bestow on Christ can be said to merit that appellation. He maintains that we must discriminate between names that characterize the eternal properties of the Second Person: those that have reference only to his relations with created beings and those that accrued to him after his assumption of the flesh, which he would not have assumed had his creatures remained unfallen. To the third class we must assign the epithets 'Christ' and 'shepherd', together with the picturesque tropes that he uses of himself in his role as Saviour (1.23.142–156). 'King' and 'light of the world' are terms of the second class, since they cannot be asserted of him unless there are subjects capable of receiving his largesse (1.25.158–166). Even the predicate 'life', which he claims for himself at John 14.6, is said in the prologue to abide in him as Word, and is therefore not primordial, even though it is a property of his essence and not only a corollary of his dominion over others (1.19.112). The one attribute accorded to him independently of his creation – the attribute on which the creation itself depends – is Wisdom,[29] personified in Proverbs 8.22 as the companion of God before the ages (1.19.111). This, then, is the beginning of which the Evangelist speaks – though, as Origen is writing in opposition to the Valentinian exegete Heracleon, he takes care that we should not imagine Wisdom and the Word who abides in Wisdom to be different entities, rather than specific representations (*epinoiai*) of the same hypostasis.

Logos is therefore the cognomen of the second hypostasis as the one by whom and through whom all things came to be. Nonetheless it would be a mistake, in Origen's view, to imagine that the Evangelist's usage is of a piece with ours, or that the Logos is no more than the speech of God, as epiphenomenal as our own speech is to us. Clement had already protested against the equation of Christ as Logos with the mere *logos prophorikos*, or syllabic utterance, of the human tongue, and there is evidence enough to show that the teachers to whom they addressed these admonitions were not imaginary, even if such labels as 'monarchian', 'patripassian' and 'Sabellian' are mere sobriquets of polemical literature. Origen is no doubt a reliable witness to the use of the verse 'my heart has disgorged a goodly word' (Psalm 45.1) as a monarchian proof-text;[30] the assumption that the Father is speaking here of the procession of the hypostatic Logos seems to him dubitable, as the same locution might be sued by the psalmist of his own labour in composition. If it must be conceded – on the grounds that it is God himself who salutes the Church as his daughter at Psalm 45.11 – that he is also the progenitor of the *logos* in verse 2, we may take the referent to be not the Word himself but the 'types' or archetypal verities which constitute Truth – 'truth' being, like 'life' and 'word' itself, a term germane to his essence, though it lacks the primordiality of the term

---

[29]   See Tzamalikos (2006), 165–172, on the relation between the appellatives Logos and Wisdom.

[30]   1.24.151; cf. Orbe (1991).

'wisdom' (1.39.287). Origen here looks back to an earlier stage in his discussion, where he argues, against theologies which would circumscribe the knowledge of the Son, that if the Son is Truth there is no truth known to the Father of which he is ignorant; to make him simply identical with that knowledge is, however, not only to misconceive his identity, his *hypostasis*, but to deny him *ousia*, or substantial being, altogether (1.24.151; p. 39.29 Preuschen).

It is harder to identify another group who, according to Origen, posited a cosmic alphabet legible to the saints.[31] Permutation of the numerical values which were conventionally attached to Greek letters was characteristic of Gnostic divination, and even the most orthodox inmates of Egyptian monasteries in the fourth century could ascribe occult virtues to alphabetic characters.[32] To Origen it was always an error to honour the visible sign at the expense of the thing that it signifies, and he declines to accept the inference that the Second Person is known under twenty-four titles. We are not surprised to find in his work no trace of the ingenuities by which others reduced the writings of the Old Testament to a total of twenty-four or twenty-two.[33] Having shown that Logos is not the self-interpreting term that many suppose it to be and that merely quotidian usage cannot account for its adoption in the Fourth Gospel, he concludes that the Second Person is called the Logos as the hypostatic expression of divine reason, and that the governance of rational beings, the *logikoi*, is the role allotted to him under this denomination. Two classes have been entrusted to him – the merely rational, of whom it can only be said that their actions have intelligible motives, and the elect, who exercise reason to better purpose in the contemplation of eternal goods. The name Logos, then, though logically posterior to Wisdom, represents indefeasible properties of the Second Hypostasis; its meaning is revealed in the economy of creation, but is not simply a concomitant of his economic role.

Visions and Epiphanies

Eikôn, 'image', is a pejorative term at *Commentary* 2.6.49, where Origen contrasts the true God with every form of copy and similitudes. No censure of the *eikôn* is implied, however, at 2.2.18, where the Logos is extolled as the 'archetype of numerous images', nor at 2.6.38, where, as the absolute truth proceeding from the Father, he is said to be the prototype of the *eikones* engendered by meditation on the truth in rational souls. Again, he can write without censure of the scriptural use of characters as *eikones*. The subject of the figure may be good or malign: against the Jews who symbolize the devotion of sound mind to God at 13.13.81 we must set the Samaritan who personifies false religion at 13.1.6 and the equation

---

[31] *Commentary* 1.31.221; cf. Fr. 7 Metzler on Genesis.

[32] Pachomius, Letter 6 in Veilleux (1982), 67–69. Cf. Bandt (2007); Matthew 5.18; Urbach (1975), 312, as in Chapter 1.

[33] See 4 Ezra 14 at Charlesworth (1983), 555; Epiphanius, *On Weights and Measures*.

of Capernaum with subjection to the devil at 13.59.412. In either case, however, it is by virtue of our creation in the image of the Word that we begin to imbibe his teaching (1.17.105), and hence the image in us is subject to a continual metamorphosis from glory into glory, the result of which is an elevation of the inward senses resembling the outward eye's discovery of ubiquitous beauty in the created order (13.42.280; cf. 2 Corinthians 3.18). Thus, it is the Word who is the true image, of whom we in turn are uncompleted images; the refinement of the image within keeps pace with the growth in our understanding of images which the Word plants in the written text of scripture, and the scripture (as we have seen) is the Word himself in a palpable guise.

Origen's account of our creation and its purpose differs chiefly in conceptual fullness and exegetic rigour from its model in Irenaeus. God proposed at Genesis 1.26 to create humanity in his image and likeness; since, however, only the image is said to have been conferred at Genesis 1.28, it must be presumed that the likeness was deferred until it could be granted as a reward for our own exertions (*First Principles* 3.6.1). Adam and Eve in paradise had the perfection that was commensurate with the perfection of the image; because they sinned, when they might have attained the likeness by their obedience, they forfeited the image, and their progeny bear the image of Satan until they receive a new seal through incorporation into the Church as the body of Christ. No physical body is, however, the true abode of the likeness or the image: here Origen departs from Irenaeus, who held that the body is created in the image, and that Christ's assumption of a human body was thus the necessary condition of his manifesting the image in its perfection. For Origen, as we have seen, the incarnation is a remedy for our trespasses, and it is not in his embodiment but in his character as Word that Christ is the image of the Father. So strong is his conviction that no visible representation of the Father is admissible that he substitutes 'invisible' for 'visible' in Paul's description of Christ as the 'visible image of the invisible God' at Colossians 1.15 (*First Principles* 1.2.6). When, therefore, he has to construe the dictum 'He who has seen me has seen the Father' (John 14.9), he scarcely observes that these are the words of the embodied Christ. It is in the Word, he declares, that we contemplate the Father who begot the Word, and those who perceive in Christ the image of the invisible God will at once behold the Father as prototype of the image. It is not so much his assumption of outward form that makes God visible as our own proficiency in auscultation.

Origen's comments on the Second Commandment in his *Homilies on Exodus* leave no doubt of his antipathy to the use of plastic images in worship.[34] Nevertheless, it might seem that he makes a concession to idolatry at *First Principles* 1.2.8, where he suggests that, to understand what it means to speak of the Son as a *kharaktêr*, or impression, of the *hypostasis* of the Father (Hebrews 1.3), we should imagine a statue infinite in magnitude and thus exceeding the

---

[34]   *Homilies on Exodus* 8.3, distinguishing the 'likeness' of a real creature from the *eidôlon*, which, as Paul declares at 1 Corinthians 8.4, has no counterpart in the world.

purview of any possible spectator. This is Aristotle's simile for an ill-wrought play, but it may have seemed to Origen that its very incongruity made it fitter than any abstract term to represent the Father's inscrutability, which is a measure of his priority, if not superiority, to the Son. The second image differs from its prototype only in comprehensibility, and thus it was that the Second Person emptied himself of his incomprehensible majesty to become an object of mundane perception. The allusion to Philippians 2.7 reveals that Origen does not separate the Son's function as image from his adoption of flesh, but does not entail that imaging and embodiment are synonymous. Christ is, as we have seen, the invisible image of the Father, and the flesh is his visible cipher.

Even the incarnate Christ was not universally seen as he was seen by those who were favoured with a more intimate revelation. The failure of the guards to recognize him in Gethsemane suggests that he had appeared in different guises to the multitude. The higher content of his teaching, too, was audible only to those who heard him with the ears of a disciple, while the rest knew only that he preached in riddles. Even of the twelve, three only were taken to the mountain where his glory was temporarily unveiled; the information at Matthew 18.1 that this disclosure occurred six days after he had prophesied the advent of the kingdom is another sign legible only to the adept: we are to understand by six days the entire span of creation, and the moral is that only those who have risen above the foppery of the world will behold the Saviour in his glory. After his resurrection, the solidity of his body was proved beyond doubt, yet we have no evidence that he was seen by those who sought him without the eye of faith, and we cannot be certain that he appeared to all who would have called themselves disciples, or held more than desultory intercourse with any (*Against Celsus* 2.62–65). It is characteristic of Origen that he offers no prescriptions for the discerning of Christ's presence, though he makes this discernment a shibboleth of true discipleship.

Among Origen's putative heresies is his equation of the angels in Isaiah's vision with Christ and the Holy Spirit. This exegesis is tendered on the authority of his Hebrew teacher (*First Principles* 1.3.4), and clearly implies not (as Jerome alleged) that these persons of the Trinity were mere creatures of the Father, but that in this passage they are depicted as angels because there was no other form under which they could have been perceived by a prophet of the old covenant. What form the Father himself assumed he does not stop to inquire, and in the remaining fragments of his *Homily on Isaiah* 6 he has equally little to say of the ocular phenomenon. We can draw a more useful lesson from the abasement of the prophet – 'Woe is me, for I am a man of unclean lips!' – which is illumined for us by Paul's ejaculation – 'O wretched man that I am!' at Romans 7.24 (*Homilies* 4.2, p. 260.13 Baehrens). The apprehension of sin is a function of the inner man, and the coal that is placed on the lips of the seer is the fire of repentance that Christ kindles in the soul that is not too moribund to receive him (4.5, p. 262 Baehrens). There is a fire prepared for each of us, but those who allow the ardour of repentance to purge them in the present life will be spared the unrelenting flame that awaits the devil and his angels. In this discursive, not to say prolix, reading of the epiphany, no reference is made either to the outward or to the spiritual senses; it is the soul itself that experiences the piquancy of contrition, which in the ordinary Christian will most often be excited simply by reading Paul or meditating upon one's past transgressions.

Conclusion

Rhetoric, as Plato said, is a species of enchantment, and in the mouth of the lover an instrument of seduction. According to the culminating speech of the *Symposium*, however, it is love who is the sophist, and the evil is not desire but the suborning of desire by unworthy objects. While Socrates, the unshod lover of wisdom, has at hand all the wiles of the sophist, he employs them not to make dupes of his interlocutors, but to disabuse them of their false convictions. To those who approach the dialogues as seekers, he is a paradigm of the inquiring spirit, a mirror to souls enamoured of the Good just as, according to the *Phaedrus*, the beloved finds the rudiments of his ideal self in the lover. Philo, in his co-option of philosophy as a handmaid to exegesis, saw the dialogues only as a mine of dogmas, since there was no historical personage in his scriptures who could stand in the same dramatic or obstetric relation to the inquiring reader as Plato's Socrates. Clement and Origen both inherited from him the belief that true philosophy is the harmonization of the human will with that of God through the study of God's disclosure of truth and wisdom in an infallible text; in the Gospels, however, they had what Philo lacked – not only a grammar to unparsed prophecies of the Old Testament, but also a record of the self-promulgation of God in a human cipher. Obedience and love were the keys with which he unlocked the meaning of the word already written; it is through the ripening of those virtues in us that we come to grasp not only the new interpretation that he gives to these ancient signs, but his own significance as the Word of interpretation. Origen, going further than Clement, argues that the word in scripture is more than an affidavit to the ministry of the Word; it is a perpetuation of this incarnate ministry, a reinscription of speaking wisdom in spoken wisdom, threefold in texture like his own humanity, the literal sense at once a veil and a vehicle to the deeper sense, as his flesh was at once the cloak and organ of his divinity. Those who can pierce the surface of the text are as few as those to whom Christ exhibited his glory on the mountain; the veil that Moses wore is torn away, the dark glass becomes luminous, and to those who can sincerely confess 'Thou art Christ, the Son of God', the transfigured Solomon proclaims that God is love.

'My *eros* is crucified' (Ignatius, *Romans* 7.2): Origen applies the words of Ignatius, Bishop of Antioch, to Christ himself, though Ignatius may have been speaking of the extinction of his worldly passions on the eve of martyrdom. Socrates, too, had died as a willing hostage to the law of his countrymen. Nevertheless, the analogies cannot be pressed without breaking. Socrates is not the Good that he holds up as an end to himself, no less than to his pupils; he is the subject of the text, but never its author or the object of an allegorical reading; whatever Plato said in his oral teachings, there was no indefectible Church to control the reading of his dialogues, and no one said of Socrates what Origen says of Christ, that 'to us he is an image, but in relation to the Father he is Truth'.[35]

---

[35]   *First Principles* 1.6.2, though the terms are transposed in variants noted by Koetschau, p. 36.

Chapter 7
Neoplatonism and the Arts

Neoplatonism is the name given by modern historians to a succession of teachers and pupils who do not in all respects hold the same philosophy. That no false doctrines can be ascribed to Plato, and that the source of all existence, though ineffable, cannot be less than perfectly one or consummately good, are tenets held in common; so, too, was the familiar conception of philosophy as the pursuit of the archetypal and essential, a turning from shadows to the thing itself. But whereas Plotinus turns away – forgetting to eat, neglecting to write – from everything that goes proxy in this nether world for the contemplation of the highest entities, his pupil and biographer Porphyry reasoned, on the contrary, that if all becoming is but the likeness of being, it should be possible for the disciplined intellect to discover vestiges of eternity in a static image no less than in a living one, in a sculpture as readily as in book. It was not in the apparatus of religion but in the abuse of it, in sacrifice and ritual invocation, that he saw evidence of blasphemy and imposture; the rejoinder that his *Letter to Anebo* drew from Iamblichus is not, as we shall see, a manifesto for unlimited superstition, and is typically Platonic in its aversion to visual trumpery, whether the artist be a daemon or a mage.

Plotinus on the Iconic Structure of Being

John Rist remarks that, whereas the 'goal of the historical Plato is to contemplate the Forms', that of 'the Plato of Plotinus is to become a Form'.[1] As like is known by like, the Forms, when perfectly known, must be identical – so Plotinus argues – with the demiurgic intellect, so that the Demiurge is no longer merely a copyist of the paradigm but the paradigm itself. Yet if this world of Forms is to be a totality, and if the contemplating subject is to be one with the object of its contemplation, we must postulate a principle of unity superior to any of the things that we have named.[2] This is the One of Plotinus, which he takes to be identical with the Good which Plato represents under the figure of the sun at *Republic* 509b–c. Since the One transcends not merely essence (as Plato says of the Good) but the contemplative activity (*noêsis*) which Plotinus holds to be one with essence, it cannot itself be

---

[1]   Rist (1964), 91.
[2]   See Armstrong (1960), with Smith (2002) for a demonstration on Aristotelian premises.

a being among other beings or an object of intellectual comprehension.[3] We can speak of it only by similes and analogies, which is to say that all our knowledge of it is iconic; ignorance, on the other hand, is the substitution of the mere *eidôlon* for the icon. The term *eidôlon* connotes not so much a weaker degree of resemblance to the origin – there being no true likeness of the unknowable – as a weaker approximation to unity. Since any physical quantity is susceptible of division and dispersion, the material realm is richer in *eidôla* than in icons; as we shall find, however, the skilful artist or mythographer, even in this realm, can excite some apprehension of higher realities in the intellect – or at least in the intellect of a philosopher, who is capable of unifying the images presented to him in a linear or plastic medium.

We may begin with Plotinus' interpretation of the *Timaeus*, in which Plato describes the visible realm as a copy of the eternal paradigm. The relation of the two is repeatedly characterized in this dialogue as that of an image, likeness or copy to its original. These terms are used interchangeably by Plato throughout the dialogue, and it is no doubt only by chance that his choice has fallen on 'image' (*eikôn*) in the most celebrated passages. Timaeus begins his account of the creation with the truism that an artist will always look to a model (28b), and pronounces it self-evident that the author of the generated universe will have looked to the most sublime of models, and hence to the eternal (29a). We have next to decide 'in the likeness of what living being' the universe was fashioned (30c): the answer must be that no pattern could be more worthy of imitation than that which comprehends every species of intelligible life. It follows that the generated world contains the likeness of every intelligible species, and that, as there is but one compendious paradigm, so there can be no more than one generated universe after its likeness (31b). Since he is bound to impose some physical shape upon his world, he makes it a sphere because this isotropic figure affords the closest approximation to the uniformity of the eternal (33b); as its paradigm is a realm of inexhaustible life, it must also be animated by a soul (34c). The perfect resemblance desired by the creator cannot be achieved, however, unless the world participates in the eternity of its archetype; since this attribute cannot be bestowed on a mere copy, he creates the 'moving image of eternity' – eternal itself, but moving according to number – which we call time (37c). His own work culminates in the creation of lesser gods whose task it is to people the generated realm with mortal creatures, framing their bodies from the elements and imbuing them with an immortal soul in imitation of their own progenitor (42e). Hence it is that the cranium which houses the reasoning faculty in human beings imitates the spherical form of the cosmos (44c). The consequence of this united labour is an exquisite harmony of ends and means, and as he contemplates this domicile of mortals and immortals in which all things, from the greatest to the least, are infallibly ordered for the best, Timaeus

---

[3]　See Charrue (1978), 256. His debt to the Parmenides is greater, as both Charrue and Halfwassen (1992) have demonstrated, but lies outside the purview of the present study.

extols it as a sensible god in the image of the intelligible, the most beautiful, the most perfect and *monogenês* – the only one of its kind (92d).

Timaeus describes his speech as an *eikos logos*, a likely account (29c). It is a maxim of his that words should be akin to the things that they denote, so that when they subtend the eternal they ought themselves to be such as could not be otherwise, whereas when the object is itself a mere copy or analogue, the relation between the word and the object will also be one of analogy (29 b–d). Most philosophers after Plato have held the perfect contrary of this, since it is surely the eternal that can be represented only by indirect means, whereas common terms are used without ambiguity to refer to common objects. To the second half of this objection one could reply that even common terms are not replicas but symbols of their referents, and are necessarily cryptic when the object is itself an arcane correspondence between the visible and the invisible. Certainly it could be held that Plato's concept of eternity as that which always is, immutably and necessarily, without change or parts or linear succession, is more perspicuous than his definition of time as the moving image of eternity. Perhaps it is for this reason that Plotinus, when he glosses this text in *Enneads* 3.7, begins by demonstrating what it means to be eternal before he proceeds to the analysis of time. After some consideration of rival theories, he decides that one would be close to a definition of eternity if one spoke of it as 'infinite life in the present by existing as a whole and expending nothing of itself inasmuch as none of it has passed or is still to come' (3.7.5.25–30; cf. 3.7.3.35–41). Regarding the nature of time, on the other hand, there is no agreement even among the admirers of Plato. Some characterize it as motion, some as measure, some as measured motion, but all alike are easily refuted. If time is motion (or a concomitant of motion) it must be either one particular motion or the aggregate of all motions: the second thesis is patently untenable, as it implies that there are as many times as motions (3.78.30–31). The first, however, leads to similar consequences, for if we ask how the motion which is time is set apart from the others, the answer can only be that they mark out equal distances *in unequal times* (3.7.8.16–19). Nor can time be measure, for time itself admits of measurement; even to define it as measured motion will not suffice, because we have no better reason to identify time with measure than with the magnitude that measures it (3.7.9.26–27). We are left with Plato's formula that time is the moving image of eternity (3.7.11.29–30): it is, so to speak, eternity diffused, the iteration in linear sequence of the life that exists as one and at once in the higher plane (3.7.11.36–43), without quantity or division. Since it is the soul that communicates life, it would not be false to conclude that time is a function of soul.[4]

Time does not resemble eternity, therefore, as a statue or portrait resembles the living prototype; on the contrary, it is the joint possession of life that constitutes the likeness. The propensity of life to manifest itself as image is explained in *Enneads* 3.8, which is commonly regarded as the first in a *magnum opus* of four

---

[4]   *Enneads* 3.7.12–13; for a longer elucidation, see Smith (1996).

chapters.[5] According to the argument of this treatise, every act is performed with a view to an end, and, since no agent acts without wishing to know the outcome, the end that is prescribed in every case is the contemplation of the act (3.8.1). If, therefore, contemplation is the act for the sake of which all others are done (3.8.3–6), it may be regarded as the supreme act, and the noblest of all agents will be one that has no proper activity but contemplation. This agent, *nous* or intellect, is constituted by nothing but the objects of its knowledge (3.8.8.26–29): there is no matter to be actualized, no substrate to be acted upon, no entity that knows in contradistinction to the thing known.[6] And yet it is still not perfectly one, so long as the objectivity of knowledge can be opposed to the subjectivity of knowing (3.8.9.8–9). A dyad cannot be the origin of its own unity, though it must have a share in unity if is to be one dyad and not many. The origin lies outside *nous*, in that principle which we call the One, not so much because it has oneness as a predicate as because it is the *sine qua non* of the unity which we predicate of every logical and grammatical subject. By contemplating the One – insofar as anything is there to be contemplated[7] – intellect approximates to unity, exhibiting the *ikhnos* or trace of its inexpressible origin (3.8.11.19–25).

The universal corollary of life is reproduction, and the contemplative vitality of intellect gives rise not only to the eternal forms, which abide within it, but to *logoi*, discursive principles of reason, which sow intimations of the higher realm in a lower plane.[8] The two *logoi* which preside over the coming to be and passing away of phenomena in the visible world are nature and soul, the latter of which is more comprehensive in its operations. Soul is the life of intellect devolved and, insofar as it sustains its contemplation of the intelligible, it approximates to the unity of *nous* and may be regarded as its *logos* (3.8.6.26). Only of the soul of the world, however, can it be said that it never averts its gaze from the higher to the lower.[9] Every individual soul is attached to a mortal body for the purpose of infusing life and form to this transient domicile; each, however, becomes to a greater or lesser degree enamoured of that which it ought to rule.[10] Forgetting its origins in the higher sphere, it is left with nothing but the *eidôlon* or simulacrum of the eternal (3.8.4.45; cf. 3.9.1.8). Thus time – which, as we saw, stands in the same iconic relation to eternity as soul to *nous* – becomes for the individual soul the only vehicle of understanding. Only by contemplation, says Plotinus, can we understand the works of contemplation; nevertheless he is forced to concede elsewhere that our approach to understanding is through myth, which allows the

---

[5]   Harder (1936).

[6]   Cf. Armstrong (1960).

[7]   On the gradual denudation of the One in the vocabulary of Plotinus, see Maijer (1992), 26–52.

[8]   See Rist (1967), 82–102, on the term *logos*. Deck (1967), 62, defines *logos* as 'the diversifying aspect of intellectuality'.

[9]   See Deck (1967), 69–70, on difficulties of interpretation.

[10]   Rist (1967), 112–129.

soul to parse by stages the truths that intellect can encompass in one simultaneous act of vision (3.5.9).

The dissolution of this synchronic consciousness – in other words, the descent from noetic to psychic apperception – and the means by which the soul can regain a primordial integrity of vision, furnish the subject of *Enneads* 5.8, the second treatise in the sequence known as the *Grossschrift*. In a tacit critique of Plato, Plotinus asks where the artist finds his original, and concludes that the Zeus of Phidias is a defective copy of the eternal form that he had grasped by the exercise of his higher faculties.[11] Plato, who had nothing to say of the representation of gods in sculpture, had mocked the painter of common things as a plagiarist who is not even conscious that he is making a counterfeit of the copy; Plotinus, on the other hand, seems willing to grant some knowledge of the archetype even to this quotidian copyist and argues that if nature can reproduce the eternal forms without blame, we ought not to blame her disciple. Of course, the material artefact is unequal to the form that it tries to embody (5.8.1.22–28); nature too, for that matter, is not the wellspring of the beauty that we admire in living creatures, but the *logos* or discursive power of wisdom (5.8.4.37) – a term denoting not a discrete hypostasis, but *nous*, instinct with life. We may be reminded of Origen's conjecture that the name 'Wisdom' signifies that which is logically prior to his function as Logos in the second person of the Trinity; nor is there any want of Christian precedent for Plotinus' observation that in the *Timaeus* the Demiurge looks upon his own works with satisfaction.[12] The analogy cannot be pressed, however, since the citation is not designed to illustrate either the goodness of the created order nor the omniscience of the Demiurge: the aim of Plotinus is rather to excite in us a desire to behold the timeless and immutable exemplar which the Demiurge sees eternally and by virtue of which he knows his own handiwork to be admirable.

Plotinus has no Bible, and his *logos* is not, like Origen's, a Word that creates by fiat. He himself opines in *Enneads* 3.8 that if nature were given a voice she would paradoxically declare that she performs her works in silence (3.8.4.1–13). If there is such a thing as a revelatory text, it will always be cryptographic. For example, the superiority of synchronic over linear understanding is attested in the writing of the Egyptians, who are able to express a concept in a single hieroglyph, whereas the Greeks are forced to employ a succession of letters (5.8.6). Again, the three gradations of reality are arcanely represented in the mythical genealogy of Zeus (5.8.10–13). As the visible world is the image and offspring of its noetic archetype, so Zeus is depicted as the son of Kronos in Hesiodic and Orphic poetry; and, as the noetic archetype is at the same time merely an image of the ineffable, so Kronos has for his parent the august, but elusive, Ouranos.[13] So long as the surface

---

[11]   *Enneads* 5.8.1.38–41. On his relation to the sophists, see De Keyser (1955), 39–41.

[12]   *Enneads* 5.8.8.7–21, embellishing *Timaeus* 37c7–d1. Cf., for example, Genesis 1.10, 1.31.

[13]   On the recurrence of this myth in the *Enneads*, see Hadot (1981).

detains us, Egyptian hieroglyph and Greek myth will be equally impenetrable; this impenetrability is in fact what is signified by the dynastic myth in which each god eclipses his predecessor. The myth, when elucidated, is found to symbolize the priority of archetype to image, which is the very thing presupposed in the exegesis of any sign.

In *Enneads* 5.5 – the third item in the so-called *Grossschrift* – Plotinus asks how intellect can be sure that it has an intuitive perception of truths which are not vouchsafed to the soul except in images.[14] The answer would disappoint a modern empiricist: the knowing intellect is its own criterion of knowledge, and no external standard of veracity can be applied (5.5.2.16–21). The function of mind is to grasp what is logically so and could not be otherwise without ratiocination; the soul aspires to a knowledge of the same objects, though it also aspires to grasp that which is beyond them since, although the contents of intellect may be logically self-sufficient, the intellect (as we have seen) requires a source of unity outside itself. Desire for the good is rooted in soul more deeply than the appetite for beauty (5.5.12.11–18), the stupefaction (*ekplêxis*) that the latter engenders may divert the soul from the proper object of its quest (5.5.12.35–38). Where Plato had likened the vision of the Good to the eye's conversion from the object to the sun, Plotinus compares the intellect, when it turns within, to an eye that gazes not at the illuminated object, but at the source of illumination (5.5.7.30–36). Just as there is no superior light which reveals the sun to us, so the One, which confers the unity of being on everything in the realm of essence, cannot partake of any quality and consequently cannot be said have any determinate essence, or even (in the common sense) to exist at all.[15]

Throughout this exposition, it is assumed that the works of the Demiurge are enlightened and benign. Plotinus barely pauses to acknowledge, let alone to canvass, the manifest presence of evil in the world, which he ascribes in other treatises to the volatility, or the mere inchoateness, of matter. He does not conceive of matter as a force antagonistic to being but, rather, as the horizon at which it vanishes: most probably an emanation of soul, it furnishes individual souls with a theatre for action and the exercise of virtue. It retains just enough reality to act as a mirror to souls engaged in the propagation of beauty; the result is that, although it is not evil in itself, it becomes pernicious to those who forget their heavenly origin, mistake the simulacrum for the archetype and drown as Narcissus drowned, pursuing his own face into a pool.[16] The task of a soul, according to Plotinus' adaptation of Plato's simile in the *Phaedrus*, is to work upon itself as a sculptor works upon a statue:

---

[14]   At 5.5.1.47 the term is *agalmata*.

[15]   On the sense in which the One can will and know, see Rist (1973). Bussanich (1996), 62, ascribes to it 'consciousness without an object'.

[16]   Enneads 1.6.8.

Withdraw into yourself and look. And if you do not find yourself beautiful yet, act as does the creator of a statue that is to be made beautiful: he cuts away here, he smoothes there, he makes this line lighter, this other purer until a lovely face has grown upon his work. So do you also: cut away all that is excessive, straighten all that is crooked, bring light to all that is overcast, labour to make all one glow of beauty and never cease chiselling your statue, until there shall shine out on you from it the godlike splendour of virtue, until you shall see the perfect goodness surely established in the stainless shrine. (*Enneads* 1.6.9, trans. Mackenna)

Where Plato had imagined the lover cultivating the beauty of his beloved, his disciple holds, as we saw above, that the craftsman loses the fullness of his vision when he tries to impose it upon an external medium. Looking into himself, the philosopher looks beyond his perishable union with the body to the realm of eternal being and beyond this to the ineffable source of unity; if he should choose instead to turn from the heights to the depths, he resembles the Dionysus of Orphic myth,[17] who was so distracted by his own image in a mirror that he was taken from behind before he knew it, to be dismembered and devoured (4.3.12.1–2).[18]

There is clearly an evocation of some mystery here, though one of whose performance we have no clear record outside the imagination of philosophers. In the earliest of Plotinus' writings, *Enneads* 1.6, the encounter with beauty is said to kindle a Dionysiac exultation in the true lover (1.6.5), while the soul is exhorted to imitate the adepts who put off their old garments in order to don new robes (1.6.7). Such metaphors – if metaphors they are – assure the reader that Plotinus is not teaching any new doctrine when he asserts that the cause of evil is not in soul or in the procession of matter from soul, but in the bondage that the soul incurs when it makes a prison of its earthly tabernacle and takes the counterfeit for the archetype. Among his own contemporaries, however, there were philosophers who had forsaken the ancient mysteries, and the fourth treatise of the *Grossschrift*, *Enneads* 2.9, is a polemical rejoinder to these erstwhile friends, as he styles them, who believe that they can release the soul by sibilant cries and wordless ejaculations. This world, as they represent it, is not the creation of an omniscient Demiurge, but of a far inferior agent who stands, like Plato's artist, at two removes from the divine. Porphyry gives this work the title *Against the Gnostics, or against those who say that the Maker of the Cosmos is Malign*. Plotinus attaches no name to his opponents, but their teachings, as he adumbrates them, coincide with those of Gnostic *Zostrianus*, the prototype of which is said by Porphyry to have been among the texts cited by the malcontents.[19] Their Demiurge is the shadowy child which Wisdom spawns after stooping towards her own luminous *eidôlon*, or reflection, in the matter which lies below the noetic cosmos; when Plotinus mocks him as

---

[17]   Detienne (1979).

[18]   See further Pépin (1970).

[19]   *Life of Plotinus* 16; see Edwards (1990).

an *eidôlon eidôlou*, the shade of a shade, he is throwing one of their own conceits in the teeth of his interlocutors (2.9.10.27). To these enemies of providence the world in which the soul now dwells is not a glorious *eikôn* of the intelligible, but a 'tragedy of terrors' (2.9.13.7), orchestrated by the inexorable malevolence of the stars. Their error, Plotinus argues, is to imagine that the demiurgic activity of the soul requires a cause and not to perceive it as an indefeasible function of her being. Stigmatizing them as Epicureans (2.9.15.8), he taunts them with the Master's aphorism that those who are not at peace with the world have the power to leave it,[20] insinuates that they (like all false readers of the *Symposium²¹*) are secretly enamoured of the bodies of young men. There can be no more perfect image of the eternal in matter than the temporal cosmos, in which 'there are not only images (*agalmata*) of the gods, but the gods themselves, keeping watch from on high' (2.9.9.20–21).

The noun *eidôlon* is used elsewhere in the *Enneads* to denote that complement in the lower realm to the higher part of the soul, which remains unfallen. Plotinus writes at *Enneads* 1.1.12 that the soul incurs no guilt when she condescends to shed her light below, and that no *eidolon* would be created were it not for the opacity of the substrate. He surmises that 'the poet' – that is, Homer – was alluding to this projection of a dark image by the soul when he contrasts the deified Heracles with his shade in the nether regions.[22] He concludes that when a soul has exemplified active rather than contemplative virtue, a part of it will remain behind when it ascends. At *Enneads* 4.3.27 he opines that the Heracles of the lower realm will retain the memories of his actions and experiences on earth and adds at 4.3.32 that even a Heracles in his heavenly abode will not, like the wiser man, renounce anecdotal memory for the knowledge of sublime and timeless objects. The words of an ancient poet may lend authority to the teachings of a philosopher, but only because the philosopher has the acumen to discover a hidden sense in the poet's words.

Porphyry and Statues

Porphyry of Tyre was among the most versatile and polymathic writers of antiquity. For a few years he was a student of Plotinus and at length became his editor, yet he left few works that would justify us in calling him a disciple. His *Cave of the Nymphs* is not, perhaps, inimical to the principles of his master, but it was not Plotinus' way to give such prolonged attention to authors other than Plato. In his treatise commending the vegetarian diet he appeals to the example of Plotinus, yet he seems to embrace a whole taxonomy of sacrifices in his *Philosophy to be Derived from Oracles*. Even the trenchant *Letter to Anebo* is not the composition

---

[20]   *Enneads* 2.9.9.17; cf. Diogenes Laertius, *Lives* 10.126.
[21]   *Enneads* 2.9.17.26–27; cf. *Life of Plotinus* 15.
[22]   See Dodds (1934), 49.

of a man who could have said, with Plotinus, 'the gods should come to me, not I to them' (*Life of Plotinus* 10.35). If we begin this survey with his tract *On Statues*, that is not because we can prove it to be the earliest of his writings, but because it expresses a characteristic faith that there are agencies at work in the lower sphere who deserve at least a portion of our reverence.

The first excerpt begins in the hieratic manner of Callimachus and the Orphics: 'I shall speak to those for whom it is lawful: adepts, shut the doors!' (Fr. 351.14 Smith). We might regard this as Porphyry's confession of the inadequacy of sculpture, which conveys no understanding of the gods until the thought of the artist is expressed in words. Yet words, too, are defective when the book is their only medium: the choice of a ritual idiom suggests that the graphic character owes its efficacy to its success in mimicking the verbal utterance. It becomes clear that the object of this proem is not to demonstrate the superiority of word to image, but to establish an analogy between two visual substitutes for speech. Effigies of the gods are to be read as one reads a book; those who cannot decipher them will, of course, believe them to be no more than wood and stone, as those without knowledge of letters will see nothing but stone in a stele, wood in a letter and papyrus in a book (Fr. 351.24).

There remains nonetheless an asymmetry between the pictorial icon and the alphabetic sign. While we construe the latter by translating it, according to fixed conventions, into a sound to which it bears no perceptible likeness, Porphyry is not prepared to admit that the correspondence between a god and his icon is equally adventitious. There are certain properties of the divine which must be honoured in the image, though the mode of illustration is necessarily oblique. The ethereal fire in which this luminous nature robes itself is invisible to our benighted organs: the sculptor will therefore represent the inscrutable light by crystal and the unsullied fire by gold, adding dark materials to remind us that the true subject of his handiwork remains hidden (Fr. 352.8f.). Differences in age, apparel or gender are once again indices of real, though arcane distinctions: white can stand for the gods of the upper heaven, the circle for time, the sphere for cosmic powers or for hope and fortune (352.17–22). The pyramid, as Plato had prescribed, is the token of fire and the cylinder of earth, while crude outlines of the procreative organs serve as hieroglyphs for the forces of generation (352.23–27).

More can be achieved in verse, as Porphyry proceeds to show by quoting an Orphic hymn (Fr. 354). It is a litany of strange and sometimes incompatible attributes, declaring that Zeus, the author of all, is also the first who came to be and the wielder of the thunderbolt, that though he was born as a man he is also a deathless nymph, that all things repose in his body – not only earth, air, fire and water but Metis the first progenitor and much-rejoicing love – that his head is the luminous ether and his tresses the stars, that the dusk and the dawn are his two horns and the sun and moon his eyes, that his mind consists of imperishable ether, that the air is his chest and the earth his sacred belly, the sea his girdle and his standing-place the nethermost parts of the earth. This is hardly an exemplary piece of metaphysics, or a classical specimen of poetry: Horace, in the famous prologue to his *Art of Poetry* (*Epistles* 2.1.1–5), had asked why, if the tail of a fish and the body of a woman do not make an acceptable picture, we should be ready to condone such incongruities in verse. Porphyry's position appears to be that, when the object of the poem is by nature inapprehensible, visual imagery may be carried to a point that beggars vision. Because his work could never be mistaken for a simple counterfeit of the original, the poet has a licence to cheat the senses, which cannot be extended to the artist in a plastic medium.

But what, then, is the relation between the artefact and the deity, since it is evidently not the case that one resembles the other as a portrait might resemble its human sitter? Porphyry does not speak of analogy, though he will sometimes use an argument of the form, 'What A is to B, so X is to Y'. The term more characteristic of this treatise is *symbolon* (Fr. 358.29, for example). The blue helmet of Hephaestus is a symbol of the azure heaven (359.14), the virile satyr a symbol of agricultural fertility (358.55). The uncastrated Adonis, in contradistinction to the emasculated Attis, is a symbol of reaping at the harvest season (Fr. 358.51–52). Gods themselves may be symbols of attributes in another deity: thus the salvific power of the sun is symbolized by Asclepius, his dance through the year by Dionysus, his impregnation of the soil by Pluto and his desiccatory heat by Pluto's co-regent Serapis. In the purple robe of Serapis, in his sceptre and in the inflexion of his hand, we discover symbols of the sun's descent, his sovereignty in the nether world and his disappearance into the unseen (359.33–55).

As this example shows, Egyptian gods are as amenable as their Greek counterparts to a symbolic interpretation, and indeed it is often study of their emblems that enables us to recognize one deity as the counterpart of another. On some occasions, however, the sacred heraldry is elucidated by a play on words. Leto, the mother of Apollo and Artemis, is a symbol of the darkened air because her name resembles the noun which signifies 'oblivion' (Fr. 356). Cerberus, the dog (*kuôn*) allotted to Pluto, signifies the *kuêsis* or gestation of the earth's fruits. His three heads correspond to the sowing, the incubation and the germination of the seed, though, since an icon admits of more than one legitimate exposition, they can also be said to represent the three phases in the sun's daily course – his rising, his meridian and his setting (359.55–58). The word is thus the key to the image – though not, if we return to the opening sentence, the written word only, for the sacerdotal exordium suggests that the lore of the icon will be imbibed by stages under the guidance of a skilled preceptor.

The *Cave of the Nymphs*

The *Cave of the Nymphs*, a work that finds no parallel in the classical tradition as we know it today, is a reading of both a poem and an artefact, since it takes for its text a passage from the *Odyssey* in which the hero wakes to find himself in a cave on his native isle of Ithaca, which shows marks of more than human workmanship.[23] Porphyry's first observation is that the text is not to be understood 'historically' (*kath' historian*), since there is no structure that resembles the cave in the known topography of Ithaca (55.15–16). To the native pronouncements of the geographers we can add the philosophical strictures of Cronius, a second-century Platonist, who opines that the cave is not so much a wonder to the eye as to the ear, since, while it can at least be represented in words, its properties and contents are too incongruous to be reconciled in a visible artefact (56.24–57.1). In the same verse, for example, we are told that it is both misty and alluring, though experience would inform him that in the presence of shadows we feel not desire but dread (56.13–14). Again, we hear of vessels, though there is no one at hand to pour anything into them, and it is all the more paradoxical to be told that they serve instead as a haunt for bees (56.16–19). If it is incredible that purple garments should be woven in such a place for the gods and that these garments should be visible to mortals, the fact that they are woven on looms of stone rather than of wood compounds the absurdity (57.1–4). That the cave should be consecrated to the nymphs, and that it should have one door for gods and one for mortals, are further mysteries, which ought to convince not only the wise but also the vulgar that an allegory and riddle are concealed in the poet's invention (56.7–8). Porphyry concurs with Cronius so far, except that, in order to avert the charge of *plasma* or fabrication, he contends that the most accurate geographers have discovered the cave to the east of Cephallenia (58.6–11). At the same time, he acknowledges that the poet would not be exonerated merely by the proof that his cave was real: so long as it appears to be a congeries of irreconcilable elements, the masons who designed it and the poet who described it are equally open to reproach. It is consequently the duty of the interpreter to show that, if the cave was truly a hallowed site of the 'ancients', they would not have failed to adorn it with mystical symbols, while on the other hand the poet must have more than casual motives for his commemoration of their handiwork (58.16–18).

Aristotle had argued that a poem can express philosophical truths which are of more import than the anecdotal facts of history. Porphyry, too, commences with the assumption that, since Homer understood all that Plato later brought to light, he would have made his cave a representative specimen of the cosmos, which he knew to have come into being by the superimposition of form on matter. As a product of matter, the cave, like the world, is tenebrous and unpleasing to the intellect; as in the whole, however, so in the part, the intertwining of form and substrate can impart a superficial beauty to objects which, on closer inquiry, prove repellent to the intellect (59.18–25). The outward form of the cave is therefore seductive to the eye, though Odysseus, who is an icon of the philosopher (79.20), will understand that his task is to escape it, just as the enlightened soul will thirst for escape from that 'strange icon', the cave of Plato's *Republic* (62.5; cf. *Republic* 514a). He is surely hinting at an analogy here between the emblematic content of the text and the *agalmata* or images which populate both Plato's cave and Homer's (57.13);

---

[23]   The text is *Odyssey* 13.102–112.

at the same time, there is nothing arbitrary in this use of a fictional edifice as the key to the iconography of a real one, since the worshippers of Mithras have built caves of palpable stone which are also legible repositories of symbols, avowedly imitating the god's own workmanship in the visible cosmos (60.7–9). Mithraic architecture is also adduced in corroboration of Porphyry's thesis that the doors to the cave are the tropics of Cancer and Capricorn, the first of which is a portal for descending souls, the other their means of egress from the material universe. The proof-texts for this teaching are supplied by the second-century philosopher Numenius; the figure of Mithras, holding the northern regions in his right hand and the south in his left, admits of a philosophical exegesis which reveals the existence of the same belief among the Persians (73.6–7). The Mithraists themselves have left no literature as a gloss on the patterns of astronomical signs which they contemplated in their sanctuaries;[24] the Platonists, on whom we rely for want of a native dragoman,[25] manifestly do no justice to the intricacy of these diagrams or the learning that informs them. The decipherments proposed by modern scholars require whole books for their justification and leave us wondering whether worshippers in antiquity were equally dependent on the word or were able to apprehend intuitively what we now grasp by discursive revelation. Although the perusal of Mithraic images is not the same thing as the *epopteia* of the Athenian mysteries, the comparison proves that there is no absurdity in supposing that for Mithraists, too, the 'thing seen' was the interpretant of the 'thing heard'.

For Porphyry it is discourse – and, more specifically, the discourse of his own philosophy – that elucidates the mysteries, though at the same time the endorsement of the Mithraists enhances the universality and hence the authority of that discourse. He has every reason not to read these painted cryptograms as the adepts did, for the motions of the stars are of no interest to him in any of his writings. Since he maintained that Plotinus had exploded the pretensions of the astrologers, he could not even say, with Origen, that the zodiac might serve as a book to superhuman beings. He does not, however, make light of the widespread propensity to find emblems of metaphysical truth in the natural order. The association of bees with springs is commonly attested, while among the Mithraists these springs can be symbolized by vessels resembling those of Homer's cave (68.16–69.4). Honey, being a salve for wounds and the putative food of the gods, may be a symbol of immortality (67.66.23–67.19); a more accurate reading of the present passage will discern in it a symbol of the catharsis or purification which precedes entry into this world, since folklore attaches the bee to such powers as Demeter, Kore and the moon, which preside over temporal vicissitude, and souls are said to be drawn into this world by its pleasant savour (68.17–69.16). The congelation of matter in northern climates, the seminal powers attributed to the north wind and the stoutness of northern peoples are all indications that the portal to the north is the tropic of Cancer, through which souls descend to the sphere of

---

[24] See now Beck (2006).

[25] See further Turcan (1975).

embodiment and generation (73.17; 74.8–9; 76.4). Water is a ubiquitous symbol of generation; the Roman Saturnalia, in which the slave becomes master for a day, takes place in January because Capricorn is the gate through which the soul returns to heaven from its captivity (72.4–11). The fabrics woven by the nymphs are dyed in red, the colour of blood, to complement the analogy between the stone loom and the skeleton which supports the soul's robe of flesh (66.2–15).

There might seem to be neither head nor tail in Porphyry's exegesis, no equivalent to the Alexandrian canon of interpreting Homer from Homer. If there is any feature of Homer's landscape that would point to a hidden meaning, it is the olive tree at the mouth of the cave, but only when we take notice of the properties which are accorded to it in sources outside the poem:

> For since the cosmos did not come into being at random or by chance, but is the product of divine wisdom and the intellectual nature, the olive, which is a symbol of divine wisdom is planted by the cave which is an icon of the cosmos. For this is the plant of Athena, and Athena is wisdom ... Nor do I think that it was beside the purpose [*apo skopou*] for those who follow Numenius to opine that for Homer Odysseus throughout the Odyssey carries the image of one who has passed through the stages of generation and has thus taken his place on the mainland beyond reach of billow and sea. (*Cave*, pp. 78.10–14 and 79.19–23)

In the language of ancient criticism, the term *skopos* signified, or was coming to signify, the import of an entire text, which must be grasped before we proceed to the resolution of circumstantial difficulties.[26] The tree that serves Odysseus as a beacon is thus the analogue of the philosophical insight which enables us to interpret the mariner's egress from the cave as the deliverance of the soul. If we may build conjectures on the assimilation of Homer's cave to the parabolic cave in the *Republic*, we may argue that, as the olive stands in the place which is occupied by the Form of the Good in Plato's narrative, it foreshadows that sublime illumination which reveals the value of all things and to which all lights that we see in this world are mere candles. It may seem paradoxical to offer, as a warrant for allegorical reading, an allegory not warranted by Porphyry's own example, but speculation is authorized by the last sentence of his treatise, in which he admits that half of his task remains undischarged:

> But let the written treatment (*to sungramma*) of this be postponed [*huperkeisthô*] to another exercise, while with regard to the matter of the cave [*tou hupokeimenou*

---

[26] Proclus, *Republic Commentary*, vol. 1, p. 11.1 Kroll; *On the Cratylus*, p. 90.24 Pasquali. Cf. Heath (1989), 132–134, though he rightly denies that Porphyry seeks a unifying *skopos* in this treatise, which is after all not a commentary on one text. If Origen employed the term – as Young (1997), 24–26, has demonstrated – he cannot have borrowed it from the Neoplatonists, his younger contemporaries.

antrou], the exposition [*hermêneia*] has reached its conclusion here. (*Cave*, p. 81.8–10 Nauck)

The term *hypokeimenon*, which connotes a substrate, suggests that the cave, or Homer's description of it, is the matter of Porphyry's treatise. Which of the two he means we cannot determine, for it had been common since Aristotle to speak of the subject of a writing as its *hule*,[27] as it was also common to speak of an author's fashioning the body of his text. Porphyry too distinguishes the body of a text, which admits of *hermêneia* or lexical anatomy, from the soul in which we look for its *dianoia* (fr. 416 Smith). In promising a new study, which will advance from *hermêneia* to *dianoia*, he adopts the complementary verb *huperkeisthô*, as though to hint that his present enterprise is only the matter or substrate of the next.

In his *Life of Plotinus*, one of his later writings, Porphyry seems to hold a different view of the representation of human beings. It is possible that, in his role as panegyrist and biographer, he has allowed his own voice to bend with that of his master, whose reluctance to sit for his portrait supplies a prologue to, and perhaps a vindication of, the literary memoir. 'Why create an *eidôlon* of an *eidôlon*' retorts Plotinus when his friends attempt to persuade him (*Life* 1.7); the consequence is that the reproduction – the *eikôn*, as Porphyry calls it (1.6) – has to be painted surreptitiously by an artist who has been smuggled into his classes. It was common both in lives of individuals and in generic adumbrations of the virtues for an author to claim the vividness of a painting for his handiwork, perhaps with a hint that the brush is not so versatile an instrument as the pen. Readers of Porphyry's *Life* who were familiar with this trope will also have noticed that Amelius, the author of this stratagem, was also the first to distribute records of Plotinus' lectures (3.47), though the illustrious critic Longinus judged them inferior to those which Porphyry subsequently prepared in collaboration with his master (19.21–31). The *Life* is his preamble to this corpus which is destined to outlast the osseous shell, preserving not the outward lineaments, but the thought that made Plotinus 'the philosopher of our time' (1.1).

Porphyry writes that the artist drew his first sketch from the *phantasiai* or impressions that he had formed of the most striking (*ekplektikas*) features of Plotinus. The term *phantasia*, as we have seen, had a chequered history in the second sophistic, while attempts to produce *ekplêxis* or stupefaction were never applauded. It is evidently not without design that Porphyry makes this story the overture to his *Life of Plotinus*, a full two chapters before he relates the little that he knows of his master's birth and early life. I have argued elsewhere that the purpose of this departure from convention is to intimate – against his rival Amelius, who not only commissioned the portrait, but also produced the first commentaries on Plotinus' teachings – that the character of a man is not to be found in the meretricious duplication of his appearance. Where, then, should we look for a true memorial of Plotinus? In the *Life* itself, or in the *Enneads* to which

---

[27]   Aristotle, *Ethics* 1094a; cf. *Poetics* 1452b1 and Heath (1989), 126–127.

the *Life* is an introduction? Most probably in the latter, which is not to say that Porphyry has no hand in the composition, for, as we have seen in his handling of the *Grossschrift*, it was he who divided the writings of Plotinus into six groups of nine, beginning with the rudiments of the ethical life and soaring at the end into the 'flight of the alone to the alone' (6.9.9).

The *Philosophy to be Derived from Oracles*

The words of a disciple, then, present a more faithful likeness than the picture, and these in turn are surpassed by the subject's own account of himself. If more persuasive testimony is required, it may be sought from the mouth of Apollo, whose omniscience has been famous since times that were already legendary to Herodotus (*Life* 22.6–7, citing *Histories* 1.47).The eulogy that follows shows us not the dead exterior of Plotinus – so leprous and malodorous in his last days that his closest friends could not endure his company – but a soul that has swum victoriously through blood-choked tides, no longer the soul of a man but a daemon, beckoned to shore by the immortal choir (22.13–63). The diction is reminiscent of Empedocles, the allusion to Homer makes Plotinus a second Odysseus, the dead are welcomed by their elders in one of Plutarch's myths: should we therefore surmise that the poem – appearing as it does two centuries after the shrines are said to have fallen mute, or at least to have lapsed into prose – is a free composition by Porphyry, not the substrate but the product of the commentary that succeeds it in the *Life*? Or might one assume more charitably – since Plotinus himself declares that we beget the gods in ascending to the One – that Porphyry thought himself entitled to speak for the earthbound gods, much as the Fourth Evangelist thought it lawful to credit the embodied Word with sayings imparted to the Church by the Holy Spirit? He himself undoubtedly believed that the gods had recovered their power to speak in verse, for among the works to which he owed his infamy among Christians was a treatise in three books, *On the Philosophy to be Derived from Oracles*. In this he does not fail to name the seats of Apollo from which he had gathered precepts for cultic practice, the aversion of wrath and even the conjuration of gods in the visible form that was characteristic of each.

In his prologue Porphyry avers that he has reproduced the oracles just as they came to him, without adding or subtracting a word except to reform the metre or relieve the text of obscurities and lacunae (Fr. 303). It is not for us to improve on the depositions of such witnesses, though we must be aware that riddling or deceitful answers are given where the truth exceeds the capacities of the inquirer (Frs 305, 340). Natural forces may also prevent gods from becoming visible to their suppliants (Fr. 339), and there is nothing in the collection to show that Porphyry had witnessed the epiphanies which are promised to other inquirers in his collection. Apollo's depiction of golden-horned Pan with a rod in one hand and a syrinx in the other was to Porphyry, as to us, a poetic figure (Fr. 307), as is Sarapis' account of his meeting with Pan as a bearded youth who has wreathed a cluster of grapes about his temples (Fr. 318). We cannot even say whether he had seen the *xoanon* or wooden effigy, adorned with the shapes of various beasts, which worshippers of Hecate had been enjoined to carve for her (Fr. 317), or another in which she wore a girdle of snakes and assumed the likeness of Demeter (Fr. 319). He seems to speak with personal acquaintance of the statues in which she bears a whip, a lamp and a sword (Fr. 320), but it is only from the oracles in which she is the putative speaker that we learn of the aery phantasms (*eidola*) which revealed her now as a maiden, now as a bull (Fr. 328), or of the benign and potent letters which were carved upon her images in silver, bronze and gold (Fr. 321). Porphyry can do no more than assemble verbal testimonies to ocular manifestations; without the ocular manifestation, however, there is nothing to corroborate the verbal testimony.

It is obvious that Porphyry is not hoping to construct a complete theology from the utterances of beings who can be bound and intimidated by their own worshippers (Fr. 308.21). When he states that the gods impose not only on mortals, but also upon daemons (Fr. 340.10), he may be assuming, with Apuleius and Plutarch, that it is these intermediate deities who act as conduits of divine revelation at local shrines. The phantasms of which Hecate boasts are certainly not commended in his *Letter to Anebo*, a sceptical interrogation of the Egyptian priests, whose tone can scarcely be reconciled with the credulous posture of the *Philosophy from Oracles*, or even with the more qualified demonolatry of the work *On Abstinence*. Since Porphyry seems to be a different man in each of his writings, we need not be surprised that he represents all astrologers as charlatans at *Life of Plotinus* 14, yet concedes in the *Philosophy from Oracles* that the gods many inscribe their knowledge in the stars (Fr. 331) and appear in person to cast the horoscopes of their votaries (Fr. 330). According to his treatise *On Abstinence*, neither the highest divinities nor the philosophers who serve them would have derived any benefit from the animal offerings which he allocates, in the first book of the *Philosophy from Oracles*, to the agents who govern the different elements of the physical universe. If words stand proxy for vision in his collection, it does not follow either that words will suffice or that vision would be the consummation of knowledge. The second book commences with a prayer to the highest god as the ineffable, eternal and hidden father of the immortals (Fr. 324.1), who is in fact no less mother than father, the form amid forms, coeternally harmony, number, soul and spirit (Fr. 324.31–33); since our finite minds can imagine him only by negation, by the juxtaposition of contraries and by metaphors of transcendence, it is impossible to form any picture of him, and we are not told that he returns any speech in answer to our prayers.

Anebo and Iamblichus

The *Letter to Anebo*, as has been noted, is an anomalous work – and one, we should add, that we have to reconstruct entirely from captious or anomalous quotations in other authors. Porphyry asks his supposed interlocutors how they can imagine that a god could be coerced or cajoled by human arts, why barbarous names should be more potent than their Greek equivalents, why an emblem of mud or some other base substance should be adopted as a cipher of the ineffable, why demons (if they are indeed the magician's gods) should require their suitors to be holier than they are, why they should be allowed to batten on the odour and blood of sacrifice, and how the soul can be free if it is in thrall to a natal daemon who is assigned to it by the stars. Since Porphyry's other works reveal that he knew how to answer a number of these questions, it is possible that he was writing in a didactic, rather than controversial, spirit and in the hope of eliciting just such a response as we possess in the lengthy treatise *On the Mysteries*, attributed to Iamblichus of Chalcis.[28] Those who denounce Iamblichus as the high priest of a new age of unreason may be surprised to note that he mentions images only to condemn them, denies the daemons any right to the worship of philosophers and does not believe that the deference of the soul to its natal guardian makes it a puppet of the stars.

Porphyry's *Letter* ascribed to Egyptian sorcerers the practice of *eidôlopoiia*, by which he appears to have meant the conjuration of ethereal forms which are said to convey a true likeness of the gods. True phantoms they are, Iamblichus retorts, with an indignation that would do honour to a Christian denouncing graven images. No one, he maintains, who has beheld the gods would turn his hand to such figments; vapid as they are, more evanescent than reflections in a mirror, they are of less worth than the charlatans who devise them, for the latter at least are children of the Demiurge, who is able to confer bodily existence upon the objects of his thought without mechanical contrivance (*Mysteries* 3.28). No 'demiurgic' art that is known to humans can be likened to his ceaseless and unhindered animation of natural forces; it is no less a misnomer to say that the conjurer has the assistance of astral powers when he avails himself of a weak and dwindling efflux from the stars which is at best a collateral product of divine purpose (3.29). We cannot presume, however, that he would have thundered with the same vehemence against the use of images in civic cults.

No Christian theologian of this age whom we now call Catholic could have held this Greek philosopher's belief in the talismanic power of barbarous locutions. The use of unintelligible terms in our incantations, says Abammon, mouthpiece of Iamblichus, may be thought irrational, but since our mode of communion with the gods exceeds both speech and reason, we cannot hope that the terms in which their acolytes speak of them will always be patient of conceptual rigour or logical analysis (*Mysteries* 7.4–5). If the rites in use among Egyptians and Assyrians are to be deemed inviolable because they have proved themselves efficacious, the same respect is due to the words that have accompanied these rites. To urge that the sense is of more account than the utterance itself (7.5) is to set our wisdom above that of our teachers. Only superficially does this position resemble the

---

[28]   Saffrey (1971).

Christian veneration of the scriptures. The churchmen who drove their opponents back to the text on all occasions did so because they thought that its meaning was, or could be made perspicuous: against both Jews and Gnostics, they maintained that neither numerals nor letters have any potency in themselves, and that it is not the jots and tittles of the law that bring salvation, but its spirit, as manifested in the Gospel of Jesus Christ the living Word. Even the Montanists, who held the same faith in most things, could be anathematized because they were thought to favour ecstatic prophecy, in which the tongue was set loose from the mind.

While he holds that the Demiurge acts by thought alone, Iamblichus needs no doctrine of creation out of nothing, since he regards 'materiality' (*hulotês*) as an abstraction from the *ousiotes*, or principles of essence, which is logically prior to all determinate being (8.3). On the matter of our own world we may impress a picture that symbolizes both the immanent principles of this world and the reality that transcends them. Thus mud may represent all that is corporeal and material, or the hidden flux in these things, or their nutritive capacities; at the same time it may subtend 'the form immanent in nature' or the 'primordial cause, pre-established as a foundation of the elements and of all the powers that surround the elements' (7.2, p. 291 Clark, Dillon and Hershbell). So long as it is acknowledged to be a picture, its polyvalency is a virtue, to be contrasted with the univocal signification of the spoken word when it signifies at all. Nor is it a demerit in the symbol that it bears no perceived resemblance to its archetype: in the semiotic, as in the ritual act, there may be a calculated deformity (*askhêmosunê*), which forestalls the risk of our taking the secondary for the primordial, reminding us that what we apprehend in the present world is never the real, but its signature (1.11).

Epilogue

The commentaries of Iamblichus on Plato are all but lost, and we know even less of his immediate successors. The most illustrious Platonist of the mid-fourth century is the emperor Julian, who preferred the hymn and the diatribe to the hermeneutic exercise, and chose his teacher not so much for his logical acumen as for his ability to animate a statue. Twentieth-century scholars have unfairly blamed this surrender to credulity on Iamblichus, though the latter would undoubtedly have scoffed, as he did when he heard that some of his pupils thought him capable of bodily levitation. To Christians, Julian was a persecutor, a patron of obscenities, a traducer of Holy Writ – in short, a standing proof that every philosopher must be an infidel. He and his admirers, for their part, looked with a satirical eye on the quarrels that had lately been engendered in the Church by the obscurity of the same scriptures – quarrels all the more ludicrous to those who knew, on the authority of Porphyry, that the being whom all Christian sects revered as the image of God in man was in fact no more than a man of godlike soul.

Chapter 8
Image, Text and Incarnation in the Fourth Century

We have seen in Chapter 5 that Christians of the second century, whether Gnostic or (as we should now say) Catholic, unanimously proclaimed that the divine cannot be known without revelation, and that no image of God can be fashioned by his creatures which is as faithful as the one that he himself infused or kneaded into the living clay of Adam. At the same time we found that, with the exception of Justin, Catholic apologists had almost nothing to say of the union of word and image in the incarnation of the Saviour. Chapter 6 was chiefly a study of Origen, whose reading of the scriptures as a continuation of Christ's threefold ministry in body, soul and spirit fused the two modes of revelation, making the text a seamless garment for the image. If the authors reviewed in the present chapter did not reproduce this synthesis, the reason is not that they had turned against Origen, but that questions had arisen for them which he had not raised or to which he gave forked answers. In asking what it means to style the Second Person the image of the First, they were asking not how God communicates, but whether one ought to worship Christ as God. Scripture was the organ of inquiry, not the object. It was necessary from time to time to warn an interlocutor that failure to note the *skopos* or goal of a text would lead to a false interpretation;[1] on the other hand, while the holiness and authority of the text were not denied by any party, it was not to the advantage of that party which maintained the most exalted view of Christ to speak of him in terms that threatened, as Origen says, to deprive him of both *hypostasis* and *ousia*. This, after all, was an age in which the New Testament was widely copied, with imperial sanction, in a form that, unlike the scroll, did not invite reverence for the text itself as a physical artefact.[2] For a time – since the controversy turned on the nature of sonship, and it is a platitude in scripture that a son should be the image of his Father – the term 'image' proved more serviceable than *logos* to champions of Christ's divinity. A later generation, however, conscious that the statue is always inferior to its prototype, was obliged to choose between giving up the word 'image' and attaching new conditions to its use.

---

[1] Young (1997), 29–30, opines, however, that the importance of the *skopos* in Athanasius has been exaggerated by such authors as Pollard (1958–1959).

[2] Young (1997), 11–14. Her argument does not require that Christians should bear a peculiar responsibility for the dissemination of the codex: see Bagnall (2009).

A New Epoch?

The Church before Constantine was aniconic, in the sense that its theologians gave no sanction to the veneration of images,[3] though the decorative use of art was not uniformly prohibited. Historians have detected a fusion of pagan and Christian imagery in the paintings of the catacombs;[4] if they are right, we have surely all the less reason to surmise that these scenes had any liturgical function, since the standard charge against Christians, in Rome as elsewhere, was atheism, or neglect of the pagan gods. At the beginning of the fourth century the Council of Elvira in Spain forbade the use of pictures in Christian places of assembly,[5] yet the wording suggests that they feared not so much the worship of the artefact as the profanation of the true object of worship by exposure to public view. Furthermore, while this condemnation was echoed by distinguished men of God,[6] the abundant remains of Christian iconography from the fourth century show that the laity could tolerate not only the depiction of Christian scenes, but the coalescence of these scenes with motifs that remained intractably pagan.[7] Eusebius of Caesarea tells the world with pride in his *Ecclesiastical History* that his church possessed likenesses of the apostles Paul and Peter; he also refers, without disapprobation, to an image of Christ himself.[8] The same Eusebius, however, is generally supposed to have been the author of a letter to Constantia, sister of Constantine, which rebukes her for having solicited a portrait of Christ himself.[9] If the letter is authentic – and it is not to our purpose here to trace its provenance, or decide which of two Eusebii is more likely to have composed it[10] – it shows once again that the visual representation of the holy was regarded as a violation of the second commandment; it does not imply that images were being employed in Christian devotions. One sect of the second century, the Carpocratians, are said to have honoured a portrait of Christ, together with those of Pythagoras, Plato and Aristotle (Irenaeus, *Against Heresies* 1.27); our witness, Irenaeus of Lyons, betrays his own prejudice when he ridicules this as worship 'in the manner of the Gentiles', but the Carpocratians, if they had any existence outside his own nightmares, were atypical even of heretics in maintaining that the soul must perpetrate every sin in order to be saved.

A new reverence for both symbolic and pictorial images was a natural, though not instantaneous, consequence of Constantine's succession to the throne of a pagan

---

[3]   Lane Fox (1986), 392–395; Grigg (1977). The material culture (intermittently) contradicts the teaching of the ecclesiastical doctors: see Charles-Murray (1977).

[4]   Green (2010), 170–206.

[5]   Canon 36 in Jonkers (1954), 13. On the date, see de Clerq (1954), 87–103.

[6]   For example, Nilus of Sinai at *Patrologia Graeca* 79.577–80, cited by Elsner (1997), 260.

[7]   Elsner (1997).

[8]   *Ecclesiastical History* 7.17; cf. Grabar (1968), 66–69.

[9]   Thümmel (1992), *Testimonium* 13, p. 282.

[10]   Schäferdiek (1980) ascribes it to Eusebius of Nicomedia.

empire. Shortly after assuming the purple, and before he became a Christian, he professed to have received Apollo's blessing in a vision (*Latin Panegyrics* 7.21); as a Christian emperor he declared that an oracle of the same Apollo had sanctioned the persecution of Christians by his immediate predecessors. Accustomed as he was to see divinities whom others knew only by hearing, he was converted to Christianity by a dream, although in this case he was in need of a voice to explain the revelation.[11] Eusebius, citing the sworn word of the Emperor, describes successive apparitions, first of a cross of light and then of Christ himself as its interpreter. Lactantius, placing the dream on the eve of Constantine's seizure of Rome, relates that it took the form of an ancient figure, the labarum, in which the Greek letter P, imposed upon an X, spelt out for Christians the first two consonants of the name of Christ. Hearing the promise 'In this sign thou shalt conquer', Constantine had the labarum inscribed upon the shields of his soldiers and gained the victory. Eusebius agrees that this was his emblem; it was not, however, the letters X and P but the Cross that became a common feature of Christian funerary art,[12] and it was the putative discovery of the true Cross that made Jerusalem a patriarchal see and a centre of pilgrimage. The legend which ascribes the excavation to the emperor's mother Helena is of no historical value, and there is no surviving account of a display of the Cross to pilgrims before the 360s; it is possible, however, that Eusebius preserves an elliptical record of its discovery in his *Life of Constantine*.[13]

The hallowing of a relic is one thing; a plastic or painted substitute for the invisible is another. The accession of Constantine nonetheless induced his Christian subjects to acknowledge the legitimacy of an artefact which had hitherto been among the forbidden objects of devotion. Violence to the emperor's statue had never been condoned by the Church, since this would be taken to mean that the iconoclast did not recognize him as the monarch ordained by God; nevertheless, it was only when the emperor had become their co-religionist that Christians could entertain a positive desire for the propagation of his image while they sought his aid in throwing down every other.[14] According to Chrysostom, Constantine knew better than to confuse the imitation with the original, and had once put aside the news of an assault on one of his statues with a jocular affectation of surprise that this grave injury had not left any scars upon his person. But this is a posthumous anecdote, designed to avert the wrath of a later emperor whose statues had been defaced by the people of Antioch. We shall see that in the first half of the fourth century the maxim that an injury to the statue is an injury to the emperor was accepted not only as a legal fiction, but also as a premiss of Christological debate.

---

[11] Eusebius, *Life of Constantine* 1.26–28; Lactantius, *Deaths of the Persecutors* 44–46.

[12] See Grigg (1977), 21, on the 'apotropaic power' of the symbol and the 'double meaning' ascribed to it by Christians. For a bibliography on the origins of the labarum, see Lane Fox (1986), 616, and Cameron and Hall (1999), 206–213.

[13] Drake (1985); Baert (2004), 39–41.

[14] On the 'potential ritual significance' of such images, see Elsner (2006), 263.

Alexander of Alexandria

One of Constantine's first acts as universal sovereign was to convene a general council at Nicaea to judge between Arius, an Alexandrian presbyter, and his bishop, Alexander. The former professed to demonstrate from the scriptures that, although the Son has the attributes of God, he possesses them only by derivation from the Father, who is God by essence and to whom alone such properties as eternity, immortality, goodness and wisdom appertain by essence and not by grace or fiat.[15] To say that the Second Person is begotten by the First does not imply that they share one nature; there is equal warrant for calling the Son a creature, with the analogous proviso that this term does not imply that he shares the frail and contingent nature of other creatures. While he is superior to time, he is not eternal; we express his superiority to the material creation when we say that he is 'from nothing', since it would be a palpable heresy to imagine that the Father himself is his substrate, as though it were possible to produce by abscission a *homoousion meros*, or 'consubstantial part' of the indivisible Godhead. Those who subscribe to Alexander's motto 'always Father, always Son' are making the two coeternal, and therefore positing two equipollent and independent deities in defiance of the biblical proclamation of one God.

Arius, as is well known, was excommunicated at the Nicene Council for his refusal to sign a creed which affirmed that the Son is consubstantial (*homoousios*) with the Father. To the reader of the early Christian scriptures this is not a self-evident tenet. It does not sit well, for example, with the appellation Logos, since the properties of speech are not those of the speaker and the two cannot therefore share a common nature. Again, if Christ, as Paul avers, is the 'image of the invisible God' (Colossians 1.15a), common sense will surely agree with Aristotle that it is precisely in the *logos tês ousias*, in the principle of its essence or substance, that an image differs from the original which it resembles in outward form. When Paul adds at Colossians 1.15b that Christ is the firstborn of creation, we observe a confusion of metaphors (since an artist does not beget what he creates), but, as neither metaphor is applicable to the Father, it would seem that this dictum favours Arius rather than those who held that the Second Person inherits the nature, essence or substance of the First. As Arius clearly takes this view of our last text, it is all the more surprising that he does not invoke the others when explaining his theology to the hostile Alexander or the sympathetic Eusebius of Nicomedia. 'Son', not 'Logos', is his preferred designation for the Second Person until he submits a new creed to the emperor some years after the Nicene Council. 'Image' is one of a catalogue of titles which connote the inferiority of the Son to the Father in his poem, the *Thalia*, as this has been reconstructed from the satires of Athanasius, but he says nothing to suggest that it is more of a stumbling-block to his adversaries than such terms as 'power' or 'spirit', which are not so clearly

---

[15]   Athanasius, *On the Synods* 16; Epiphanius, *Panarion* 69.7. For a recent history of the conflict, see Behr (2004), 123–161.

repugnant to the affirmation of a common nature. What is more surprising still, perhaps, is that Alexander, in letters written before the Nicene Council, assumes that the common nature is as fully attested by the terms 'Word' and 'image' as by those, like 'son' or 'firstborn', which imply that the divinity of the Second Person is inherited rather than conferred.

The Creed of Alexander of Alexandria

The whole of Alexander's case against Arius is condensed in a brief encyclical which is commonly known by its opening words words 'ενός σωματός, 'of one body'.[16] Even if, as has more than once been argued, it was drafted on his behalf by Athanasius, his deacon and lieutenant during the last years of his tenure,[17] the encyclical would not have been published under his name had it not expressed the doctrine that he was willing to hold in public disputation. Against those who deny that the Son is God and coeternal with the Father, he asseverates that the scriptures prove the Son and the Father to be like in essence (as he expressly says[18]) and hence gives the lie to Arius' belief that he is a creature who exists only as an instrument for the creation of lesser beings (Socrates, *Church History* 1.6.10, 1.6.12–16). How can there have been a time when the Word was not, when the Gospel tells us that he was with the Father from the beginning (John 1.3)? How can the one through whom all things have come into existence be a creature? How can he be from nothing, when the Father says of him 'My Heart has disgorged a goodly word' (Psalm 45.1)? Can he of whom it is said that he is the same yesterday, today and forever (Hebrews 13.8) submit to any change? If he were unlike the Father in essence (1.6.16), would it be said that he is the Father's perfect image or his radiance? Can he for whose sake all things were made be made for the sake of another, and can his knowledge be circumscribed when he himself declares 'as the Father knows me so I too know the Father'? Alexander concludes in a lengthy peroration that one would not have thought such perversity conceivable had not the apostle warned of heresies in days to come (1.6.24–26, citing 1 Timothy 4.1).

The other surviving work by Alexander of Alexandria is a voluminous epistle to his namesake, Alexander of Byzantium, which has never been ascribed to another hand. More than four times as long as the 'ενός σωματός', it is scarcely broader in scope or more prolific in argument.[19] Its strictures on Eusebius of Nicomedia, the formidable ally of Arius outside Alexandria, are eked out by comparison with both Paul of Samosata, the first great prelate to be deposed by an assembly of his peers from the neighbouring provinces, and Lucian of Antioch, who was known to have been the common teacher of Arius and Eusebius of Nicomedia, though

---

[16] Socrates, *Kirchengeschichte* 1.6, pp. 6–10 Hansen.

[17] Stead (1988).

[18] Socrates, *Church History* 1.6.10, 8.1–2 Hansen.

[19] Theodoret, *Kirchengeschichte* 1.4, 8–25 Parmentier and Hansen.

not regarded on all sides as a heretic. It is in this letter that Alexander expressly declares the Son to be 'from the Father' (Theodoret, *Church History* 1.14.45) in opposition to those who (as he complains repeatedly) suppose him to have been created in time and out of nothing. He now asserts not so much a likeness of essence as a community of nature (1.4.31), which he appears to deem equivalent to – we ought not to say, reducible to – a parity of honour (1.4.40). Nor is it any diminution, either of his Godhead or of his majesty, to style him the peerless image of the Father, for if the archetype is eternal so is the image (1.4.27f., 1.4.48).The one prerogative which is denied to the Son is that of being unbegotten. It is by virtue of being born without mediation from the Father that he shares the Father's nature; the birth is affirmed, and the unity of nature is not concealed, when he confesses that 'the Father is greater than I' (1.4.52; John 14.28). In expounding the words and acts of the Son on earth, we must beware of losing the manhood in the divinity and of burying the divinity in the manhood: to uphold the integrity of the incarnate Christ is not to confound the two natures in the one hypostasis (1.4.36–38).

Alexander therefore finds the terms 'word' and 'image' no more inconsistent with the affirmation of a common nature than the term 'son'. He is not afraid, as Origen was, that to speak of the Son as a word or *logos* issuing from the Father's heart belies his identity as a distinct hypostasis; and although the term 'image' clearly carries no intimation of filial procession, he finds it no less useful than the term 'ray' as a phylactery against Arian misreading of the Gospel. His prime concern is not to show that the Son and the Father are equal in all respects – 'subordinationism', as it is now styled, was not then a recognized heresy – but to call down the anathemas of scripture on any argument for the temporal priority of the First Person or the creation of the Second 'out of nothing'. It was therefore very much to his purpose to couple the notion of sonship – which, taken alone, might seem to invite the first mistake – with those of a ray, a word or an image, all of which imply the ontological dependence of one person on the other, without entailing that the First existed when the Second did not.

The insertion of the adjective *homoousios* into the Creed of the Nicene Council in 325 was not accepted without dispute, although, according to Eusebius of Caesarea, it was the emperor himself who had demanded the innovation. The defence of it, however, was undertaken by an unnamed party of bishops whom we may guess to have been its original proponents:[20]

> Now as to the phrase 'from the essence', they affirmed that it signified that, while he is from the Father, he does not exist as a portion of the Father … Likewise, after scrutiny, it was established that the expression '*homoousios* with the Father' was not to be understood in the way that applies to bodies or similarly to mortal animals … The expression '*homoousios* with the Father' signifies that the Son of God bears no resemblance to creatures that have come

---

[20]   Theodoret, *Kirchengeschichte*, 51 Parmentier and Hansen.

into being, but uniquely resembles in all respects the Father who begot him. (Theodoret, *Church History* 1.12.9–10 and 12)

The evidence gathered above suggests that 'they' would have included Alexander of Alexandria when it had to be proved that the Son is 'from the *ousia*' of the Father. While it is conceivable that we have to do with a miscellaneous party in which each man upheld his own watchword, the most natural reading of Eusebius' words would imply that a single party defended a particular constellation of beliefs. Defenders of the locution 'from the essence' would therefore also be advocates of the *homoousion*. The gloss which is supposed to have been supplied by the interlocutors of Eusebius – the homoian explanation, as we may call it, that to share the same *ousia* is to possess identical properties – is perfectly reconcilable with the doctrine of Alexander in his letters. To some members of the Council it would imply that perfect likeness cannot amount to *less* than identity of *ousia*; others would draw the inference that identity of *ousia* need amount to nothing *more* than perfect likeness. Either construction may have been satisfactory to the patriarch, so long as it reconciled two hundred bishops to a formula that no Arian could sign.

Eusebius of Caesarea

Eusebius, bishop of Caesarea, whose letter is the one surviving record of the Nicene Council, is often said to have taken the part of Arius against his Alexandrian superiors. Yet less than an iota separates him from these putative adversaries after the Council, at which Alexander of Alexandria added the word *homoousios* to his public vocabulary and Eusebius acquiesced after hearing a gloss on the term which was consonant both with Alexander's theology and with his own. Even in his *Demonstration of the Gospel*, which is likely to have been written before the eruption of the controversy, Eusebius differs from Alexander not in anything that he affirms or denies, but in the little that he fails to affirm. That is, he does not maintain that the Son and the Father are identical in nature, or even that they are like in essence, although he does treat 'image', 'word' and 'offspring' as equivalent terms which can be adduced to illustrate the divine character of the Son. The purpose of this lucubration, a sequel to the author's *Preparation of the Gospel*, is to show that Jesus of Nazareth is the Christ who was foretold in the Word of God revealed to the Jews, and hence the destroyer of every idol which the nations, lacking the guidance of the Word, have erected in place of the true Creator. It is in the fourth book that he undertakes to explicate the meaning of the title Logos, or word, when this is applied not only to the Old Testament (*Demonstration* 3.7.40), but to Christ as the subject, consummation and interpreter of its prophecies.

Eusebius commences with the obvious truth that 'he who is', the God of Moses (*Demonstration* 4.1.7), is also the unacknowledged God of the nations, the beginning of all existence as the Platonists hold, ineffable, inexpressible, immaterial and predisposed, as the Good must be, to communicate his goodness to all other beings (4.1.4–6). To this end he brought into being his 'firstborn wisdom' (cf. Proverbs 8.22), the perfect workmanship of the perfect, and bountiful offspring of the bountiful, (4.2.1) who differs from the unbegotten Father insofar as he is begotten, yet deserves the appellation 'God' insofar as he resembles him in every attribute (4.2.2). For this reason he is styled the image of God (4.2.2), yet he falls short in no respect of his original and progenitor. Whereas the second god, or second mind, of Numenius the Platonist was merely *agathos*, or good, in contrast to the first who was *autoagathos*, good itself, the second person of Eusebius' Trinity is not only *autonous*, *autologos* and *autosophia* – mind itself, Logos itself and wisdom itself – but *autokalos* and *autoagathos*, the beautiful itself and the good itself without further discrimination of these epithets (4.2.1). Plato had maintained that, as the intelligible world is one, its unity must be evident in the material imitation; Eusebius, baptizing his logic, argues that the one God can have only one perfect offspring, just as light can have no progeny but its own radiance. This metaphor, drawn from Hebrews 1.3, implies, for him, that the Son is an 'image of the Father's goodness' (4.3.3); it also implies that the Father begets the Son as inevitably as a light sheds radiance (4.3.5), though this cautious theologian adds at once that the Father, in contrast to the light, is subject to no necessity but his own will and choice (4.3.7).

The Son, then, is one, the companion of the Father before all ages, and, like him, superior to every paradigm, as Plato held the Good to be superior to all existence (4.3.9–10, 13); being perfectly immaterial, the Word who is God from God cannot be produced from him by fission or separation, and the mode of procession must be pronounced inscrutable and ineffable (4.3.13). For all that, it is he who performs the mediating role between the Father, in his indefeasible and the irreducible multiplicity of the created order (4.6.2). If we observe a constant harmony in the play of elements (4.5.5–7), if day follows night and the stars perform their revolutions according to a fixed order of vicissitude (4.5.8), if the reasoning faculty in human beings is one despite all variance in climate and physiology (4.5.9), the reason is that one and the same artificer shows her handiwork in all created things (4.5.5). In us he displays not merely his cunning but his image and likeness, and through his own assumption of our flesh he has drawn us closer to his own nature, and has thereby made us aware that the image and likeness are perfected not in the flesh, but in the intellectual and immaterial element of our being (4.6.6–7). The Word is the sun of the intellectual cosmos, as Plato and prophets combine to teach us (*Republic* 509c; Malachi 4.2); adapting another Socratic conceit, already domesticated in Christian usage, Eusebius explains that, as our eyes cannot look directly upon the sun without relapsing into blindness and confusion, so the frailty of our natures make it impossible for us to sustain an unmediated vision of the Godhead (4.6.5). One connotation of the term 'image', therefore, is that the incarnation reveals to us the nature of God which is also the paradigm of our human nature; one meaning of the title Logos, easily grasped by a student of Heraclitus or Origen, is that the Second Person acts in the cosmos as a hegemonic principle, whose work is mirrored in the coordination of our own members by the demiurgic faculty within.

But, of course, it also betokens the revelatory function of the Second Person. The prepotence of God and the ubiquity of his revelation are illustrated by Eusebius' marriage of Platonic and biblical diction in the fourth book; at the same time, he believes that the Hebrews alone were set apart as the trustees of the revelation and has no tolerance for the impostures of the pagan world or the arguments advanced in their defence by Porphyry. As he urges in the long invective prefaced to his fifth book, it is impossible to believe that the Creator has placed the daemons in the oracles as his own servitors, for why would such ambassadors lure mortals into misfortune by their ambiguous responses, or listen without demur while their mortal subjects put about stories of their lewd escapades and fickle cohabitations? Only to the Hebrews did God communicate the true *logos* (5, proem 29); only the prophets received from the Holy Spirit the capacity to see God and to know his purposes, insofar as he permitted them to be known before the full sense of the prophecies was disclosed in the incarnation. The prologue fittingly ends with a transition from the *logos* of the prophets to the evangelical *logos* in which the Logos who was with God in the beginning steps at last from behind the veil (5, proem 32–33).

To say that Christ the Word is the summation of the written word does not imply, however, that he has made plain all that was hitherto obscure. After all that has been said in previous books of his perfect likeness to the inscrutable Father, anyone who tries to elucidate the biblical text with his own analogies is making an impious use of image and likeness (5.1.12). Such idolaters should be warned that, if Christ is described by Paul as the Father's image, this does not mean, as the quotidian sense of the noun would imply, that he differs in form and 'in substrate according to essence' (5.1.21); he is, rather, the pure form, the living image and ineffable similitude of the Father who is *autoousia*, essence in itself. When Eusebius proceeds to liken the relation between the Father and Christ to that between the emperor and his statue at 5.4.10, with the proviso that the statue is not a second king but the image of an unrepeatable archetype, his aim is not to disparage the Second Person but to demonstrate that parity of honour need not compromise the unity of the Godhead. In the same way, though he repeatedly characterizes the Son as *deuteros*, or second to the Father, this adjective does not seem to connote inferiority unless it is tempered by another phrase, such as 'after the Father' (5.33.3; 5, proem 23); by itself it rather suggests an unqualified iteration of the Father's attributes. The subordinationism of Eusebius, though every scholar feels it, is elusive, masked as it is by his strong conviction that the attributes of the Son are no more perspicuous to the finite intellect than those of the Father. If he was as wary of the *homoousion* as of Arius' doctrine that the Son is 'out of nothing', it was because both opinions seemed to him to trespass upon the silence of the scriptures, which opposes to all our reasonings the unfathomable question 'Who can declare his generation?' (5.1.25, citing Isaiah 53.8).

The same arguments are recapitulated in his writings against Marcellus of Ancyra after the Council of Nicaea. According to Eusebius' account of him, Marcellus thought it impious to speak of the word as an image except with reference to the flesh that he had assumed for his earthly ministry (*Against Marcellus* 6.4 Klostermann). To say otherwise is to make common cause with Asterius, the 'Arian' sophist, who contended that because the Word is an image, he cannot be of the same substance as the Father (24.10–16). Both, in Eusebius' view, forget that the image and likeness of Adam was communicated to Seth, his natural son (Genesis 5.3), so that when the same noun is applied to the Son, it is not a denial but an accentuation of his divinity (25.17.24). The honours paid to a statue are not inferior to those which we accord to the king himself (106.13–16); the original is expressed in the image just as the light is present in the ray (25.21–24 and 106.18–20). If it were by virtue of his flesh that Christ is the image of the Father, would not all flesh be his image (49.7)? Marcellus, falling victim to his own rhetorical imagery (77.30), argues that the Logos is so called because he came forth from the paternal intellect after ages of silence (5.32–34). To imagine the Father existing without his Logos is, however, a manifest blasphemy (115.9–13); and if this is the Wisdom that was with him before the foundation of the world and therefore ages before the assumption of the flesh (47.12, for example) it is equally blasphemous to think of him as no more than a transient icon. To be the image of divinity is to be God (63.29–30), and if the Father is *autotheos*, God in essence (115.16), the Son is *autos theos*, God on his own account (115.22).

Although Eusebius is often called an Origenist, he does not see an adumbration of the Trinity in the vision of Isaiah. The angels he takes to be nothing but angels, creatures like ourselves but for their incorporeality, and equally unable to bear the radiance of the Lord, who, as the theology of Eusebius dictates, is identified here as the 'only-begotten'. We may be reminded of Origen by his comment that the wings are no mere phenomena, but the sensuous form under which an inward faculty clothes invisible powers, functioning analogously to the organs of the body. Characteristic of Origen again is his conclusion that this veiled epiphany is itself a parable, in which the stupefaction of the Lord's retinue prefigures that of the nations when they witness his resurrection from the dead. The second god is a visible yet cryptic iteration of divinity, the glory discreetly presaging the mission of the image, holding a cipher within a sign.

Athanasius of Alexandria

It was after the death of all the more eminent signatories to the Nicene Creed that Athanasius, deacon and successor to Alexander of Alexandria, set his face against half the world by holding up the *homoousion* as the sole test of orthodoxy. For the decade and more of exile and forensic persecution that lay behind him he had come to blame not only the late Eusebius of Nicomedia but his namesake, Eusebius of Caesarea. The theology of the latter was, however, not so easily impugned as that of the former, since he had signed the Creed after hearing it expounded by Alexander, or at least in accordance with Alexander's public response to Arius. Athanasius parts company with Eusebius when he argues, in his *Orations against the Arians*, that it is blasphemous to speak of the Son as a creature except with reference to his assumption of the flesh, and he rejects the Eusebian concept of the Word as an intermediary whose presence is more easily sustained by the world than that of the infinite Father. They are at one, nonetheless, and at one with Alexander, in their insistence that the Son is no less a Son if he is the image of the Father. His equality is not compromised in Athanasius' works on anthropology and the plan of God, where he undertakes to show that it is the character of the Son as Word and image that necessitates his incarnation as man.

The exordium to the treatise *Against the Nations* proclaims that the Cross has overthrown the idols erected by the pagan world in honour of spurious gods (1.5). These are the progeny of the erring soul, which, having wilfully turned its gaze from God to the carnal realm (4.1), proceeds to abuse its natural mobility (4.2) by setting up plastic images to imagined benefactors (8.2). All our vices flow from this defection, since, as the scriptures tell us, idolatry is the beginning of fornication (9.4, citing Wisdom 14.12). The argument is embellished with the customary discourses on the folly of worshipping our own confections (13), the iniquities of the gods who are represented in Greek statuary (11, 17) and the failure of the nations to concur in the representation of divinities who are supposed to be identical (23). The gods are credited with the invention of the arts of life (18.1), and yet their statues, if they portray them faithfully, show them to have been men like us (18.4); if the statues lie, they testify that the artist owes his skill not to the gods, but to a native faculty of imitation (18.2). Echoing Philo, Athanasius scoffs that if the beauty of the artefact could induce the god to dwell there, it is the sculptor who deserves our veneration (20.4). The image of the true God resides in the incorporeal soul, the existence of which is proved by our ability to recall images of things no longer accessible to vision (30.5). These veridical memories are no doubt to be contrasted with the forgetfulness to which the world seeks a remedy in the creation of false gods. The character of God is also manifest in the concord of the elements and the immutable procession of the seasons, which could not be sustained by chance or by a mob of warring deities (35–39). The crowning proof of benevolence is the incarnation of the creative Word (40.2, 47.2) in whose image and likeness we have been fashioned; from the writings of his prophets and apostles (45–46) we learn that the cosmos is the one material testimony to God that can be admired without profanity, but only if we remain true to the axiom that the artist deserves more reverence than the products of his art.

The sequel to this work, the famous tract *On the Incarnation*,[21] is not so much a continuation of the argument as a redaction of it for those who are already Christians. For such believers the exaltation of Christ is more comprehensible

---

[21]   For differing views of its date, see Anatolios (1998), 26–29, and Kannengiesser (1970).

than his abasement; although the idol no longer obscures the image, they have still to learn why the Cross is the only antidote to the deformity that the image has sustained after Adam's fall. 'God made man the image of his deity' says the Book of Wisdom, 'but by the envy of the devil death entered the world' (Wisdom 2.23–24; *On the Incarnation* 5). What will become of the image if it is abandoned to corruption? And what becomes of the Word of God if humankind does not die, as God foretold, on the day when it eats from the tree of knowledge (*Incarnation* 6–10)? Suppose, Athanasius says, that this very Word becomes incarnate, that the image of God after whom our sinful race was modelled sinlessly descends to our condition. In the breaking and restoration of this image the entire race would be involved, or at least all those who willingly turned to him as their fathers had turned from God. The Cross is now perceived to be an attestation rather than an occlusion of his majesty. It exacts a death by violence from the one man who could not have paid it as a debt to nature; by making that death a spectacle to the world it leaves no doubt of his resurrection; it raises him into the air where he can wrestle with the daemons and extend his victorious arms to embrace humanity (*Incarnation* 25–26). This is the Word that silences the oracles, the glory that illumines the darkness of the scriptures; God, in this new creation, has become one of us in order to make us gods.

Christ redeems by exercising the revelatory function which is connoted by the term Logos; this term acquires a sense familiar to the Greek schools when Athanasius argues that, if the harmony of the cosmos can be ascribed to an immanent *logos*, it is reasonable to imagine that this *logos* can inhabit a single body (41.4, 42.3). While his role as image in this treatise is to exemplify human nature in its fullness and perfection, it is a standing presupposition of the argument that this image is in no respect inferior to its archetype. In his writings against the Arians, Athanasius assumes that it is they, and not the partisans of the Nicene *homoousion*, who will be at a loss to reconcile the word 'image' with their own theology. If God is one, he reasons in *On the Nicene Decrees*, his image too must be one (17); if, as the Nicene prelates have intimated, he is in all things like the Father, it is a palpable subterfuge to reply that all human beings are made in the image and likeness of God according to Genesis 1.26, ignoring the more apposite testimony at Genesis 5.3 that a true son is the image and likeness of his Father (20). In the *First Oration against the Arians*, it is said to be as inevitable that the Father will have his image as that light will project a ray (20, citing Hebrews 1.3). If the Arians marshal sophistries to prove that he is as much the Father's creature as we are his creatures, they have turned a sacred utterance into an empty vocable, slighting the similarity of essence which is implied by his status as image (21). This image was the very form of God which, when it took on the form of a slave, prostrated the idols and dispelled the mirages of demons (41–43, citing Philippians 2.6–8). There are some, as Athanasius concedes at *Against the Arians* 2.43, who insist that all images are created; but a son, as we have seen, is his father's image (2.2), and it was surely his image that God beheld in the Wisdom who was his mirror before the foundation of the world (2.82, citing Wisdom 7.25–6). As the faithful image of God, the Son enjoys the parity of honour that we accord to an emperor's statue (3.5); it is only in his spontaneous effulgence that we see that light which is the essence of God (3.11). No doubt the title 'image' is itself a specimen of that verbal imagery which tempers the word of God to our understanding; rightly understood, however, it signifies that, the original being God, the image cannot be less than God or other than he is. It is only when we depart from scriptural usage, misconceiving the Word as the Father's tool or instrument, that notions of contingency, inequality and transience take on a specious hue.

Critics of Athanasius alleged that he could not hold these positions without condemning the most illustrious of his predecessors, Bishop Dionysius of Alexandria, who had likened the relation between the First and Second Persons of the Trinity to that between a carpenter and his ship. Athanasius retorts that the Great Confessor had availed himself of a simile that suited the occasion in an age when the present controversy could not have been foreseen. If he is to be tried by modern scales, such anachronisms will be outweighed by his own assurance that, whatever he may have said in passing, he understands the First Person to be properly not the maker but the Father of the Word (On the *Teaching of Dionysius* 21). The passage in which he styles the Word a creature will be found, when cited in full, to be a gloss on the opening of Psalm 45, 'My heart has disgorged a goodly word': Dionysius infers that, as intelligence cannot exist without speech or speech without intelligence, so the issue of the Father's heart cannot fail to express itself as an utterance, his creature by analogy with our own speech but more accurately his Son, symphonic in content though distinct in form and proclaiming that he and the Father are one, each present in the other (23). Noting that the office of the Word is to 'gain a lodging in the soul of the hearer', Dionysius intimates that the Logos must be rightly heard to be rightly understood. Athanasius duly reminds us in his preface of the written text which declares that the Word who springs from the Father's heart was with the Father in the beginning (2), and it is a perennial refrain in his *Oration*s that the Arians disparage the Son because they have failed to grasp the full sense of the scriptures in which he bears witness to himself.

Nowhere is this more apparent than in their threadbare interpretation of Proverbs 8.22 – 'The Lord created me in the beginning of his way' – as a proof of the Son's contingency and inferiority to God the Father. Those who build so much on this one text forget that in scriptural usage 'beget' and 'created' are synonyms only when 'beget' is used in its proper sense and 'create' as a loose equivalent (*Orations* 2.60). They make a creature of Wisdom who, by her account, was daily in the sight of God before he laid the foundations of the earth (for example, 2.56, citing Proverbs 8.30); they defraud the very name 'Wisdom' of its meaning when they fabricate a distinction between the framing of the universe by the Father and the creation of its denizens by Wisdom under his guidance (2.27–29). They ought instead to discriminate between the essence of Wisdom and her image, not construing the image as anything less than the spontaneous and eternal manifestation of the original, but remembering that all disclosure is for us (2.78; cf. 2.46, 2.49). The beginning 'for which' (not 'in which') Wisdom declares herself created was the incarnation, the masking of God's glory in the flesh as a revelation of his benevolence (2.52–53). In the flesh we see him grow in wisdom, suffer pain and confess his ignorance, though none of these infirmities is germane to the Word as God. The circumscription of the Word in flesh and the self-inscription of God in the written word are two forms of enciphered revelation: each acts as an interpretant to the other, the flesh unveiling the double import of the text and the text enabling us to winnow what is said of the Word as God from what is said by him as man.

The Later Fourth Century

Thus, although Eusebius, Alexander and Athanasius may not have concurred at all points in their reading of the Nicene Creed, it seemed to all three that the biblical designation of Christ as the Father's image presented fewer difficulties to defenders of the Council than to its critics. In the latter half of the fourth century, the self-professed champions of the Nicene faith take a different view; they no longer find it possible to assume that the image inherits all the attributes of its paradigm, and are more apt to explain the term away by reference to the manhood than to adduce it as a scriptural affidavit to his divinity. It is only part of an explanation to say that after Constantine it was possible for Christians to frequent the philosophical schools, and hence to draw lessons from Aristotle's logic, without suspicion of apostasy; it was only in the sixth century that churchmen began to treat Aristotle with scholastic deference, and even then they dissented freely from his theological positions. The tenet that a substance and its copy must differ in *logos tês ousias*[22] was of less moment, even to philosophic Christians, than the rulings of a series of ecclesiastical councils in the 350s, which supplanted the *homoousion* with the formula that the Son is like the Father; the Council of Sirmium in 357 went so far as to anathematize the use of the unscriptural term *ousia*. It was thus no longer possible to argue that the doctrine of the Nicene Fathers was adequately conveyed by a comparison of the Father to a king and the Son to his statue. When new teachers, taking up a position once invidiously attributed to Arius, maintained that, since the Father alone is ingenerate while the Son is the first of generated beings, they are not even alike but contrary in nature, the wiser representatives of the Nicene faith did not try to restore the old phylacteries. Imitating the strategy of their adversaries at Sirmium, they rebuked the presumption of those who professed to define the essence of God by human epithets and maintained the ineffability of both Father and Son with a diligence that threatened to render obsolete all discussion of their likeness, since their essential traits were equally unknown.

The first postulate of an apophatic, or negative, theology is that predicates drawn from human language cannot be true in the strictest sense of God. Eunomius, who reduced the Father's essence to a single attribute, his ingeneracy, was accused by

---

[22]   Aristotle, *Categories* 1a1–3; Zachhuber (2000), 71–73.

Basil of Caesarea of failing to distinguish negation of predicates from predication of negatives. No more than 'wise' or 'just' will the term 'ingenerate' suffice to characterize the Father's essence; even a privative epithet can be no more than an *epinoia*, an artificial notion standing for the *ennoia*, or true conception, of his essence which is not vouchsafed to mortal intellects.[23] Gregory of Nyssa writes in a similar vein to pre-empt the false inferences that might be drawn from a legitimate analogy between the three divine persons and three men. If *theotês* or divinity were an essence – whether we take this to mean a class, a genus or an ensemble of properties – then Father, Son and Spirit would be three gods, just as Peter, James and John are three men. Since, however, *theotês* is a term signifying not the essence of God but his providential operation in the cosmos – signifying, in other words, not God in himself but all that he is for us – there are not three gods at work but one when the Father, Son and Spirit are united, as they always are, in a single operation.[24] Gregory does not conclude that knowledge of God is unattainable, only that it cannot be attained through ratiocination or through dalliance with images, whether these be intellectual or corporeal. To speak of God, with Plato and Eusebius, as the sun of the intellectual world, is once again to confound the operation with the essence. Those who would know God as Moses did must follow him into the cloud at the peak of Sinai (*Life of Moses* 162–163); we must gird ourselves in the purity of the high priest to enter the Holy of Holies (184–201), where darkness is our light. Echoing Philo, the Gnostics and Plotinus rather than Plato, Gregory conceives God as a fathomless immensity, whom the soul comes to know by increments as she matures in virtue. The inner man is a mirror to the divine, but only because the mind, too, is infinite; even after death and liberation from the body, progress in knowledge will be inexhaustible, and infinitely more will remain to be won than has been acquired.[25]

No Christian apology for the veneration of images has come down to us from the fourth century, and Gregory was not the only man of his time to hold that mental phantasms were as alien to the worship of God as the idols of the nations, which were being cast down on all sides with the connivance, and at last with the open sanction, of the emperor. Evagrius of Pontus, though he may not have gone so far as to hold that God is best known through a species of unknowing, exhorted monks to cultivate prayer without images,[26] while hostile reports inform us that the Messalians starved the senses by excluding even the sacraments from worship.[27] Hilary of Poitiers, too, introduces a treatise in twelve books *On the Trinity* by disavowing all positive knowledge of God. Hilary, however, makes a

---

[23]   Basil, *Against Eunomius* I.5–8; on the history of the term *epinoia*, see Vaggione (2000), 252–256.

[24]   On the letter to Ablabius and its interpreters, see Zachhuber (2000).

[25]   *Life of Moses* 219–255; see Corrigan (2009), 176–197, and on the relation of Gregory's eschatology to his teaching on the image of God, see Ludlow (2000), 50–63.

[26]   *On Thoughts* 41; see Corrigan (2009), 113–132.

[27]   See Plested (2005), 30–45.

notable attempt to produce a Catholic theology of the image, though this term, to him, is no longer a shibboleth of orthodoxy, but a rune which must be deciphered by the Catholic according to his own lights and that of God.

Hilary, who was no stranger to the Platonists, will have been aware that Plotinus had distinguished the living icon – which expresses a superior plane of being in a lower one, so that intellect is an icon of the One and time the living image of eternity – from the *eidôlon*, which is merely the dead simulacrum of the visible.[28] Marrying this antithesis with the familiar polemic against idolatry, he contends that, while the smith can reproduce the colour and aspect of the original, no lifeless image can represent a sentient being; still less could the Father be represented by anything but the living image who bears the indelible tokens of divinity (*On the Trinity* 7.38). These properties cannot be taken from the Son because 'a perfect birth engenders a perfect image' (9.1). A consummate likeness repeats exactly the traits of the original (8.48), and we see in Jesus Christ not the faint impression of the stronger on the weaker (as Hebrews 1.3 might suggest to some), but the fullness of the Godhead stamped on flesh (8.45). Lest we should imagine that, because God has communicated his image and likeness to one of his creatures, it is possible for the Word to be an image and yet lack the divine perfections, we must remember that we do not yet see the consummation of God's image in us, and that this will be realized only when godliness has restored us to immortality (11.49). Hilary thus maintains as vigorously as Athanasius that the concept of representation does not entail, but precludes inferiority to the archetype; in his new circumstances, however, the parity of image and model must be proved repeatedly and can never be assumed.

Epilogue

As we have noted, Christian iconography is abundant in the fourth century, though the ecclesiastical use of images, even for mere adornment, is not commended in any theological treatise of the period. Painting as an art is not despised, and it was possible for Chrysostom to liken the growth in a reader's understanding of a biblical text to the painter's transformation of an outline into a portrait. Plato's metaphorical description of the lover as a statue taking form under the chisel of the beloved was borrowed by Gregory of Nyssa; in adapting it, like Plotinus, to the disciple's education of his own soul, he could also avail himself of a biblical tenet unknown to Plotinus, that the inner man is the image of his Creator:[29]

> Just as those who are transfiguring marble into the shape of some animal use the chisel to scrape and cut away from the stone those things without which the likeness assumes the figure of the original, so with respect to the beauty of the

---

[28]   For other references see Smulders (1944), 190–191.

[29]   Cf. Plato, *Phaedrus* 252; Plotinus, *Enneads* 1.6.9.

hands of the ecclesiastical body, many things must be pared away by the chisel of instruction, so that the hand my become truly golden and without blemish. (*Song of Songs Commentary*, pp. 407–408; Jaeger, commenting on Canticles 5.14)

Does it follow that the outward form that the Word assumed, as creator and archetype of the inner man, is a proper study for Christian artists? A letter by Epiphanius of Salamis, self-appointed tribune of orthodoxy in the last quarter of the fourth century, records his violent tearing down of a veil that he judged idolatrous;[30] nevertheless, it is only in Jerome's translation of his letter that this veil is unequivocally said to have borne an image of Christ. Whatever his opinion, it would seem that the majority of churchmen in his time were not offended by the pictorial representation of scenes and characters from sacred history. The visible representation of the invisible – the depiction of any person of the Trinity in his character as God – would have raised another question and was not, so far as we know, essayed by any Christian artist of this epoch. Perusal of the scriptures, and especially of the life of Moses, taught the theologians that no discrete form could manifest the true nature of God to the senses. The soul that seeks this knowledge, according to Gregory of Nyssa, must follow Moses up the mount into the unfathomable darkness from which God, without showing his countenance, had dispensed his Law to Israel. The way of ascent was not by the inspection of outward forms or by the contemplation of our maturing faculties within, but by a humble and assiduous meditation on the text which is our one material remnant of the enlightened soul's communion with the incommunicable.

---

[30] Thümmel (1992), *Testimonium* 34, p. 293. On the authenticity of other documents ascribed to Epiphanius, see Ouspensky (1992), 141n.

Chapter 9
Myth and Text in Proclus

From its inception, Christianity was a religion of the book, if by the book we mean the Old Testament. Platonism, by contrast, could not be called a philosophy of the book until the third century of the Christian era. Plato himself would not have wished it to be so, if the soul of his dialogues is the figure of Socrates, personifying a spirit of restless inquisition that carries the reader beyond the uncertain results of his own inquiries. This spirit survived in the Sceptics, but they lost sight of the man, and it was left to the Church to make a pagan Christ of Socrates as a man who had been obedient unto death in the service of truth.[1] Platonists of a more dogmatic stamp seem to have cherished a scheme of doctrine which they could verify by proof-texts and occasionally by the protracted examination of recognized obscurities; since it was held, however, that any intellect had only to disenthrall itself from the body and its passions to know all that Plato knew, it was possible to acquire a great reputation as an expositor without offering a sustained and minute interpretation of any dialogue, let alone of the whole Platonic corpus. Fragments survive of early commentaries on the *Theaetetus* and the *Parmenides*, and the treatises of Plotinus often proceed by meditation on select passages, but Iamblichus would appear to have been the first to produce a series of commentaries on texts that he himself had arranged to form a syllabus. Almost all of his work is lost, but his method and some of his matter survive in Proclus, a pagan born in a Christian era who contrived to remain, on the surface at least, wholly ignorant of the dominant theology. He also left behind him a corpus of writings which, despite its incompleteness, exceeds in volume the surviving remains of any Greek philosopher with the exception of Aristotle. The bulk of this is commentary on Plato, in which he flatters his author from time to time by applying to him the allegorical tools that were characteristically reserved for sacred writings. By parity of reasoning he permits himself to engage in a remedial application of allegory to other texts which Plato himself had regarded only as mines of error. Plato's coy description of his own parable of the cave as a verbal icon has been taken up by his student as a hermeneutic canon, with results that could have been held up by Plato himself as a sovereign illustration of the impotence of the book to explain its contents once the reader has taken it out of the author's hands.[2]

The extant works of Proclus include a commentary on the *Elements* of Euclid, commentaries on the *Parmenides* of Plato, the *First Alcibiades,* the first part of the *Timaeus*, and some portions of the *Republic*, a series of readings in the *Cratylus*,

---

[1] Frede (2006).

[2] Cf. Derrida (1981).

a systematic treatise entitled *The Elements of Theology*, a compendious (though incomplete) *Theology of Plato* and a number of smaller treatises and hymns. Even in works that are not expressly dedicated to Plato, his thought is a mosaic of quotations from the dialogues, though, like Plotinus, he holds that every tenet which a faithful gloss can elicit from the text should also be demonstrable by reasoning alone.[3] The same logic that entailed the postulation of the Forms will lead the careful reader of Plato, in the footsteps of Plotinus, to a principle transcending form and essence, which is not itself an entity at the head of a chain of beings but the logical presupposition of all being, the ineffable source of the unity in which everything, from the forms to the infinitesimal particular, must participate if it is to be at all. In agreement with Plotinus, he styles this the One or the Good without implying that these are predicates which it enjoys by participation in the simpler and more universal Forms of oneness or goodness. Nothing is simpler or more universal than the One, and for this reason we cannot properly assert even that it *is* one, or indeed that it *is*.

More austere at times than Plotinus himself in his denudation of the first principle, Proclus is nonetheless aware (as Plotinus also is) that when we say of a thing in the world, or of the world itself, that it is one, its unity is as tangible as its being and we have no sense that either predicate is of lower order than the other. Therefore, he believes, we must also posit a One that *is*, posterior to the One that is above being. Here it is that philosophy joins hands with exegesis, for in the latter half of the *Parmenides*, the audience is perplexed by the promulgation of eight or nine contradictory theses, the first of which affirms that the One *is not*, the second that it *is*. Plotinus intimates, and Proclus roundly maintains, that these propositions are reconcilable only on the hypothesis that each has a different subject. The subject of the first is the unparticipated One, while that of the second is its homonym which manifests itself in the realm of being. In accounting for the subsequent propositions in the dialogue, Proclus arrives at his doctrine of henads, or self-constituted unities, which preside over chains that penetrate every level of existence, thus enabling such an entity as a soul to remain one even as it descends into multiplicity. The term 'self-constituted' indicates not that they depend on nothing above them, but that the essence of the henad (as a thing of a certain kind) and its existence (as a discrete thing) can be perfectly reunited by the *epistrophê* or reversion which accompanies its procession from the source. Proclus is both a monist and a polytheist, as all Neoplatonists are, and it is equally true to say that the One is God for him and that the henads are his gods.

Below the One and its namesake lies the intellectual realm, which for Plotinus occupies a single tier, in which the knower is coterminous – and even, one might say, identical – with the essence that constitutes the object of his knowledge. It is, for all that, the residual duality of knower and known that requires us to posit a source of unity transcending essence, and we also discern in the *Enneads* the rudiments of an 'intelligible triad', in which the object is conceived as absolute

---

[3]   The following summary of his thought owes much to Steel (2010), 637–641.

being and the knower as simple intellect, while life represents the movement by which the knower grasps the known. While the triad originates in the *Sophist* of Plato, the Neoplatonists after Plotinus found it again (or at least a close equivalent) in a body of oracular verse, passing under the name of Julian the Chaldaean, a thaumaturge of the second century, who was supposed to have written it under inspiration. According to the Chaldaean system, the planes of existence form a triad of triads, in each of which the father, or being, is set above power and power above intellect. In the vocabulary of Neoplatonists, from Iamblichus to Proclus, being is assigned to the noetic plane and intellect to the noeric, while life (as they preferred to call it) occupies an intermediate plane, at once noetic and noeric. Proclus, so far as our evidence goes, was the first to add that that which is highest in ontological rank is also widest in scope of action. Existence, he observes, is predicated even of inanimate subjects, whereas only plants and animals partake in life and only certain animals are endowed with intellect.

Philosophy, when pressed to its goal, is the knowledge of the unknowable. The fact that it is unknowable and the necessity of the fact are capital elements in this knowledge, and we achieve the greatest approximation to truth when we are most conscious of inadequacy in the means of approximation. The first approach to truth is the reading of Plato under the guidance of a master who has understood the symbolic or analogical relation between the text itself, as a representative medium, and its unrepresentable object. We shall be following Proclus' own method if we commence with the first of his extant works, the *Commentary on the Timaeus*, in which he finds analogues for three orders of demiurgic activity in the discourses of the principal speakers. Next we shall consider his reflections on analogy, symbol and myth in his dissertations on the *Cratylus* and the *Republic*;[4] the *Commentary on the Parmenides* and the *Platonic Theology* will complete this study, as they are the works in which Proclus consistently tests the bounds of epistemology, warning his readers not only against the confusion of the secondary with the primordial, but against mistaking language for acquaintance when the best that we can aspire to is an adequate confession of the inadequacy of speech.

Text and the Texture of Being

In the proem to his commentary on the *Timaeus*, Proclus finds that the process of coming to be, as Plato adumbrates it, is subject to a dynasty of causes. In Aristotle's nomenclature, these are distinguished as the final cause, *for the sake of* which all things come to be; the formal cause *in relation to* which they come to be; and the efficient cause *by which* they come to be (p. 3.13–14 Diehl). Plato's usage suggests that we should style the first of these the Good to which all things tend: if there were no such tendency, a thing in the world could not retain even the fickle and tenebrous being which belongs to it, since the Good is also the principle of unity,

---

[4]   See Dillon (1975a) for a comparison with the semiotic theories of Charles Peirce.

which counteracts the inevitable fall of the contingent subject into dissolution and multiplicity. Aristotle's formal cause is the paradigm of the *Timaeus*, in which are enfolded the lucid archetypes of the phenomena which we apprehend indistinctly and under a mutable guise in the present universe: these archetypes, forms or essences are invisible to the senses, but perspicuous to the intellect which has risen above the changeable and contingent. The latter exist, so far as they can be said to exist, by virtue of the third cause, which is represented in Plato under the figure of the Demiurge: he does not work in opposition to his superiors, for it would not be possible even to grasp the phenomenon as a phenomenon were it not for the latent presence of the archetype in all its simulacra, and the continual reversion of both archetype and simulacrum to the inscrutable source of unity. Since nothing in the gross world has any claim to being except by the imitation of its archetype, the phenomenal can be said to be paradigmatically existent in the intelligible, while the latter is iconically present in the phenomenal; if the mathematicals are to be posited as an intermediate category, they, too, are present iconically in the sensible and paradigmatically in the intelligible (8.14–24). For this reason it can be said that the mathematical speculations of the *Timaeus* are mystical or symbolic ciphers of immutable realities (7.29–30); the iconic relation in which the cycle of vicissitude stands to the realm of essence is expressed in Plato's dictum (*Timaeus* 37c) that time is the moving image of eternity (6.27). Since time is said to coexist with the heavens in the same passage, Proclus clearly understands this saying to mean not that time has a shorter span than eternity, but that, since the temporal order is not governed by the same logical necessity that reigns in the intelligible order, the intelligibles will always be known (to philosophers at least) with greater clarity and certitude than the inhabitants of time.

The procession of the lesser from the greater is a corollary of the necessary truth that what is good will desire to communicate its goodness. As we have seen, however, this superabundance will inevitably entail a decay of power, a loss of integrity, an occultation of original causes. The descent of every rational soul is a recapitulation of the same tragedy, since each is a microcosm of the whole (5.8–12). The same process is writ large in the revolutions of human history, which have constantly buried the records of previous epochs; only in Egypt have some permanent records survived the catastrophes which have blotted out the remembrance of the past among other nations. The Athenians have forgotten the most glorious of their past victories; just as the soul's forgetting of her origins may be corrected by an act of anamnesis or recollection, so the evanescence of the past can be overcome by a written memorial if its truth is guaranteed by an unbroken chain of custody. Nevertheless, the story of Atlantis, the memory of which is supposed to have been kept alive in Egypt by just such a tradition, is, according to Proclus and many of his predecessors, an *eikôn* or stochastic representation of truths which are metaphysical rather than historical. Plato has located his fictitious realm of Atlantis in the far West, which was regarded by Numenius and Porphyry (whether literally or iconically we can hardly say) as the home of malevolent daemons who tempt the soul into dissipation and illusion; the Athenians, on the other hand, represent higher beings inhabiting a plane that is free of malice or disorder. Even if the daemons are left out of the interpretation, Proclus seems to agree that the belligerent Atlanteans represent the tumult of the sensible order, while the triumph of Athens confirms the supremacy of the intelligible. If the tale is fictitious, so is the record that is supposed to attest it; the *Menexenus*, as Proclus adds, has also been read as a humorous admonition to those who imagine that a text can afford an accurate representation of the past.

Now if texts can lie about empirical matters, one can hardly expect that a metaphysical truth and the discourse which purports to represent that truth will be equipollent. It was a principle for all the Neoplatonists – who in this respect were equally true to Plato and to Aristotle – that our knowledge can never exceed in precision the ontological purity of its object; that is to say that, if the object is not purely and immutably what we deem it to be, nothing that we assert of it can be strictly or irrefragably true. The sensible cosmos stands in a confusedly iconic relation to the supernal order; philosophical myth is the icon[5] which a 'father of discourse' constructs in the hope that words will prove a more diaphanous veil than the material phenomena under which the Demiurge has been obliged to conceal the Forms. The correct interpretation of the mythical war between Athens and Atlantis is one that justifies the obscurity of the mythical Form itself: if the sensible were perfectly submissive to the intelligible, the icon would be a perfect representation of the paradigm, and the philosopher's embodiment of the truth in words would in no respect fall short of the thing itself. In our present state of exile from the higher realm, however, the thing to be signified will always exceed our powers of representation. Socrates in the *Timaeus* grants the philosopher an advantage over the poets, who can offer us only specious imitations of the familiar (19d–e); Proclus is inclined to concur with those predecessors who held that Plato did not mean to include Homer in this arraignment and does not share Porphyry's view that Homer could not rise above magnificence to a state of philosophical intellection (p. 647–11 Diehl). To find evidence of this power, it is, of course, necessary to make use of the same tools that that one would bring to the reading of a Platonic myth.

In the *Timaeus* Solon the Athenian is reminded by an Egyptian that his city ascribes its fortune to Athena. In the *Euthyphro*, Plato had noted that her own deeds were commemorated in the *peplos*, or robe, which was carried once a year in a great procession by the women of the city. The war between gods and giants which the robe depicted is obviously an analogue of the putative war between Athens and Atlantis; the mode of representation, however, is visual rather than verbal, and the myth is inherited rather than invented. At the same time, it is not the robe itself but his own description of it, with interpretative concomitants that Plato has handed on to his succession. The verbal representation of the robe is not identical either with the robe itself or with the truths that are represented in the

---

[5]   In the *Commentary on the Republic* it is also a veil, as Lamberton (1989), 185, observes.

robe, although those truths must be represented in words for those who either do not possess the robe or cannot decipher it. According to Proclus, the lowest level of signification is the pictography of the robe; higher than this, but camouflaging truths still more arcane, is Plato's account of the conflict which is depicted on the robe (and also, perhaps, of the emulation that it inspires among the people). We reach a higher level again in the Panathenaic festival which celebrates the exploits of Athena, but this is a poor facsimile of the conflict between the intelligible and the sensible which permeates the cosmos. Loftier than all is the robe that Athena herself weaves among the paradigmatic causes, which the goddess encompasses in a single act of intellection. It will not have escaped the readers of Proclus that weaving is a common poetic figure, in Greek as in Latin, for the construction of that verbal artefact which we, retaining the metaphor, still call a text.

The practice of the sophist is invidiously compared, in Plato's dialogue of the same name, with that of the weaver. The excursus on the nature of true being which accompanies the unmasking of his fallacies is prompted by an Eleatic disciple of Parmenides, and it is in the *Parmenides*, if anywhere, that the promised sketch of the philosopher is executed. In the Socratic dialogues, as we have seen in Chapter 3, it often appears that Plato is less concerned to impart a particular doctrine than to personify the spirit of philosophy in his hero. But if Socrates is the paradigm, what should we make of the other characters? Ancient commentators on the *Timaeus* seldom doubted that Plato had some weighty motive for dividing the conversation between three speakers, each of whom, according to the unfinished plan of the trilogy, was to set out his own design for a constitution. The commonwealth which Socrates depicts in his recapitulation of the last day's dialogues resembles the one that he and a different group of friends imagined in the *Republic*; in the equilibrium of classes we see, according to Proclus, an icon of the counterplay which sustains the diverse elements in the cosmos. Socrates, as the initiator of dialogue, is a 'Father of *logoi*', and, since the term *logos* denotes not merely a word but a seminal principle, he is the counterpart of the universal Demiurge who, as Proclus was to explain in the *Platonic Theology*, fathers a triad of demiurgic agents in the intellectual realm. This triad is represented in the dialogue by Timaeus, Critias and Hermocrates; since, however, the latter is absent, others had argued for a correspondence between the three present speakers and the Aristotelian triad of productive, paradigmatic and final causes. Even these interpreters could not agree in their correlation of causes and interlocutors. None of them, however, would have disagreed with Proclus when he argues that, in the human microcosm, the higher nature is able to imitate the paradigm while the lower observes the rhythms of the natural order; nor would they have doubted his peroration that the natural world cannot be studied without an internal discipline of the character, which will be complete when the contemplative soul has been transformed into the likeness of the object contemplated.

The Figure of Socrates

We have noted above that for Proclus the human soul is a microcosm of all that is, and that at its most august it is a mirror to the Good. Proclus understands this to be not merely one theme but the repeated burden of the *First Alcibiades*, a dialogue now widely deemed to be spurious, though perhaps on inadequate grounds. To Proclus, as to most of his fellow-Platonists, this dramatic representation of Socrates' courtship of Alcibiades – the future statesman, turncoat and desecrator of the mysteries – was a model of all pedagogic condescension. The munificence of Socrates is indeed but one expression of the largesse which universally flows from the higher to the lower; in his role of lover, the philosopher is an emblem of the Good to his disciple; in the latter's imitation of his master we see in miniature that reversion to the One which is disguised in the fickle and centrifugal existence of the soul that is one among many. The dialogue, Proclus tells us, has no other goal than 'to reveal the essence of man and to turn each of us back to himself from the propensity to look outwards' (p. 14.2–5 Segonds). The goal of the lover is always 'assimilation to the beautiful' (48.9–10), and it had been explained by Plotinus that this object is attained by the progressive realization of a higher self, or daemon, at each new stage of the soul's deliverance from the external. According to Proclus, the philosophical lover is the daemon (45.36), holding the middle ground between the beloved and the god whom he himself imitates (53.9; cf. 73.19), so that his gathering of the discrete things that come 'after him' can in turn become an offering of the 'second things' to the first (53.1–8). Just as intellect works ubiquitously upon the tumult and vicissitude of the lower word, allaying our passions and secretly diffusing the light of reason, so will the constant presence of the 'divine lover' guide the beloved,[6] though at first in silent tutelage until the time comes to impart the *logos* or teaching that will acquaint the beloved with his true identity (44.12–45.5). Whereas the *Symposium* and the *Phaedrus* had maintained that desire is kindled in the lover by the perception of transcendent beauty in that which is only partially and deciduously beautiful, Proclus finds repeated proofs in the *First Alcibiades* that it is in the nature of the lover to exercise providential care in the sustenance of the beloved (55.14–15) and that when the lover is able to perform these offices without mingling openly in the affairs of the beloved, he has assumed the daemonic role (62.19–24). A candid reader will not be persuaded that *erôs* in Proclus signifies only acquisitive love, and it would not be absurd to suppose that his thought has been modified by the intercourse which Neoplatonism had been obliged to maintain with Christianity. But, of course, Neoplatonism is no more prone than Christianity itself to the indiscriminate contraction of thoughts that are alien to its first principles, and Proclus can find precedents in the

---

[6]   Rist (1964), 215–216, maintains that the downward-tending *erôs* of *Alcibiades Commentary* 2 (p. 23 Segonds) is anticipated in *Enneads* 6.8, where Plotinus attributes a non-acquisitive *erôs* to the One.

mythological amours of Zeus (55.13–14) and in the unstinting superabundance of the Platonic Demiurge.

Proclus ascribes to Socrates three modes of intellectual conversion, the erotic (that of the lover), the maieutic (that of the midwife) and the dialectic (that of the teacher in cross-examination). The erotic directs the pupil to the beautiful, the maieutic discloses in each of us a wisdom of which we were ignorant, and the dialectic reveals the ascent to the Good (29.1–7). The *First Alcibiades* is predominantly a specimen of the erotic mode, and since this resembles the rhetorician's medium of persuasion, it is not surprising that Socrates should sometimes adapt his teaching to the vanity of his pupil. The latter possesses a soul whose defects are veiled by its specious virtues (101.16–19); likewise, the encomium of Socrates, when inspected, proves to be no more than a mimicry of a young man's praise of himself (102.23). Moreover, the bodily vigour and extraneous nobility on which he prides himself are mere *eidôla* or effigies of their noetic archetypes (108.18; 111.11; cf. 49.13 and 22); even Socrates' commendation of his parents is thus not so much a conventional eulogy as a reminder that no soul can prosper when it forgets the originals that it ought to imitate (24.12–25.21). Socrates is offering himself as an archetype to Alcibiades, having proved what his interlocutor has yet to learn – that the soul achieves autarchy or self-sufficiency as it grows into the likeness of intellect, discovering the Good within itself. If instead it supposes the Good to reside in its outward properties and material possessions, its imagined self-sufficiency is a figment, a *phantasma* (106.21–107.5). It should therefore be apparent that no merely dramatic effect is being pursued in the infusion of rhetorical colour: this proem to all the dialogues subordinates every word to its goal like a rite in which all actions are designed to effect the 'universal consummation of the things that are looked for' (18.15–19.9). In the benign machinations of the teacher we see 'a wonderful image (*eikona*)' of the sacred performance, in which the more perfect assumes something of the less perfect in order that it may draw to it the souls that are not yet perfected, at the same time setting them apart from souls of higher desert.

Names and Images in the *Cratylus*

Proclus distinguishes four modes of being in nature, perhaps intending each to correspond to a section of Plato's divided line in the *Republic*. First comes that of *ousia* or essence, next that of *dunamis* or *energeia* (power or energy), third the natural apparition in shadow or reflection, and finally the artificial copy (*Lection* 17). This inclusion of plastic images among natural objects intimates that we are not obliged to choose between the thesis of Cratylus, that names are allotted *phusei* or by nature, and the Aristotelian teaching (prefigured in the *Cratylus* by Hermogenes) that a name is only an arbitrary *sumbolon* (*Lection* 47) which owes its semantic force to social custom (49). Passages in other Platonic dialogues allow us to differentiate the mere vocable, which is the product of law and custom, from the paradigmatic object in the natural realm to which it corresponds (51). In the coining of names (as distinct from their application), the salient contrast is not to be drawn between the natural and the artificial, but between the eternal and the transitory; only the names that are given to eternal objects can be said to proceed from deliberate legislation, for the naming of chance existents is itself subject to chance. Many a short-lived human has borne a name that connoted immortality or length of years.

The bestowing of names is not purely the work of a legislative faculty. *Eikasia*, the representation of the visible world in painting and statuary, is a natural propensity of the human soul, which, when it desires to represent the essence of things in abstraction from their matter, takes the faculty of speech as a coadjutor in order to bring forth the 'essence of names' (51). Just as telestic or ritual art makes use of ineffable symbols and devices to shadow forth the invisible nature of the gods, so the same assimilative power enables us to fashion *agalmata* of visible things by lexicographic fiat. The verbal legislator is the counterpart of the Demiurge, who is the first to name the two circles that he entwines in his creation of the soul. Now, demiurgic activities are of two kinds: the dissemination of universal *logoi*, or rational principles, is attributed to the Demiurge, while the lesser gods are held responsible in the *Timaeus* for the discrimination of particulars (52, 55). The *eidos* or universal form of the human is implanted in each of us from above, while the lesser gods determine the physical attributes and circumstances of the individual (55). The curious allusion to a shuttle in the mind of God at *Cratylus* 389b–c is a cryptic index of the likeness between the work of the Demiurge and that of his human imitators. Each is capable of effecting the synthesis which is presupposed by the very existence of the particular, but without depriving the particular of its specific qualities (56). In its ideal (that is to say, transcendent) form the activity of the Demiurge remains inscrutable, but that is not to say that the metaphorical image of the shuttle is capricious: it is a truth, and not an arbitrary conceit, that 'what a shuttle is to weaving, such is discernment in the creation of the forms' (56). The relation of object to name is not that of *idea* to *eidôlon*, but a symbolic one such as (once again) we observe in the performance of a mystery.

Noting that both Plato and Aristotle had distinguished the artisan who is conscious only of the artefact from the expert who has the skill to use it (60, 62), Proclus surmises briefly that the dialectician excels the vulgar practitioners of speech much as the Demiurge excels the lesser gods (63). Further meditation suggests, however, that even the philosopher has not yet achieved the cognizance of the essential that would enable him to grasp all truth in its wholeness and that therefore he, like the lesser gods, is aware of the partial rather than the eternal, exercising only the shadow of true intellection (64). Since names may be true or false, since they are as apt to denote the *eidôlon* or mere similitude as the thing itself, an intellectual winnowing is required, which cannot be furnished either by Cratylus, who opines that all names are natural, nor by Hermogenes, to whom they are baseless tokens (68). In the triad of speakers, Socrates is the counterpart of intellect, Hermogenes of *doxa* or opinion seeking the Good without the aid of reason, and Cratylus of the carnal understanding which cannot free itself or its objects from the envelope of matter (67). Even to a Socrates there are names that remain unknowable: behind all names is the silence of the divine realm, in which appellation and essence coincide (71).

Symbol, Myth and Allegory in the *Republic*

We have noted above that Proclus credits the mysteries with the power of representing the invisible in symbols. Commenting on an intermittent differentiation of the symbol from the icon in other works by Proclus, John Dillon has proposed that, whereas the icon is palpably a representation and could not be interpreted, even superficially, without reference to its original, the symbol is not so readily seen to point beyond itself and will yield an interpretation even to those who study it with no sense of its hidden import. The evidence of the *Cratylus* would suggest that the distinction is not so much one of form as of reference. If the object signified is invisible, the signifier can bear no resemblance to it: the opaque is the currency of the obscure. The term *sunthêma*, a synonym of *sumbolon* in Proclus' commentaries on the *Cratylus* and the *Republic*, is said in the latter work to imply the manifestation of that which is not manifest, the seeing under definite forms of that which has no form (II 242.24–26 Kroll). The resemblance to the biblical definition of faith as 'the substance of things hoped for, the evidence of things not seen' (Hebrews 11.1) may not be wholly adventitious but can certainly not be traced to direct borrowing. The mysteries to which Proclus alludes throughout his commentary on the *Republic* are the same rites which he commends for the use of *sumbola* in his readings of the *Cratylus*, and his references appear to betoken a genuine belief in the possibility of grasping the ineffable by other means than speech.

His principal aim, however, in the exposition of Book 3 of the *Republic* is to rescue the poets (or at least the best of them) from the charge of deceiving the public through mimesis. His first shift is to urge that Plato intends his strictures to fall on only one of three kinds of poetry,[7] since he accommodates the didactic poet even in the tenth book of the *Republic* and praises those who sing under inspiration in the *Phaedrus*. Even mimetic poetry may be further subdivided into the eikastic and the phantastic, the first of which offers faithful representations of the object, while the latter flatters a puerile taste by substituting fancy for perception (I 188.28–192.5 Kroll). While this distinction is indeed applied to painting at *Sophist* 235d, it is clear that Proclus is trying to make a wig out of a split hair, since the eikastic in Plato excels the phantastic only as the bad excels the worse. Proclus himself is seeking only a palliative, not a remedy, since he readily confesses that the mimetic kind is inferior to the others and that the palm must be given to the

---

[7] See Sheppard (1980), 95–103, on the originality of Proclus' division of poetry into three kinds.

poetry of inspiration. As Plato associates the inspiration of the poet with that of the hierophant who orchestrates the mysteries, we might suppose that the symbol would be the characteristic medium for both. This, however, is only intermittently true of the bard, and in other instances it would appear that the prerogative of inspired speech, be it that of the poet or of the philosopher, is to express with a peculiar directness that which is wholly inexpressible to others.

For the better understanding of myth, we must add analogy to symbolism as a mode of speech that is innocent of mimesis. We have seen that in the *Cratylus* the term 'shuttle' admits of an analogical usage which does not imply any likeness such as obtains between an *eidôlon* and its paradigm. A variant of the same teaching occurs at *Commentary on the Republic* I 86.5–8: the creators of myth dealt not in icons and paradigms but in symbols and analogies, communicating not by signification but by sympathy. Proclus was not the first admirer of Plato to defend him against the protest of the Epicurean Colotes that only a charlatan would create his own myths as vehicles of instruction after denouncing the use of the same trope in the sophists and elder poets. This, for an Epicurean, was conventional persiflage, as the master himself had enjoined his disciples to 'shun poetry like the sirens': Colotes finds in Plato what Epicurus found in Homer – an admission that his own literary medium lends itself easily to the purpose of deceit.

The rudiments of an answer to Colotes are already visible before Proclus begins to paraphrase his strictures. As an Epicurean, Colotes has no place in his philosophy for a disembodied soul or the providential interposition of the gods. For a Platonist, on the other hand, the survival of the soul after separation from the corpse was no conceit but a dogma proved beyond controversy, and it would be equally unphilosophical to deny that it will be called to account for all its deeds on earth at a celestial assize. Nor is there any caprice in the transition from the seen to the unseen world, for in the foregoing dialogue Socrates has designed a commonwealth which, as he himself confesses, could exist only in the heavens; when he divides the inhabitants of the upper realm into three orders, corresponding to the three castes of his imaginary city, he is to be taken at his word. It is not therefore the substance of the myth but its picturesque garb that requires apology, and this is easily furnished once we admit that there are truths that cannot be directly communicated to the unenlightened soul. Myth can implant a dusky intimation of such truths through images drawn from the sublunar realm, but without pretending to the veracity of a historical record. Once our irrational faculties have been stirred by the specious elements of myth, it is for intellect to penetrate the veneer:

> That myths exert an effect upon the multitude is evident from the mystic rites. For they too, making use of myths to ensure that the truth about the gods remains beyond speech, give rise by their performance to sympathetic affection in souls by means unknown to us and divine. The result is that some of those who are bring initiated fall into consternation, being filled with divine terrors, while others, making themselves conversant with the holy symbols and standing out

of themselves, are ensconced among the gods and look upon them. (*In Rem Publicam* p. 17–24 Kroll)

Myth is thus an alloy of the 'shown' and the 'contrived' – these being complementary terms which denote respectively the epiphany of the real and its symbolic representation. The contrivance remains inferior to the disclosure, but, since the myth is a symbol rather than a simulacrum, it will not mislead us, like the work of the artist, into taking the counterfeit for the reality. We find no such emollients in the *Republic* itself, but some defence of this kind must be offered if the philosopher is not to fall victim to his own critique. Porphyry (if Proclus is to be trusted) had undertaken a similar refutation of Colotes, while Heraclitus the Stoic had commended allegory as an antidote to the Epicurean disparagement of poetry. That these notorious libellers of the gods were also enemies of Homer was, for a Platonist, sufficient proof that the Muse deserved a hearing, and that myth, when duly interpreted, had a place in the ideal commonwealth.

The End is Silence

The interpretation of myth depends, of course, on the disposition of the soul, as Proclus explains in a striking image:

> Myth that is wholly fictitious is germane to those who live only according to the phantastic faculty, and whose intellect is entirely receptive; that which is revelatory of knowledge and a natural medium of noeric cognition [is germane to] those for whom pure meditation is the seat of their whole activity. That which is externally fictitious and internally noeric remains as a helpmeet to us, who are composite and possess a twofold intellect, one that is what we are and the other that we have assumed in our coming forth. For pleasure accrues to the twofold intellect in us, and if one of us is nurtured by the things within he becomes a spectator of true things, while the one who has been dazzled by externals has been prepared for the route to knowledge. If, however, we exercise the phantastic faculties, it nonetheless behoves us to make use of the phantastic in its pure form, unsullied by vicious phantasms,; in the same way the outward vesture of myths should be suited to the noeric images (*agalmasin*) within. (*In Rem Publicam* II 107.27–108.13 Kroll)

A number of Platonic antecedents can be cited for the notion that the reader's soul is the seat of *agalmata* or sacred images. We may think of the teacher honouring his beloved like the statue of a deity in the *Phaedrus*, of the beautiful figure within the ugly Silenus to which Socrates is likened in the *Symposium*, of the mobile *agalmata* which cast their shadows on the wall before the prisoners in the cave. Speech of a kind is germane to all these similes in Plato: it is by solicitation and instruction that the teacher will bring out the godlike element in his pupil, it is the conversation of Socrates that illustrates the beauty of his soul, and tongues must be exercised both in the manoeuvres of the *agalmata* and in the efforts of the prisoners to construe them. In Proclus the living characters of Plato have become timeless and voiceless ciphers of the eternal: there is no room for the durable antinomies and Protean negotiations in which sceptics of antiquity and a host of modern readers have professed to discover the true pedagogic import of the dialogues. To us it may seem that Proclus commandeers the texts as a loom for his own ingenuities; to him it was already a finished tapestry, and he would have been of one mind with the young contemporary who urged, in his *Prolegomena to Plato*, that every dialogue is an image of the world.

Speech and movement seem to our morbid souls to be marks of life; to a Neoplatonist these are the last, anarchic waves in a stream that wells from the plenitude of silence and repose. Like any pagan adept, Proclus keeps a becoming reticence in his allusions to the mysteries;[8] we know enough, however, of these performances to be sure that the consummation was not the thing said (the *legomenon*) nor the thing enacted (the *drômenon*) but the thing revealed to the eye, the *horômenon* or *epopteia*. Christians who endeavoured to profane these rites were apt to halt at the superficial obscenities; if they got further, they came away with nothing more than 'an ear of wheat sown in silence'. In the Valentinian system, as we have seen, it is with the assistance of his consort Sige or Silence that the Father begets the aeons; we have seen again that Nature, when she is given a voice by Plotinus, declares paradoxically that she fashions all things in silence. It was only to be expected, then, that Proclus would celebrate the discipline of silence when he prefaced his demonstration of the knowable with an anatomy of knowledge in the second volume of his *Platonic Theology*. Here he undertakes to show how the mind can learn to set aside the fickle or fraudulent bulletins of the senses by abstraction, by analogy or (hardest of all) by absolute negation. It is in the description of this final process that he leads us through a verbal replication of the mysteries, concluding with a vision, the *epopteia*, which is plainly supposed to transcend the formulaic terms in which it is conveyed:[9]

> Let there be stillness for us, not only of opinion and fancy, not only of the passions that impede us in our movement towards the one as it draws us upwards, but let the air be still, let this All be still; and let all things with unshaken power elevate us to fellowship with the ineffable. And as we stand there, having transcended even the intelligible, if such a thing there be in us, and having adored it with sealed eyes like the sun in its rising (for it is not right for us to look directly upon it, nor for any other being) … let us, as it were worship it, not on the pretext that it created earth and heaven, or souls and the generations of other living things – these indeed it created but in the last stages – but that before all this it brought to light the whole intelligible race of the gods and all that is intellectual

---

8   See further Sheppard (1980), 145–149.
9   Translation from Edwards (2009a), 212.

> ... and when after this we come back down from our intellectual hymnody and putting aside the irrefutable science of dialectic, let us consider in the wake of this vision of the first causes how far the first god is raised above the sum of things. (*Platonic Theology* 2.11, p. 65 Saffrey and Westerink)

The ear within must be deaf before the eye within can see. We have observed that the same rule holds for Plotinus in his one reminiscence of mystical rapture at *Enneads* 4.8.1. It is not so, on the other hand, in the ecstasy which Augustine shares with Monica at Ostia, where the stilling of outward voices is the prelude to an audience with the ineffable. The relation of truth to the soul in Augustine is always that of master to pupil, never that of the quarry to the hunter. He imbibed both truth and falsehood in youth by reading; it was the books of Mani that decoyed him into heresy and the writings of the Platonists that revealed a higher notion of God; from these he was introduced to a subtler form of his mother's creed first by the injunction 'take up and read' (*Confessions* 8.12.28), then by the diligent perusal of the scriptures to which this led him. From this time on, all revelation was in the imperative mode, and progress in wisdom was measured by the deepening of obedience; at the root of this equation of philosophy with service was a veneration of the written text as the medium of disclosure, and at the root of this in turn was a belief that the eternal Word and Wisdom of God had assumed the tangibility of flesh.

To a Platonist the text may be an icon of the universe, the history that it recounts may be a symbolic representation of a metaphysical truth, and analogues to the ordering of different planes of knowledge or of being may be discovered in the juxtaposition of characters; the doctrine that the truth itself is immanent in this text and no other would, however, be entirely at odds with their conception of the book as a seed and an icon. Even when the sower of thoughts appears in the figure of Socrates, it can be said at most that the action of the book upon the reader resembles that of the sage upon his interlocutor, not that the book is a continuation of intercourse with the sage and that our only duty is to understand it. The purpose of Socrates' speaking is to promote the illumination of the soul: the student becomes a philosopher when he can add his own experience to another's testimony, hearing in order that he may see. Augustine, for his part, holds that the reward and culmination of fidelity to the one Master is a more intimate acquaintance with the Master through the same means that were given to him at the outset. He does not inherit the words of a dead preceptor as a stimulus to internal discipline; he joins the saints before him in a practice of discipleship that will bring him into everlasting communion with the Word.

Positive and Negative

Can we then say that for Proclus silence is all that can be communicated of a concealed epiphany? His reply is to warn the reader not to imagine the negation as a kind of proposition, which expresses the truth that was wanting in the ascription of positive qualities to the first principle. Nothing said of this principle, whether positive or negative, can be absolutely true, since, if we understand truth as the perfect coincidence of thought with the object of thought, we can speak of such a coincidence only at the noetic or intelligible realm which is immediately posterior to the One. It is here that we find the ideal, the paradigmatic and everything of which it could be said, in the parlance of a later epoch, that its essence is identical with its existence; of the One itself we can predicate neither existence nor essence except by accommodation to our own weakness. Proclus explains, at *Platonic Theology* 5.27, that even the noetic has three 'hypostases', the first 'according to being and the one', the second 'according to the intellectual life', while the third contains the intelligible in their multiplicity. The author and presiding god of each noetic tier exists at the level of the noeric, in which there is perfect adequation, but not identity, between the knowing subject and the object of its knowledge. When Plato's Demiurge contemplates the paradigm, he can be said to subsist noetically in the object of contemplation, while the latter subsists noerically in him (5.27; p. 101, 19–21 Saffrey and Westerink). Commenting on Plato's famous dictum that it is difficult to find out the Father and Maker of the universe and impossible to reveal him to all, Proclus concludes (if it is a conclusion) that we are capable of grasping the noetic only in silence, whereas a certain understanding of the noeric can be vouchsafed to the handful of minds that have been prepared for the disclosure:

> The race of intelligible gods takes pleasure in silence and rejoices in symbols beyond speech, for which reason Socrates in the *Phaedrus* also describes the contemplation of the intelligible as the most holy of rituals, since it is wrapped in silence and the knowledge of it is beyond speech. The race of intellectual [gods], on the other hand, can be spoken of, but not to all, and it can be known but with difficulty; for it is on account of its subordination to the intelligible that it has come down to the plane of the speakable from silence and a sublimity apprehensible only to intellect. (*Platonic Theology* 5.28, p. 105 Saffrey and Westerink)

In his *Commentary on the Parmenides* – perhaps his most tenacious essay in synthesis – Proclus undertakes to show that the Demiurge, in executing his copy of the paradigm, also vindicates the teaching of the sophist that whatever exists partakes at once of likeness and of unlikeness. The *Sophist* had postulated, in addition to the forms which are exemplified in particular species such as horse or man, five 'principal kinds' (*megista genê*) in which all these forms participate, as also do the individuals (*atoma*) over which each form presides. Being, as Proclus explains, is the most universal of these categories, since when we hold any predicate to be true we are presupposing the existence of the subject to which we ascribe it. The antithetical pairs that are subjoined to being – rest and motion, likeness and unlikeness – are not so catholic in scope, since contradictory properties cannot be truly asserted of the same thing in the same respect. It is true nonetheless that likeness is exemplified in all concrete existence, since everything is a thing of a certain kind, and, insofar as it represents that kind, it resembles both the archetype and all its individual exemplars. It is equally true that all the exemplars have a share in unlikeness, since no two are similar in all their properties, and none belongs to the same order of being as the form or archetype which they all resemble. The forms themselves are subject to the same reasoning: by virtue of the mere fact that they are forms they are alike, yet they remain unlike inasmuch as each is perfectly itself and not another. At the same time, their unlikeness is one predicate that unlike subjects have in common, and therefore, simply because they are unlike, they have a share in unity – not the transcendent oneness which the *Parmenides* has shown to be anterior to being itself, but in a monadic devolution of unity which the commentator pronounces to be an icon of a higher monadic state that admits of no participation. There is nothing in the noetic realm or any realm below it which exhibits either likeness or unlikeness without its contrary; there is nothing, however diffuse or heterogeneous, which exists without some share in unity.

This logical interpenetration of contraries is inherent in all procession. When the lower proceeds from the higher, a difference is inevitably established between the product and the source of the procession; conversely, the *epistrophê* or reversion of the product to the source annuls duality, and where there are no longer two they cannot differ. One might infer that likeness is a corollary of reversion and unlikeness of procession and one might even proceed to argue that, as the end can never surpass the beginning, the supervenient likeness must be inferior to the unlikeness in which the product originated. Yet this would lead us into an antinomy, for that which partakes of oneness in a higher degree is superior to that which partakes of oneness in a lower degree, and we cannot doubt that likeness partakes of oneness in a higher degree than unlikeness. The solution to this paradox is the withdrawal, or at least the modification of the premiss that unlikeness is a corollary of procession. While the effect must differ from the cause, it cannot be wholly devoid of likeness, for that would mean that it had received no properties from the cause. The cause, then, cannot fail to communicate a certain likeness in conjunction with the unlikeness: the rule, as we have seen, is that the effect is paradigmatically in the cause and the cause iconically in the effect.

Dissimilitude is greatest where the greatest resistance is offered to the power of the causal agent. With each descent to a lower plane the power of the cause diminishes, while the viscosity or turbulence of the medium increases. It is for this reason that the work of the Demiurge surpasses that of every sublunar artist, who can manufacture only facsimiles of his own conceit from rebellious matter. The world that the Demiurge fashions – 'generated' in the sense that it is contingent and therefore subject to vicissitude – is nevertheless an everlasting icon of the paradigm, the one object in the realm of generation that has neither beginning nor end in time, exempt alike from increment and decay. Between the noeric realm that he inhabits and the noetic realm that he contemplates there is not such a gradient even as that which separates the noeric from the sensible, and, while noeric depends upon the noetic as its cause, the relation is not that of icon to paradigm. Still less is it possible to speak of the One as the paradigm of the noetic or the latter as the icon of the One. The abstraction of the concept from particulars will equip the finite intellect with an icon of the form, but the form itself is not an icon of anything that transcends it. This term is confined, as Proclus understands the usage of Plato, to that sphere in which our senses are beguiled by the hostages that we entrust to chance and time.

Epilogue

Proclus, though he poured libations to many a forgotten god of Athens, is no apologist for images, and no image-maker in prose. Following and enlarging upon the precedent of Iamblichus – perhaps moved to emulation by the example of his Christian contemporaries who were still throwing down the old images with the temples – he builds his philosophy by exegesis,[10] and he is certainly at one with the theologians of the Church in his assumption that a commentator ought to revere his text. There is this difference, however, that he reveres the philosophy more than the philosopher, since the former is the soul's path to deliverance, while the latter is only a pioneer and guide to the soul so long as she cannot find the path for herself. The text is in no sense to be identified with the Good to which it leads us; nor can it be, as Origen thought, a sufficient viaticum for the soul, for there would then have been no need for Proclus to cultivate the coercive arts of rhetoric and theurgy. Nor, as we shall understand more clearly at the end of the following chapter, would he have recommended the practice of absolute quietude, in which every voice is stilled and the soul deprived of all companionship, as a necessary overture to the vision of the Good.

---

[10] Parallels are learnedly collected by Bendinelli (1997), though they are not proof of borrowing either by Platonists or by Christians.

Chapter 10
The Christianity of Christian Platonism

Proclus was a younger contemporary of Augustine of Hippo and probably an older contemporary of the author whom we know as Denys or Dionysius the Areopagite. Both had more than a second-hand acquaintance with Platonic thought, and Dionysius has often been regarded as a disciple of Proclus, at least in his vocabulary. For all that, he and Augustine wrote as Christians who, because they knew the Platonists at first hand, were all the more conscious that their own faith rested on evidence that was not perceived to be evidence in the Greek schools. For both, the highest principle was God, the seeker of souls, who was not to be known but by his own speaking. This speaking took two forms, the word of scripture and the enfleshment of the Word in Jesus of Nazareth. These two are one, as the first is our testimony to the second, and the second the clue to our reading of the first. Reverence for the Word precludes the use of painted idols or even, for Dionysius, the espousal of verbal images as substitutes for that blindness which is knowledge. If we allow, with Augustine, that some direct commerce of God with the soul is possible, it will take the form of hearing rather than vision, even if the latter term is taken in its most elevated sense..

Augustine of Hippo

Two tenets of Augustine's moral theology were anomalous in his own day, though they would now be widely regarded as platitudes of Christian thought. First, he maintained that the cause of Adam's fall was not the capitulation of intellect to the passions, but the corruption of intellect by *superbia* (pride), a baseless faith in its own sufficiency, which resulted in a darkening of reason and the prostration of the will. Next, he affirmed that among the ordinances to which Adam's fallen progeny is still subject is an absolute prohibition of lying, even when the motive is to avert another sin or promote the victory of the Church. These postulates – that pride, rather than duress, is the root of sin and that it is always a sin to lie – condition Augustine's view of the origin of sin among the nations. He believed, like any Christian, that we are constantly exposed to the guile of demons, but he does not appear to have held, like some before him, that they were able to cause disease, let alone to bring about the natural visitations that certain philosophers had attributed to them. Demons owe their ascendancy in the pagan world to their immemorial cunning, their capacity to assume false shapes and, above all, their collusion with the propensity of the natural man (as we call him) to belie the image of God within and set up his own effigy in the place of worship. Playing upon the vanity of mortals, they have beguiled them into reading as signs the lights that God set in the sky to give us light (*On Christian Doctrine* 2.22.34); the consequence is that their benighted eyes cannot read the plain characters in which God has inscribed the moral law and the history of salvation.[1] Augustine, though more learned, is no more judicious than any other churchman in his satires on the multitudinous gods who cannot subsist without their idols; what is new in his *Confessions* is the presentation of the whole Roman Empire as a theatre of idolatry, in which dens of fornication, arenas of bloodshed, temples of imposture and the unwitting worship of matter are merely local manifestations of the universal pleasure of the deceiver in being deceived.

Looking back on his childhood in the *Confessions*,[2] Augustine found that he had drunk in vanity with the rudiments of education. Plays depicting non-existent gods were his grammatical textbooks (1.16.26); when he ought to have been lamenting his own sins he was taught to shed tears for the fictional woes of Dido (1.13.20–22). This Roman, and Christian, variant of the question of the Cynic Diogenes – why do grammarians study the wanderings of Odysseus, unconscious of our own vagaries?[3] – insinuates that even the philosophic critique of the pagan world is one more of its fopperies. In the second book he turns sin into a *ludum* –'game', but the word is cognate with *illusio* – when his juvenile playmates challenge him to steal a pear for the mere love of transgression (2.4.9). When in Book 3 the term *imago* makes its first appearance, it refers first to the illusions of the stage (3.2.2), then to games much bloodier than those of Augustine's youth (3.2.3), which, as he later reflected, blinded him to the only legitimate representation of God, his image within (3.7.13). Next, it was the phantasms of the Manichees that decoyed him (3.6.10) – phantasmal not only because their books were fabulous and their eloquence rouged with sophistry, but also because they had a false idea of God and therefore misconceived the nature of Christ. Their error, in Augustine's eyes, was not the docetic heresy that Christ had only the semblance of a body, but a failure to grasp the incorporeality of God. Confounding spirit and matter, they imagined him as an extended domain of light and had no notion of any light but the physical radiance of the sun.

After nine years of apprenticeship to the Manichees, Augustine was delivered from these nightmares by the Platonists, who taught him that the divine has neither shape nor palpable substance, and that the only kindred properties below the moon are those of intellect. The *Hortensius* of Cicero had already made it clear to him that the purpose of philosophy is to liberate the intellect by subduing the flesh (3.3.6) – not, in Manichaean fashion, to abandon the body to its own sinful courses. He now learned from the Platonists (or from one, whom we can identify as Amelius, the

---

[1]	On signs in Augustine, see Markus (1996), 1–44.

[2]	On the *Confessions* as an exercise in self-discovery, both for the author and for his reader, see Stock (1998), 21–121.

[3]	Diogenes Laertius, *Lives of the Philosophers* 6.27.

companion of Plotinus)[4] that a Greek could affirm, with the prologue to the Fourth Gospel, that *the Word had been with God* in the beginning and that *all things were made through him* (John 1.1–3). Proud sons of Adam as they were, however, they could not understand the saying 'the Word was made flesh' (*Confessions* 7.9.13, citing John 1.14). In consequence they, and Augustine as their disciple, strove for deliverance without seeking the Deliverer; the depravity of the will became ever more burdensome to Augustine, and his efforts to cultivate a Platonic attachment to the beautiful in the company of Christian sympathizers nurtured only a self-consuming love of love. His own conversion, as he later recounted it, was not a deliberate turning of the eye of the soul to the Good, but a providential accident. Like Paul, he received a peremptory command, though not, like Paul, a command from Jesus; in the legendary past of Rome, an unknown voice from a wood or the joke of a child had been accepted as an oracle,[5] but Augustine was the first to obey the voice of an unknown child. Even the song of the infant – 'take up and read' (8.12.29) – was unfamiliar, but the passage in the Epistle to the Romans (13.13) to which it led him touched his soul with a power beyond that of the philosophers. In retrospect, he perceived that the covert ministry of the Word had brought him home to the word of scripture, which in turn had taught him to throw himself on the mercy of the Word.

At the end of his autobiographical narrative, Augustine devotes the tenth book to the nature of memory, pondering the hypothesis that happiness and God can be known because we have some latent recollection of them, corresponding to the latent recollection of the Forms which supplies the foundation of knowledge in Plato. Discovering that it is hard to answer this question in the affirmative, he proceeds in the next three books to develop a Christian understanding of the creation. In rebuttal of the Manichees, he equates the light of the first day with the intellectual heaven (13.8.94); at the same time, he insists, against the Platonists, that the occupants of this heaven, be they angels or ideas, exist by divine fiat, not by logical necessity. These books contain the nucleus of his subsequent meditations, over a period of three decades, on the nature of God, the origin of knowledge and the anatomy of the soul. A brief consideration of these writings will enable us to write the commentary that the mature Augustine might have wished to append to a celebrated passage in the *Confessions* which commemorates the naked encounter of the soul with God.

Human and Divine Image in Augustine

In the fifty-first of his *Diverse Questions*, Augustine asks whether the being who was created in the image and likeness of God is the outer man of flesh and blood or his invisible homonym, the inner man. As though it were not enough that the outer

---

[4]   Augustine, *City of God* 10.29; Eusebius, *Gospel Preparation* 11.19.
[5]   Virgil, *Aeneid* 7.116; on Augustine and the *Aeneid*, see Bennett (1988).

man is said to be perishing, while the inner man is undergoing renewal day by day, he notes that for the apostle this renewal consists in putting away 'the image of the earthly' which we have worn hitherto, and putting on 'the image of the heavenly' (1 Corinthians 15.49). Reasoning that this could not be said of the body before the resurrection, he deduces that the image of the earthly is the moribund state into which the soul falls by sinning, while the image of the heavenly is the transfigured life that she comes to enjoy by dying to sin and being reborn in the righteousness of God. As the image is above all the conformation of the mind to the mind of God, we can give this appellation not only to the Son, in whose image and likeness we are made, but also to the Holy Spirit, who 'knows the things of God' (1 Corinthians 2.11). The corporeal can never exhibit the perfect likeness of the incorporeal, but, if we defer to those who contend that scripture would not use two nouns to denote one thing, we may allow that a certain likeness resides in the body also, insofar as it takes the soul for its guide and pattern. Augustine revives the ancient commonplace that our erect posture is evidence of our desire for heaven and our propensity to worship, but maintains that, while the term 'likeness' (*similitudo*) can be predicated both of soul and of body, the soul alone is the seat of the image, since this term subsumes every likeness while the converse does not hold.

Augustine's Greek contemporary, Cyril of Alexandria, was not so ready to countenance a distinction between the 'image' and 'likeness', perhaps because he saw this as a characteristic tenet of Origen, who had been condemned without quarter by Theophilus, his uncle and immediate predecessor in the Alexandrian see. While Augustine's usage is not entirely at one with that of Origen and Irenaeus, he agrees with both in holding that the first humans fell before they had attained the perfection that God intended for them. In his view this is a failure, not to consummate the image or the likeness, but to develop the *sapientia* or wisdom which would have guaranteed the proper use of wisdom, thereby rendering it impossible to sin (*On Free Will* 3.72). The divine image in the soul has been impaired by Adam's fall, yet not so utterly as to conceal from us the existence of a Creator whose benign and sovereign power is still conspicuous in his works. The Christian, to whom more has been revealed, is conscious also of an image of the Trinity in his own intellect, though the purpose of the great work *On the Trinity,* in which Augustine demonstrates this at length, is not so much to prove that God must be three as to induce the soul to compare itself with its Archetype, and thus to promote the growth of that divinely-ordered wisdom which the natural man too happily renounces in his pursuit of *scientia*, or worldly knowledge.[6] The notion that the mind is a 'lesser image' (*impar imago*) of the Deity is canvassed at length for the first time in the ninth book (9.2.2), where the mind's love for itself, as the most adequate of all created objects, is discovered to be a reflection of the love that constitutes the essence of God before all creation. The mind that loves itself is subject and object in one, while the love makes a third, inhering in both and yet

---

[6]   Hanby (2003), 27–47.

distinct from either (9.12.18). The Father who loves, the Son who is loved and the Spirit who unites them – the Spirit whose name connotes the substance of the Godhead, as love is its essence[7] – form a triad to which nothing can be added and which finds its counterpart in the self-awareness granted only to the noblest of their creatures (9.1.1).

Augustine believes, or affects to believe, that even the pagan philosophers had an inkling of this doctrine. He had read, in a work by Porphyry, now known only from his own strictures, of a paternal intellect, a filial intellect and an intermediary whose function he confessed that he was unable to determine, though to him this was all the more reason to identify it as the Holy Spirit.[8] He is not without excuse, since even now the role of 'power' or 'life' in the 'noetic triad', whose other terms are certainly the mind's knowledge of itself and the mind as object of its own knowledge, is but imperfectly understood. Whether or not we can trust him to speak for Porphyry, Augustine's presupposition in the next stage of his argument is the familiar maxim of Plato that whatever is fully loved must be fully known. The corollary in Plato is that, as knowledge on earth is the fruit of the soul's aspiration to retrieve forgotten objects of desire, we can no more fail to love what is truly known than we can love what we do not know. While the corrosive effects of the Fall entail that both the mind's knowledge of itself and its love of itself must be incomplete or corrupt in the present world, there is no vice or impediment in the love of the Holy Spirit for the Father and Son, or in the knowledge (*notitia*) which the Son brings to light from the bosom of the Father. To Augustine this second image of the Trinity seems preferable to the first, which disguised the equality of the Spirit and the Son (9.12.18). Like the first, and in contrast to Plato's myths, it is not a speculative or artificial analogy, but is grounded in the natural analogy between creature and Creator. Moreover, it elucidates the relation between the Father and the Son, which is the prototype of the creaturely relation, just as the Son himself is the prototype of the creature. The Son is the Word, giving voice to the *imagines* which populate the mind of God, and is thus himself the *imago* or image of the Father with whom that mind is identified in Augustine's simile (9.11.16). This application of the Stoic antithesis between *logos endiathetos*, the unspoken proposition, and the expression of this as *logos prophorikos*, or external speech, does not assume successive phases in the existence of the Word, as many apologists for Christianity did before the Council of Nicaea: the term 'image' implies distinctness from the Father, while the term 'Word' excludes disparity of nature, so that in conjunction they indicate that the Son is by nature the full expression of all that the Father is, without deficit or confusion. And to say that human beings are made according to the image of the Word who creates all things is to say that, by virtue of his inalienable possession of the image, he was able to

---

[7] *On the Trinity* 9.1.1, citing 1 John 4.8.

[8] *City of God* 10.29 at Bidez (1913), appendix 1, 37. Augustine is, however, not a disinterested informant: see Clark (2007).

stamp his viceroy in creation with a lesser image that centuries of wrongdoing may deface but not wholly occlude.

The use of the term *imagines* for the contents of the mind is warranted only by analogy, for in Augustine's lexicon the knowledge afforded by imagination is at best provisional and too often deceitful. The equivalent nouns in Greek, *phantasma* and *phantasia*, denote the trace or impression which survives in the memory after the object ceases to be perceived.[9] Plotinus, metaphorically assuming a bifurcation of the soul in its descent, opines that the higher, or unfallen, soul retains at all times a true image of the ideal realm, while the lower plays host to the vestiges of empirical perception (*Enneads* 4.3.31–32ff.). While it is the joint working of the two that transforms these traces into memories, they are merely by-products of incarceration, to be abandoned when the two halves of the soul are reunited and we come home to the plane of *nous* or intellect. Porphyry, following Aristotle,[10] teaches that words communicate by exciting in us the *phantasma* of the object which they customarily signify, and that intellect completes the interpretation by comparing this vestigial reminiscence with the form.[11] Like Plotinus, however, he holds that no abiding knowledge can be imparted by *phantasmata*, and according to his treatise *On the Styx* the soul that clings to them in the present world is weaving a coil for itself in the life to come.[12] Augustine, who accepts this theory of knowledge without subscribing either to Porphyry's eschatology or to his theory of recollection, admonishes his readers (more than once) that it is one thing to dream and another to perceive. On the other hand, he cannot agree with the Platonists in disparaging the phenomenal world, which God himself created as a home for embodied souls, or the remembrance of acts performed by its inhabitants, since it is these that will be judged by God on the day of resurrection. In the *Confessions* he hesitates to return an affirmative answer to his own question, whether God can be found in the memory (10.17.26), since this would imply the captivity of the Infinite in the finite, but he proposes that the memory of teachings received in the present life may expedite the return of the soul to God. Memory is the stomach of mind (10.14.21), the depository of all that can be known.[13] While God's knowledge is not of a piece with ours – he does not lay up information day by day, to be retrieved from this dark silo as occasion demands with labour and not always with success – Augustine thinks that the Trinity may be conceived without irreverence as the archetypal intellect, in which whatever is knowable is already in the memory and all that has been remembered can become knowledge again at the summons of the will.

---

[9] See, for example, *On Genesis according to the Letter* 12.15.31 and 20.42.

[10] See Whitaker (1996), 15–17, on Aristotle, *On Interpretation* 16a 3–4 and *On the Soul* 428b11–16.

[11] Fr. 78 Smith. See further Finan (1992).

[12] See further Watson (1988), 103–109; Lamberton (1989), 115–119.

[13] See further Vaught (2005), 55ff.

Memory, understanding and will complete the anatomy of the human intellect (*On the Trinity* 10.11.17), because humans can think only in time and time for us is always the past, the present or the future. In the omniscient Trinity, the memory, the knowledge of things remembered and the will to remember are coeternal and equipollent, severally and jointly containing the substance of the whole intellect, and distinguishable in their activities, though all three act in every case as one. Will supplants love as the faculty of desire, though love returns in place of will in the later books of Augustine's treatise (for example, 14.5.8). Of all his triads this is the one that recognizes the parity of Father, Son and Spirit, and the identity of each with the entire Godhead, by likening them to three covalent powers, none of which can be said, like love in the first, to have a merely epiphenomenal status, or, like mind in the second, to act as a substrate to the other two. Augustine cannot eliminate, and would not wish to disguise, the incongruities that accompany any assimilation of the created order to the Creator. These are accentuated, or so it appears, when Augustine, on the plea that every human is a composite of the inner and the outer man, proceeds to analyse the perception of natural phenomena as a synergy of three elements which mirrors the cooperation of our internal faculties in the mind's knowledge of itself. Where there is seeing, there must be first the thing seen, then the power of vision and finally the exertion of that power, the *intentio voluntatis* (11.1.1). The object, once perceived, leaves its impression in the memory; the perception of it enriches the understanding, and the direction of the eye towards the object requires an application of will. This homology will elude the Platonist, so long as he refuses to see that the body, too, is destined for immortality and is capable is exhibiting the likeness of God in the measure of its conformity to his image in the soul.[14]

According to the Gospel of John, it was God the Word who reclaimed this likeness by becoming flesh. Augustine, as we have seen, held that the Platonists could echo the opening verses of the Gospel – could believe, that is, that the Word was God with God in the beginning, and the one through whom whatever exists has come into existence – but stopped short at the incarnation. A Platonist would have understood by 'Logos' not the speech of God but the demiurgic intellect, whose timeless and indivisible contemplation of the eternal affords a paradigm for the more discursive, if still harmonious, orchestration of the lower elements by Soul. Plotinus speaks of a world-soul which is the *logos*, or ruling principle, of the cosmos, though he can also characterize the individual soul as a *logos*, or determination of intellect.[15] This soul is governed by a finite intellect, but since every unencumbered intellect contemplates the same noetic objects, every denizen of the supercelestial realm is a second self to every other, knowing all and known of all. Augustine might be thought to be upholding a picturesque variant of the same doctrine when he writes, in his book *On the Teacher*, that no truth could be known with certainty were it not that the Word, from whom we received the

---

[14] See further Gioia (2008), 232–296.

[15] See Helleman-Elgersma (1980), 32, 77 and *passim*.

capacity to reason, dwells within us without our knowing it as a universal standard of veracity. It may be that he is more indebted here to the Stoic conception of the Logos, but he is neither Stoic nor Platonist in his dialogue *On Free Will*, where he explains that the Fall has blinded us to the presence of the Word, and that it was only his appearance 'in humility outside us' that enabled us to rediscover 'the one within, whom we forsook in pride' (*On Free Will* 3.30).

Even the unrighteous, inasmuch as they know and love themselves, confess the unseen tutelage of the Triune God, and even an embryonic faith in the teaching of Christ bears witness once again to his threefold character, since the precepts of the Gospel must be impressed upon the memory before they can afford matter for reflection, and unless we adhere to them in love, the mere cognizance of them cannot be described in faith (*On the Trinity* 14.2.4). To know God as Creator is to know that he has made all things according to number, measure and weight, so that all, when faith seeks God in them, cry out in threefold harmony, 'He made us' (*Confessions* 10.6.9). At the same time, it cannot be said that this world which lies about us is his image: matter is the icon of divinity, but the substrate which he created for his handiwork. The image resides in one of his creatures only and, in the strictest use of terms, it cannot be said to be fully present even in us, so long as the mind is merely a receptacle of fleeting apparitions. Love of self, inchoate faith and the science of external things are no more than presentiments of the true image, for the true image of the immutability must itself have the attribute of immutability (14.14.20). According to one of Augustine's earliest treatises, the capacity of the human mind to embrace the eternal forms is proof that it has a claim on eternity; what we have lost in the Fall we can recover, and this time in an indefeasible form, by acquiring the image and likeness of God in accordance with his own design at Genesis 1.26. Since we are told by one apostle that the change will be accomplished in the twinkling of an eye (1 Corinthians 15.52), and by another that 'when we see him we shall be like him' (1 John 3.3), it is clear that assimilation is perfected by the self-disclosure of God to the inner eye (14.18.25).

Nevertheless, we must not suppose that only the inner man will live again, for the Gospel teaches that the resurrected body, too, is immortal, as the body of Adam was when God created him in his image. It was in order to restore this immortality that the Word took flesh: as a churchman of the fifth century, however, Augustine deprecates the inference that the Second Person is more amenable to this confinement than the First, or that the man on the Cross was less divine than the Son before incarnation. Christ is not a godlike man, or God camouflaged as man, but God in man's own flesh. For that reason he is also the perfect image of divinity, and it is when we are so like him in mind and body as to be one with him that we have become true images of God. Because Augustine admits no gradations of divinity, he cannot concur with those who held that every divine epiphany of the Old Testament was a manifestation of the Son alone. In his view, any manifestation of God is an act of Father, Son and Spirit in unison; the 'sending' of the Spirit and the 'Son' by the Father does not imply pre-eminence in dignity or nature, and the term 'image', when applied to the Son, accords him the status of a plenipotentiary without stigmatizing him as an inferior, let alone a created, agent. If we deny the presence of the Father, we must deny that of the other two, and construe the theophany as an angelophany. Moreover, since it is only the gratuitous assumption of flesh that sets the Son apart from the other persons as a visible representative of divinity, Augustine cannot follow Origen in distinguishing the Son, as the proper image of the Father, from his inferiors who are merely created 'according to the image'. What more can it mean to be the image if the test of life 'according to the image' is perfect assimilation to God (14.16.22)?

It may be Augustine's fear of thinning the blood of Christ, of turning an unrepeatable prodigy into a daily sacrament, that deters him from speaking openly, with Origen, of a continuing incarnation in the scriptures. Yet, of course, it did not escape him, any more than it escaped his predecessor, that the text is now the sole means of revelation for those who have not the vision of God that Adam had, or the first-hand knowledge of the risen Lord that was granted to Paul and the apostles. It is as true for him as for Origen that all scripture is the gift of Christ the Word, who is also its ubiquitous subject, and that every word in the text is written for the edification of the believer. As the Word himself is the beloved of the Father, the Second Person of a Godhead whose essence is love, we may be sure that every text inspired by the Word is replete with the love of which the consummate manifestation is his own death on the Cross. The translation of the Word into flesh is analogous to the translation of a thought into verbal utterances: the form changes, but the content is preserved without any loss or deformation of the original (*Christian Doctrine* 1.13.12). And so it is with the scriptures: if it cannot be said that every word is Christ, it can be said that he is present in every word insofar as God is love and love is the sovereign test of exegesis. No reading can be sound if it fails to evoke the love that the Word displayed in becoming man. Conversely, it is possible that an erroneous, though charitable, reading will bring us closer to God than one that satisfies the mere grammarian (ibid. 1.36). If the Bible itself is not the Word made flesh, it is the reinscription of his love and wisdom which, when read with love and wisdom, prints his image and likeness in the human soul.

The scripture, as Origen reads it, abounds with cryptographic references to the practice of exegesis, and talk of seeing or tasting God is commonly glossed as an exhortation to more assiduous study. Allusions to the ecstatic knowledge of God occur parenthetically, and infrequently, in the course of exposition, and it is likely enough that nothing would have been heard of such experiences if scripture had given Origen no occasion to recount them. For Augustine, as we have seen, the Word is not quite identical with the word that he inspires; conversely, the text is not the characteristic domain of the spiritual senses or a necessary stimulus to their exercise. In an early work *On the Measure of the Soul* he can describe, with the clinical zeal of a philosopher, the deliberate approximation of the soul to ideal beauty by seven stages. The first three stages – animation, sense and artifice – answer to the vegetative, sentient and hegemonic workings of the soul through bodily organs; the next two, virtue and tranquillity, are interior disciplines which the soul pursues without a carnal substrate; the sixth and seventh, ingress and contemplation, equip her first for access to God and then for eternity in his presence (*Measure of Soul* 35.79). Recalling his own experience of such transports in the *Confessions*, however, Augustine celebrates not his own fervidness in seeking God, but the unforced love of God in seeking him. We are God's prize; he is never ours, and we meet him only at his own summons. Augustine's own conversion was effected (as he tells us) by a child's voice of unknown origin, crying 'Take up and read' and turning him from philosophy to the scriptures. Although it was preceded by incipient visions, these are not ascribed to the deliberate cultivation of his own faculties, and the crowning ecstasy – not so much a vision as an audience– takes him almost unawares as he communes with a kindred soul:

> We were saying, therefore, if the tumult of the flesh subsides for a moment, if the fantasies of earth, and the waters and air are silent, silent too the poles, and the soul is silent in itself, and passes out of itself by thinking not of itself, if dreams are silent too and imaginary revelations, and everything else that must be surpassed if one is to experience total silence … if they fall still because they have strained their ear toward him who made them, and he alone should speak not through them but through himself, and we should hear his voice not through the tongue of flesh or the voice of an angel, nor through thunder in the cloud [Exodus 19.16] nor through an enigmatic likeness [1 Corinthians 13.12], but his very self whom we love in these, himself we should hear without them. Is this not to enter into the joy of the Lord [Matthew 25.21, 23]? (*Confessions* 10.9)

In the rapture described by Proclus, more than half a century later, the One appears 'to sealed eyes like the sun rising' and is saluted as though with hymns; no voice is heard, and the intellect of the philosopher (or what is above the intellect) is the seat of the whole revelation. In Augustine's narrative, it is hard to say where the human dialogue ends and the higher experience begins; the object of adoration remains external to the intellect, and, while silence gives way to hearing, there is no mention of an internal or metaphorical act of vision. In Augustine as in Proclus, we may speak of an unmediated presence, inasmuch as all physical senses are put to rest and ineffable communion supersedes the metonymic knowledge of God as the Creator of all things visible. Yet even at the summit of the ascent – if there is an ascent – it is not the elevation of the intellect that makes this communion possible, but the condescension of the eternal Word, who is a mediator in Paul's sense, not an intermediate being as historians of religion commonly understand this term, since he is neither sub-divine nor superhuman, but the fullness of divinity and humanity in one.

Dionysius the Areopagite

The provenance date and aims of the pious impostor who affects to be Paul's disciple, Dionysius the Areopagite, will be disputed for years to come.[16] Whether he was a converted pagan, a Christian apologist for philosophy, a Christian trying to dispossess the philosophers or a philosopher masquerading as a Christian, he is among the recognized founders of the mystical tradition in Christianity,[17] and his *Mystical Theology* is a cornerstone – or to some the coping-stone – of that tradition. As a lucid and cogent summary of his negative theology, which (as he held) must be the bedrock of any positive theology, it will serve us as a preface to his thought, though it is not the earliest writing in the corpus. At the same time, the celebrity of his shortest book must not be allowed to conceal the fact that his usual theme is not the unknowability of God but his knowability – more precisely, the divinely-ordered use of the divinely-furnished tools by which this knowledge is attained.

The Word Without and the Image Within

After an invocation of the Trinity, the *Mystical Theology* distinguishes and condemns two opposing falsehoods. Some, who will not believe in any obscurity that their own wit cannot penetrate, deny the existent of a transcendent being; others, who profess to believe in such a being, imagine none the less that he can be adequately characterized by images derived from the natural world (142.13–143.3). Thus the disciple of Paul condemns idolatry, but it soon becomes apparent that wood and stone are the least insidious media of false religion. The word too, even the very words of scripture, may deceive us, since no epithet that we apply to God can be true of him in the sense that it bears when applied to his creation. From the fact that Moses ascended only to the place where God awaited him and did not enjoy the vision of God himself (143.17–144.5), he will conclude that even authorized representations of God, as we meet them in the scriptures, can possess only symbolic truth, and would become blasphemies if literally construed. Referring us on this point to a lost or fictitious work, the *Symbolic Theology*,[18] Dionysius proceeds to define two modes of predication, the negative and the positive (147.4ff.). The positive, or cataphatic mode, begins with adjectives such as good or wise, which can be predicated of God as the fountainhead of these qualities in created beings. The negative, or apophatic, mode begins by setting aside the literal sense of passages which are manifestly unbecoming to God, for it is surely more true that he is just or wise than that he has hands and feet or is prone to inebriation (147.20–21). For all that, the negative mode will triumph at

---

[16]   Ritter (1994), 19–30.

[17]   Louth (2007).

[18]   Rorem (1993), 197.

last over all affirmation, for, as the mind approximates to a closer knowledge of God, it becomes aware that even the loftiest predicates fall far short of his essence:

> [The cause of all] is not truth or kingship or wisdom, neither one nor oneness, neither deity nor goodness; nor is he spirit as we know it, nor sonship, nor fatherhood, nor any of the other things that are known by acquaintance to us or to any other being. Nor is it one of the things that are not or one of the things that are; things that are know it not as it is, nor does it know them insofar as they are; of it there is neither speech nor name nor knowledge. (149.8–150.4).

The way of negation is thus the one that affords the fewest opportunities for error, yet those who follow it ought not to be content with a state of nescience. The prayer of the true disciple, matching the prayer to the Holy Trinity at the outset, should be that he will find his way into the super-eminent darkness, so that the cloud becomes his light.

The longest work in the Dionysian Corpus, *On the Divine Names*, is a guide to the understanding of those cataphatic predicates which are used of God in the scriptures. God himself, as the essence of all that is and the life of all that lives (I, p. 112.3 Ritter), cannot be known by inquiry from below, but only by his own accommodation to discursive speech, which breaks his ineffable unity into concepts more amenable to the comprehension of finite intellects. The elevated sense of the terms vouchsafed to us in the scriptures is discernible by analogy (109.3), which implies some correspondence between the unfathomable wisdom of God and our own capacities; once again, however, it lay with God himself to perfect this correspondence by a paradoxical revelation of his own multiplicity in the simplicity of Jesus (113.9). The descent of the Second Hypostasis from glory to humiliation opens for a way of return to the likeness of God, though we cannot hope to follow it, after all that can be achieved by prayer and hymnody (111.8; 112.11), unless our minds are permeated by an illumination from above (109.1; 110.11–15). This act of grace, enabling us to 'strain upward' (110.19) to the invisible God who has planted his visible image in the lower realm (113.8: *anatitheisa*), is clearly more than an exercise of hermeneutic insight. It admits the lover of God to mysteries not to be divulged to the uninitiated (121.10–13), teaching him to see with the eyes of angels in accordance with Christ's promise to the elect (116.10; 115.3–4, citing Luke 20.36). The ascent from type to reality in scripture (114.4; 120.14) is possible only for those who are willing to undergo a metamorphosis (114.11), to allow their inward faculties to be shaped (*tupoumenoi*) by the imitation of God, which brings us to union with him (11.9, 112.14). The rest of the treatise is a compendious glossary to the tropes employed in biblical representations of divinity, commencing with the most perspicuous – 'God is good', 'God is light', 'God is wisdom' – and coming at last to those which are most opaque – or, to borrow the author's term, 'symbolic' – because they appear to credit God with human members and the pomp of an earthly monarch (121.1–3). For our purposes, however, it is more useful to examine two other works, in which the legibility of the written symbol is shown to depend upon our willingness to take the constitution of the angelic realm as a model, and its ectype in the Church below as a lathe, for the reproduction in the inner man of an image and likeness of the living God.

The Celestial Hierarchy

The author of the Dionysian corpus wrote at a time when the pagan temples had been ruined or converted to Christian use, so that it was possible at last for the Church to sanction the use of images without fear of a return to polytheism. Nevertheless, it was generally held that the Decalogue proscribed not only the worship of false deities, but also the representation of that which was truly holy in a base medium, and it was evidently futile to seek in wood or stone the likeness of the God 'whom no one has seen at any time' (John 1.18), 'dwelling' as he does 'in the light that no one can approach' (1 Timothy 6.16). The author shares with all Christians the belief that the pagan multitude had mistaken the coruscation of precious metals for the radiance of the gods themselves (II, p. 13.6–13 Heil and Ritter), The Christian is secured against this error by the knowledge that all knowledge of God is mediated by analogies and types (11.12), and that only statements denying him any mundane predicate can be true without qualification (13.1). Cataphatic or assertoric statements can never be commensurate with his hidden attributes (13.1–2), and therefore it behoves us to speak of him only in enigmas, which communicate all that that can be properly be known by revealing the impossibility of communication (11.17). Where there is no pretence of likeness there is less danger that the intellect will be worsted by the senses (13.3 and 16–17). The principle that the inadequacy of the icon is a measure of its utility will, however, be more intelligible if we contemplate the image of God in the angelic hierarchies which he created to reflect his glory, each in the measure allotted to it in accordance with its capacity to receive.

Foremost of the nine orders are the thrones, the cherubim and the seraphim, to whom are entrusted in sequence the tasks of cleansing the lower creation, of imparting the light of knowledge and of bringing the illuminated creature to perfection (26.15–18; 28.1–12). Likeness to God was the purpose of other creation, as of ours (17.10; cf. *Theaetetus* 176b, Genesis 1.26), and they already occupy the mansion to which we aspire. To be pure in this transcendent sphere is not only to be free of sin and blemish, but also to be innocent of all traffic with the lower realm (28.25); knowledge by illumination flows directly from fellowship with Jesus and is manifested not in external hieroglyphs but in the acquisition of his likeness by theurgy or divine service (29.9–11); perfection is not the consummation of discursive knowledge, but the plenitude of 'all-surpassing divinisation according to the knowledge of divine offices, as among angels' (29.17–18). Second to this primordial triad of thrones, cherubim and seraphim is a triad of dominions, virtues and powers. The name of the first order signifies indomitable freedom (32.17–33.3), that of the second a steadfast and undaunted imitation of God (33.8–12), and that of the third a disciplined administration of all inferior things for the common good (33.19–24).

Angels of higher rank employ their subalterns as emissaries, and encounters with the seraphim and cherubim of the first triad have been rare since the days of the prophets, when Israel lived under the direct superintendence of the Father (34.16–17 and 22, 35.3–4 and 18–20). God himself remains inapprehensible, and the sapphire which appears to bespeak his presence in Ezekiel (1.28, 10.1) is transferred by Dionysius to an angel who is 'first after the cherubim', the captain of six other angels bearing weapons, whom the prophet had been content to describe as 'men' (35.5–11; cf. Ezekiel 9.2). This regiment is a sign to us that 'good order in our own hierarchy' is the image and likeness, so far as we can achieve this, of an angelic concord which, both by example and by tutelage, assists the assimilation of the orders below to that heavenly dispensation which transcends all hierarchy (35.22–25). Once we have grasped that the liturgy on earth is a microcosm, and only a microcosm, of the divine economy, we shall be equipped to discover the resemblance hidden within the incongruity of a scriptural metaphor. Dionysius urges the reader to lower the 'eye of the intellect' from the 'august and unitary contemplation which befits the angels' to the 'pluriform and divisible plane in which the angels appear under a protean multiplicity of forms', and then to return 'from these as from icons to the simplicity of celestial intellects' by the method of analysis, or diremption, of sensible properties from the image (50.13–51.1). Again, it is assumed that the inscrutable God cannot reveal himself in the sensible sphere except through angels. It is often by seizing the essence of the phenomenon that the term denotes that we understand its figurative import: thus, it is in the nature of fire to be powerful and active, to pervade all things without mixture, to renew them by its warmth, to draw matter into itself, to irradiate them with 'beams that cannot be hidden', to refine them by attrition, to be invisible and without form, to rise to an altitude where it depends on nothing, to be kindled suddenly and to burn unabated, and in all these peculiarities we discover a 'visible icon' (52.10–11) of some attribute that can be predicated of God without dishonour (52.11–53.2). If eyes are ascribed to an angel, they symbolize his all-seeing vigilance (53.24–25); shoulders and arms betoken power in execution (54.4–6); the heart is an emblem of life-giving benevolence (54.6–8), the breast of protective steadfastness (54.8) and the feet of his eternal orientation to 'things divine' (54.9–11). The wings on his feet connote swiftness, heavenly origin, alacrity in the performance of his office and indifference to earthly traffic (54.12–16), while he goes unshod as a sign that he is free of adventitious cares and qualities that would mar his imitation of God's simplicity (54.16–19). It is when we have weaned ourselves from a lowly attachment to symbolic representations (59.7) that we come to know what is meant by joy in heaven (Luke 15.10), participating, as only the holiest of mortals can, in the ineffable jubilation of the angels over the homecoming of the lost (58.22–59.4).

This is the germ of an answer to the perennial question 'Was Dionysius a mystic?' The customary response that it depends on what we mean by 'mystic' is more than apposite, as it is not the ostensible purpose of any writing in the corpus to induce a state of rapture, or even a quiet sense of intimacy with God. *The Divine Names* and the *Mystical Theology* are cathartic exercises in hermeneutics and the use of religious language, teaching readers how to speak of God and construe the speech of prophets and apostles without succumbing to anthropomorphism or belittling the authority of the scriptures. The student of the *Celestial Hierarchies* learns what to make of angelic epiphanies to the same authors, but, although he must take these to be real events, it is nowhere assumed that he himself could enjoy a similar visitation. The book is another guide to the interpretation of scripture, not to the analysis or cultivation of internal states. Yet, just as in Origen's *Commentary on the Song of Songs*, an appeal is made to experience as the only sufficient gloss on a text that would otherwise be as elusive as the Bridegroom, so the *Celestial Hierarchies*, having proved that the scriptures must be read with the mind of an angel if they have any meaning for us, are felt to be incomplete without a conclusion intimating that if we read them thus, we cannot help but feel a measure of what the angels feel. While references to Genesis 1.26 are oblique at best in the works of the Areopagite, it was certainly one of his axioms that the refinement of the inner man is a necessary prelude to the extraction of the inner sense of scripture from its anthropomorphic husk. It is not by chance that the term 'anagogy' signifies both the therapeutic action of the text upon its readers and the upward path of an angel or a soul to its place before the throne of God.

The Ecclesiastical Hierarchy

Whereas, however, Origen is above all a scriptural exegete, Dionysius holds that the neophyte must be prepared to learn from those whose wisdom has not been committed to 'holy scripts and theological tablets' (II, p. 67.8–9 Ritter). He reminds us at the beginning of the *Ecclesiastical Hierarchy* that even the aspiring love which quickens in us the aspiration to union with God must proceed from Jesus, who draws into one divine life one sacred energy, the diversity and otherness of our bodily condition. At the same time, taking a different view of a text applied to the commentator in Origen's meditations on the Song, he warns that the soul which tries to leap the hills before its eyes can withstand the light of the intelligible realm will fall into sorrow and dismay. Between Christ and the young believer stands the hierophant, as a member of that order which has been established on earth as a type and analogue of the celestial hierarchy. It is the office of the priest not only to teach, but also to administer the rites that initiate, sustain and cement the soul's communion with the divine. In baptism the nakedness of the candidate proclaims his emancipation from ignorance, vice and carnal passion; his immersion is a simulation of death, and his new white robes are a fitting wardrobe for the illuminated soul.

The author now proceeds to describe and explain the rite of communion, with the caveat that a full apprehension of the noetic import of the liturgy is impossible for those who have not yet been admitted to spiritual communion (78.16–19). The many who perceive nothing but the symbol, seeking only the delectation of the senses (81.10–11, 87.8–11) are described, in calculated allusions to Plato, as victims of sorcery (86.5), lovers of *phantasia* or illusion (87.18, 89.23) and mere connoisseurs of outward beauty (87.21; cf. *Republic* 475e4). Plato would have rejoiced to hear that the teaching of the novice is a process of *maieusis* or midwifery (85.12) which conducts him from the image to the archetype (81.15–16); he might have conceded also that for those who are still on the stairway to perfection, the variegated apparatus of signs is 'not without profit' (81.18), and that a teacher may at times allow the integrity of vision to be concealed by a 'plethora of sacred riddles' (83.6). He would not have allowed, however, that comprehension can be assisted by the congregational intonation of hymns, and there is no Platonic counterpart to the Dionysian argument that theurgy is the completion of theology, as the New Testament fulfilled the expectations of the prophets (84.15–21). The author commends the hymns of the Church as products of *hierographia*, or sacred writing, (84.2), paying no more attention to Plato's strictures on the deadness of the letter than to his condemnation of those who debauch the intellect by flattering the ear. To Plato, as to Origen, it would be obvious that no good can accrue to those who carry out a liturgical performance without reflection on its spiritual import; it would not be so clear to either that, without participation in the liturgy, the believer cannot hope to attain his goal of likeness to God. Platonists could imagine an imperfect sketch of the city of God on earth, but it was the biblical acclamation of the Church as the Bride of Christ that allowed this philosophic Christian to portray it as a spiritual commonwealth, whose structures were designed not only to mirror the eternal realm but to furnish each of its citizens with an efficacious means of assimilation.

Equally foreign to Plato, though purposely reminiscent of his most celebrated doctrine, is the author's explanation of the Eucharistic formula 'do this in remembrance (*anamnesis*) of me' (92.13; Luke 22.19). *Anamnesis* in Plato is the soul's recollection of an ideal form that it contemplated before its fall into the body; Dionysius, as a Christian, maintains that each of us begins his embodied life as a victim not of his own sin, but of the trespass of Adam and Eve. Turpitude and misery were the inevitable lot of their descendants until God united himself to the frailty of our mortal flesh in order to pour his light into our impoverished souls (91.19). *Anamnesis* is the reproduction in each of us of the Godlike pattern that Christ has set before us (92.14) – a process likened first, after Plotinus, to the self-fashioning of a statue, then to the painter's sedulous duplication of an object that has completely engrossed his vision (96.2–11). To Porphyry at least, this would not have seemed an ignoble simile, and no Platonist could demur when the author exhorts us to fix our gaze upon the noetic, to the exclusion of all other objects, in order to fashion within ourselves an *agalma* of divinity. But the prototype of this *agalma* is itself a visible image, a man of flesh and blood with a definite origin in history. The image, as he writes elsewhere, is not to be contrasted with its archetype in heaven, as though a man performed the works of man while

God performed the works of God, for the Word imbues his adopted flesh with a single, 'theandric' energy, in which the divine and the human are indissolubly at one (Epistle 4 at II, p. 161.8–10).

The necessity of the Church as a conduit of grace is illustrated in the second half of the treatise. The sacrament is a symbol, and the priesthood an icon, of the divine economy (105.13, 20). The priest enacts the rite that decodes the symbol, but the symbol remains an indispensable adjunct to the rite. As the polity of the Church mirrors that of heaven, each sacerdotal order discharges on earth the office allotted to the corresponding rank among the angels. The lesser clerics purify the ungodly, the priests illuminate the 'holy people', and the perfection of the spiritual athlete (that is, the monk) is the business of those whom Dionysius calls the archpriests (108.5–116.23). The Church, therefore, performs the anagogic role which a commentator of Origen's school performs for himself by pondering the canonical arrangement of the Solomonic books. Dionysius does not suggest that even a monk could encompass in his own meditation the purgative, illuminative and unitive ways that make up the itinerary of a mediaeval mystic. We can join the company of the angels in the present life, and the image of God is shown to us in its perfection by the burial of the godly amid the orisons and thanksgivings of the saints (120.13–123.15).

Conclusion

For reasons explained in Chapter 8, it will not have been so common in the fifth century as in the third for a Christian teacher to hold that images had no place in his religion. Even in this period, however, the cult of relics is more widely attested than any devotion to the images which accompanied or went proxy for the more tangible remains.[19] There is certainly nothing to show that either Augustine or Dionysius would have countenanced the veneration of images; both insist that the faithful soul seeks only the knowledge and love of God himself, and that the true image of the God is the incarnate Christ, of whom nothing now remains to be touched and handled but the scriptural record of his ministry. As Augustine intimates, however, it is possible for his likeness to be fashioned anew in every discerning reader of the scriptures, as every reader carries within him the sullied image of his Creator. The voluntary descent to our condition of the God against whom we have sinned rekindles in the elect the love which affords their only means of knowing him – a love that is not like any earthly love, but an impassioned renunciation of all in heaven and earth that stands between them and God.[20] The true reading of scripture is always one that disposes us to charity, and thus reveals the character of the living Word who, as the written word testifies, has been at

---

[19]   On the origins of the cult of martyrs, see Barnes (2010), 21–31; for Augustine's sentiments, see Straw (1999).

[20]   Burnaby (1938); O'Donovan (1980).

work for our salvation, together with the other two persons of the Triune Godhead, from the beginning of the world.

Dionysius, while he agrees that God is love, and not to be known but through a love that extinguishes every carnal or earthly desire, addresses himself primarily to the cognitive faculties of the untutored reader. Augustine had maintained that we understand words because we have learned to associate them with the imaginative phantom of the form that is apprehended by the intellect; Dionysius performs a similar operation on the pictorial vocabulary of the scriptures, leading the reader in the steps of Moses to a summit beyond the highest reach of the imagination, where the lustre of every visual conceit is eclipsed by the incandescent darkness of the God who is knowable only through the denudation of knowledge. Moses as a paradigmatic figure may be likened to the Socrates of Plato, who is at once the author's mouthpiece and a model to be imitated by the inquiring reader. For Dionysius, as for Augustine, Christ is more than a model: as a person of the ineffable Godhead, he is himself the object of inquiry, and the purpose of the text that contains his own witness to himself is to bring inquiry to an end. Not that it is designed to forestall reflection; on the contrary, the very opacity of the text inspires, desiderates and at last assists reflection on the unspeakable truths that would otherwise escape all understanding. Because, however, both Dionysius and Augustine hold that God is discovered only through his self-disclosure, both assume that the understanding of him will always be a hermeneutic enterprise. Augustine may hold that the human mind is an image of the Trinity, and Christian mysticism is no doubt the legitimate offspring of the *Mystical Theology*; neither, however, offers the mind any other ladder to knowledge of the divine but the divine scriptures. Neither appears to go so far as Origen in the identification of the Word himself with the word that speaks of him, but neither falls into that idolatry of the human intellect to which the Greeks succumbed when they imagined that the soul, once disencumbered of the appetites and sensations of the body, will be free to pursue its own vision of the Good.

Conclusion

This book has been a series of studies, discrete and necessarily selective; a summary at this point would add nothing to what has been said in the concluding paragraphs to successive chapters. By way of conclusion I offer a series of theses, which, if true, will show that Christianity owes its peculiar character, in the ancient world at least, to a triangulation of person, word and image which was never mirrored even in that diverse and evolving school of Greek philosophy with which it has most in common.

1. Christians regard the scriptures as an archive of salvific truths that could not have been known otherwise. For Platonists the truth is already present to the soul as a latent memory of the forms perceived in a higher sphere to which it can be restored by the practice of philosophy. The text of Plato or Homer may reanimate the memory, but cannot bring into the world any other truths than those that have already been imparted to the soul.

2. Faith in the inerrancy of scripture implied belief in its veracity wherever it purports to be a record of historical events. The events themselves may presage events of loftier significance or adumbrate great mysteries, but if they had never taken place in fact, we should have no assurance that there is any truth corresponding to the symbol. The text is iconic, therefore, in the sense that it is a representation, in plain though pregnant words, of real occurrences; for Platonists, by contrast, the text is iconic in the sense that it is an imaginative construct – a myth or sometimes merely a plausible account, an *eikos logos* – of realities that cannot be adequately conveyed in words.

3. For Christians, the one historical fact that confers significance on the history recounted in the Old Testament is the incarnation of God the Word in Jesus Christ of Nazareth. Had this not happened as it is narrated – had there been no birth of God, no crucifixion, no resurrection – the human race would still be dead in sin. Origen can maintain that we should seek the one Word everywhere, not only in body but in soul and spirit, beneath the many words of scripture; from the scriptural maxim, 'God is love', Augustine inferred that we find the true sense of the scriptures only where we find the love that was manifest in the incarnation of the Word. It cannot be said that any figure, even that of Socrates, plays the same role in the dialogues of Plato or in the writings of his commentators: Socrates is a pioneer, an apostle of the examined life, a pattern for all disciples, but it can never be said that he, and he alone, is the truth communicated by the text.

4. Christians seek in the Bible not only a record of God's dealings with humanity, but prescriptions for a life that will make them worthy of salvation. As the heir to the fruits of Christ's obedience in the world to come, the body must be at his service in the present one, whether or not it is thought to participate in the image and likeness of God that was revealed in its plenitude by his incarnation. For Platonists, salvation is the deliverance of the soul from its material encumbrances; although the world is an icon of the realm of forms or ideas (*Timaeus* 92c), it is in the soul alone that the 'likeness to God, so far as is possible' (*Theaetetus* 176b), can be attained.

5. If Christ as Logos is the eternal image of the Father, while humanity has been fashioned in Adam according to the same image, it might seem to follow – and would indeed have followed before the Fall – that all human beings have a capacity for the immediate knowledge of God. To the effete posterity of Adam, however, such knowledge is granted only through the incarnation of God's word and image in Jesus of Nazareth, and remains accessible after his ascension only by virtue of his continuing embodiment in the scriptures. The text is therefore the living Word insofar as it is the vesture of the Image; there is no unmediated knowledge of which it is merely an index, whereas the function of Plato's text can never be more than indexical, even to the most scholastic of his commentators.

6. Plato and his followers use the term 'mysteries' to refer sometimes (as in Iamblichus) to the practice of certain esoteric rituals or (more frequently) to the ineffable stupefaction that the soul can hope to enjoy when she is freed from the importunity of the senses. The experience transcends the text, and only by a metaphor can the deepest meaning of the text itself, or the elucidation of this, be styled a mystery. Christians spoke of the sacraments as mysteries, but made no provision for any private experience of the mystical outside the practice of scriptural commentary. We hear of ecstatic and erotic transports which cannot be reduced to a sense of hermeneutic illumination, but all such episodes are parentheses to the exegesis of canonical texts, and we have no right to surmise that one could enjoy such states without equally prolonged and reverent study.

7. The end of the Platonist's quest is an encounter with the Good that Plato likens to a vision of the sun. Ocular manifestations to the prophets and apostles are proper subjects for Christian commentary, but when the theologian describes his own sense of communion with divinity, it is not so likely to take the form of light as of hearing or the eclipse of vision.

8. Holding as they did that the world is a creature and not a copy of God, whose image resides in Christ and in the saints whom he is bringing to perfection, Christians wrote with the animus of Hebrew prophets against the lifeless images to which pagans addressed their prayers and sacrifices. Even theologians of the fourth century have little to say of the Christian sculpture and painting that was beginning to surround them as they preached that the Word alone was the true instructor of the Church.

Plato yielded to none of them in his contempt for the visual artefact, but he is equally contemptuous of the written word and of oral declamation; his successors devised apologies for all three, and none subscribed to the Christian assumption that the picture is by nature more mendacious than the word.

9. While Christians were at one with the Jews in their reverence for the word and their aversion to plastic images, their doctrine that the true Word is the incarnate Logos seems to have precluded any veneration of the book itself. The scroll was supplanted easily by the codex, and no eminent Christian teacher of antiquity joins the rabbis in imagining creation as a form of divine calligraphy or in attributing magical properties to the characters of any alphabet. To them, as to Paul, the worship of the mere letter of the law was no less idolatrous than the pagan cult of the elements (Galatians 4.9). The script and the papyrus were the mere garments of the word, and to make them objects of devotion was to share the error of those who knew Christ only after the flesh (2 Corinthians 5.16).

None of these propositions entails that there can be no such thing as a Christian icon. If it is lawful, or rather mandatory, for those who confess the Trinity to worship the embodied Christ as God, it would seem to be equally logical to argue either that all representations of his physical form should be prohibited or that, if they are permitted, they should receive the worship due to the original.[1] The third position, that images may be made but must not be worshipped, is perhaps the one that sits least easily with the Decalogue. Nevertheless, this third position has been held in almost every church where the second is denied: pictures of Christ and his saints outside the Orthodox communion are accepted both pedagogic artefacts and as tokens of devotion, but are not deemed to possess the holiness that is almost universally accorded to the scriptures.

I am aware that little reference has been made in the present volume to the material culture of late antiquity. The opportunity seldom arose, as equally little reference is made to actual works of art in Christian or philosophical reflection on the use of images. The Zeus of Phidias is no longer extant, and in any case the sophists who praised it in the second century were not so much describing what they had seen as striving to outdo what they had read. A stronger case might be made for the inclusion of a chapter on Christian liturgy, since there is no doubt that this fusion of the visual, the dynamic and the oral has furnished many of the laity with a more legible and comprehensive inventory of signs than words alone or pictures alone could have afforded. It would, however, have been all but impossible to make comparative use of such material, since our evidence for the content of pagan mysteries is a chequer-board of philosophic reverie and Christian objurgation.[2] Furthermore, no record of an early Christian liturgy has come down

---

[1] See Cameron (1992).

[2] See now Burkert (1989); Bowden (2011).

to us without adulteration, and the rationale of such elements as survive must be sought in the writings of Hippolytus, Hilary, Cyril of Jerusalem, Ambrose and other theologians, most of whom also hold an eminent place in the history of dogma. With such guides we shall never find more in liturgy than a dramatic counterpart to the rhetorical promulgation of the word.

My project was conceived before the delivery of a seminal paper by Frances Young as the keynote to the National Conference in Patristic Studies, held at Cambridge in 2009.[3] It was largely complete before the publication of the paper, and it is therefore all the more gratifying to find that my eighth chapter agrees in many points with Professor Young's conclusions. It seems to me barely possible to quarrel with her proposal that the Arian and Origenist controversies should be regarded as serial phases in the ripening of the Christian theology of the image; nor am I aware of any evidence to contradict her thesis that Athanasius was the first to perceive the mutual interdependence of the rejection of idolatry, the adoration of Christ as the image of God and the doctrine that humanity is created in this image. I have, however, undertaken a longer and more capacious narrative in the hope of showing that this theology cannot be divorced from the primacy of scripture. It was in the text that the Word who had been made visible to a few became apprehensible to all, or at least to all who could glean the true sense from its grammar. Such hearers and readers, not presuming to seek out the invisible light of God (1 Timothy 6.16), but allowing the Word to quicken within them the light of the first creation (2 Corinthians 4.6), were destined to become live mirrors to the God who made them (2 Corinthians 3.18), strangers alike to the scribe's cult of the sign and the philosopher's deification of the soul.

---

[3]   Young (2011).

Bibliography

Primary Sources

Albinus, *Isagoge*, and Alcinous. *Isagoge* or *Didascalicus*, ed. C.F. Hermann, in *Platonis Opera*, vol. 6 (Leipzig, 1880), 147–189. Text (as *Epitome*) with French translation: J. Whittaker (Paris, 1990). Translation: J.M. Dillon (Oxford: Clarendon Press, 1993).

Aristotle, *Categoriae et Liber de Interpretatione*, ed. L. Minio-Paluello (Oxford: Clarendon Press).

Aristotle, *Ethics* (*Ethica Nicomachea*), ed. I. Bywater (Oxford: Clarendon Press, 1920).

Aristotle, *Metaphysics*, ed. W.D. Ross (Oxford: Clarendon Press, 1927).

Aristotle, *On the Soul* (*De Anima*), ed. W.D. Ross (Oxford: Clarendon Press, 1956).

Aristotle, *Poetics* (*De Arte Poetica*), ed. R. Kassel (Oxford: Clarendon Press, 1920).

Aristotle, *Rhetoric* (*Ars Rhetorica*), ed. W.D. Ross (Oxford: Clarendon Press, 1959).

Athanasius, *Contra Gentes and De Incarnatione*, ed. and trans R.W. Thomson (Oxford: Clarendon Press, 1971).

Athanasius, *Orationes contra Arianos* I–III, 2 vols, ed. K. Metzler, D. Hansen and K. Savvidis (Berlin: De Gruyter, 1998, 2000).

Athanasius, *Werke*, vol. 2, ed. H.-G. Opitz (Berlin: Preussischen Akademie der Wissenschaften, 1935–40). Contains *On the Decrees of Nicaea* and other historical writings.

Athenagoras, *Legatio*, ed. W.R. Schoedel (Oxford: Clarendon Press, 1972).

Augustine, *Confessions*, ed. J.J. O'Donnell, 3 vols (Oxford: Clarendon Press, 1992).

Augustine, *On Christian Doctrine* (*De Doctrina Christiana*), ed. I. Martin (Turnhout: Brepols, 1962).

Augustine, *On Diverse Questions* (*De Diversis Quaestionibus octoginta tribus*), ed. A. Mutzenberger (Turnhout: Brepols, 1975).

Augustine, *On Genesis according to the Letter* (*De Genesi ad Litteram*), ed. J. Zycha (Leipzig and Vienna: Hinrichs, 1984).

Augustine, *On the City of God* (*De Civitate Dei*), ed. B. Dombert and A. Kalb, 2 vols (Turnhout: Brepols, 1955).

Augustine, *On the Measure of Soul* (*De Quantitate Animae*), ed. W. Hormann (Leipzig/Vienna: Hinrichs, 1986).

Augustine, *On the Teacher* (*De Magistro*), ed. K.-D. Daur with other works (Turnhout: Brepols, 1970), 157–203.

Augustine, *On the Trinity* (*De Trinitate*), ed. W.J. Mountain and F. Glorie, 2 vols (Turnhout: Brepols, 1968–2001).

Chaldaean Oracles, ed., with translation and commentary, R. Majercik (Leiden: Brill, 1989).

Cicero, *On the Nature of the Gods* (*De Natura Deorum*, ed. and trans. H.A. Rackham (Cambridge, MA: Loeb Classical Library).

Clement of Alexandria, *Excerpta ex Theodoto* (*Excerpts from Theodotus*), ed. and trans. R.P. Casey (Cambridge: Cambridge University Press, 1934).

Clement of Alexandria, *Protrepticus*, ed. M. Marcovich (Leiden: Brill, 1995).

Clement of Alexandria, *Stromata* (*Werke*, vols 2 and 3), ed. O. Stählin, 3rd edn (Berlin: De Gruyter, 1960 and 1970).

Cornutus, *Compendio di teologia graeca*, ed. I. Ramelli (Milan: Bompiani, 2003).

Dio Chrysostom, ed. and trans. J.W. Cohoon and H.L. Crosby, 5 vols (Cambridge, Mass.: Loeb Classical Library, 1932–1951).

Diogenes Laertius, *Lives of Eminent Philosophers*, ed. and trans. R. Hicks (Cambridge, MA: Loeb Classical Library, 1925).

Dionysius Areopagita, *Corpus Dionysiacum*, ed. U. Heil and A.M. Ritter, 2 vols (Berlin: De Gruyter, 1991).

Epiphanius of Salamis, ed. K. Holl and J. Dummer, 3 vols (Berlin: De Gruyter, 1916–1985).

Eusebius of Caesarea, *Contra Marcellum* (*Against Marcellus*) and *De Ecclesiastica Theologia* (*Ecclesiastical Theology*), ed. E. Klostermann (Berlin: De Gruyter, 1972).

Eusebius of Caesarea, *Church History* (*Kirchengeschichte*), ed. T. Mommsen, E. Schwartz and F. Winkelmann (Berlin: Akademie der Wissenschaft, 1999).

Eusebius of Caesarea, *Preparation for the Gospel* (*Praeparatio Evangelica*), ed. and trans. E.H. Gifford, 5 vols (Oxford: Clarendon Press, 1903).

Gregory of Nyssa, *Opera*, ed. W. Jaeger and others (Leiden: Brill, 1921–).

Heraclitus. *Allégories d'Homère*, ed. F. Buffière (Paris: Belles Lettres, 1962). Text and translation: D.A. Russell (Atlanta: Society of Biblical Studies, 2005).

Hermetica, ed. A.D. Nock and A.-J. Festugière, 4 vols (Paris: Belles Lettres, 1946–1954).

Hesiod, *Theogony, Works and Days, Testimonia*, ed. and trans. G.W. Most (Cambridge, MA: Loeb Classical Library, 2006).

Hilary of Poitiers, *Opera*, ed. P. Smulders, 2 vols (Turnhout: Brepols, 1979–1980).

Hippolytus. *Refutatio Omnium Haeresium* (*Refutation*), ed. M. Marcovich (Berlin: De Gruyter, 1986).

Homer, *Iliad*, ed. and trans. A.T. Murray and W.F. Wyatt, 2 vols (Cambridge, MA: Loeb Classical Library, 1999).

Homer, *Odyssey*, ed. and trans. A.T. Murray and G.E. Dimock, 2 vols (Cambridge, MA: Loeb Classical Library, 1995).

Horace, *Opera*, ed. F.W. Garrod (Oxford: Clarendon Press, 1963).

Iamblichus. *De Mysteriis* (*On the Mysteries*), ed. (as *Les Mystères d'Égypte*), E. Des Places, (Paris: Belles Lettres, 1966). Translation: E.C. Clark, J.M. Dillon and J.P. Hershbell (Leiden: Brill, 2003).

Ignatius of Antioch, ed. and trans. (as *The Apostolic Fathers 2: Ignatius and Polycarp*), J.B. Lightfoot, 3 vols (London: Macmillan, 1885).

Irenaeus. *Adversus Haereses* (*Against Heresies*), ed. with French trans. (*Contre les Hérésies*) A. Roussell and L. Doutreleau, 10 vols (Paris: Cerf, 1965–1982).

Isocrates, trans. G. Norlin and L. Van Hook, 3 vols (Cambridge, MA: Loeb Classical Library, 1928–1961).

Josephus, trans. H. StJ. Thackeray and others, 9 vols (Cambridge, MA: Loeb Classical Library, 1927–1963).

Justin Martyr, *Apologies*, ed. and trans. D. Minns and P. Parvis (Oxford: Clarendon Press, 2009).

Justin Martyr, *Dialogus cum Tryphone*, ed. M. Marcovich (Berlin: De Gruyter, 2005). Translation T.B. Falls (Washington DC: Catholic University of America Press, 2003).

Lucian, *Lucian*, ed. and trans. A.M. Harmon, 8 vols (Cambridge, MA: Loeb Classical Library, 1919–25).

Maximus of Tyre, *Philosophoumena*, ed. H. Hobein (Leipzig: Teubner, 1910).

Minucius Felix, *Octavius*, ed. with French trans. J. Beaujeu (Paris: Belles Lettres, 1964).

Nag Hammadi, *Codices* (including *Gospel of Thomas, Zostrianus, Allogenes, Apocryphon of John*), ed. and trans. J.M. Robinson (San Francisco: Harper Collins, 1990).

Novum Testamentum Graece, ed. W. Nestle and K. Aland (Stuttgart: Deustche Bibelgesellschaft, 2012).

Numenius. *Fragments*, ed. E. Des Places (Paris: Belles Lettres, 1973).

Origen, *Commentary on Genesis*, ed. (as *Die Kommentierung des Buches Genesis*) K. Metzler (Berlin: De Gruyter, 2010).

Origen, *Commentary on John*, ed. (as *Johanneskommentar*) E. Preuschen, (Leipzig: Hinrichs, 1903).

Origen, *Contra Celsum* (*Against Celsus*), ed. (as *Gegen Celsus* with other works) P. Koetschau, 2 vols (Leipzig: Hinrichs, 1899).

Origen, *Homilies on Genesis and Exodus*, ed. W. Baehrens (Berlin: De Gruyter, 1920).

Origen, *Homilies on Isaiah*, see Baehrens (1925) below.

Origen *Homilies/Commentary on Song of Songs,* ed. (as *Homilien/Kommentar zum Hohenlied* with other works) W. Baehrens (Leipzig: Hinrichs, 1925).

Origen, *On First Principles*, ed. P. Koetschau (Leipzig: Hinrichs, 1913). Also published as *Traité des Principes*, ed. H. Crouzel, 4 vols (Paris: Cerf, 1976–1980).

Origen, *On Prayer*, appears as *Die Schrift über Gebet* in Koetschau, *Gegen Celsus*, vol. 2 (below).

Origen, *Philokalia*, ed. J.A. Robinson (Cambridge: Cambridge University Press, 1893).

Panegyrici Latini, ed. R. Mynors (Oxford: Clarendon Press, 2006).

Philo, *Works*, ed. and trans. F.H. Coulson and G.H. Whitaker, 12 vols (Cambridge, MA: Loeb Classical Library, 1896–1930).

Philostratus, *Life of Apollonius of Tyana*, ed. and trans. C.P. Jones, 2 vols with appendix in vol. 3 (Cambridge, MA: Loeb Classical Library, 2005–2006).

Photius, *Bibliothèque*, ed. R. Henry (Paris: Belles Lettres, 1960).

Plato, *Opera*, ed. J. Burnet and others (Oxford: Clarendon Press, 1963).

Plotinus, *Enneads*, ed. E. Bréhier, 7 vols (Paris: Belles Lettres, 1924–1928); ed. P. Henry and H.-R. Schwyzer, 3 vols (Oxford: Clarendon Press, 1964); ed. and trans. A.H. Armstrong, 7 vols (Cambridge, MA: Loeb Classical Library, 1966–1988).

Plutarch, *Moralia*, ed. and trans. various hands, 15 vols (New York: Loeb).

Porphyry, *Fragmenta*, ed. A. Smith (Leipzig: Teubner, 1993). Includes *De Statuis* (*On Statues*), *De Philosophia ex Oraculis Haurienda* (*Philosophy from Oracles*), *De Styge* (*On the Styx*), *Quaestiones Homericae* (*Homeric Questions*).

Porphyry, *Lettera a Anebo*, ed. A.R. Sodano (Naples: L'Arte Tipografica, 1958).

Porphyry, *Opuscula Selecta*, ed. A. Nauck (Leipzig: Teubner, 1886). Includes *Vita Pythagorae* (*Life of Pythagoras*), *De Abstinentia* (*On Abstinence*), *De Antro Nympharum* (*Cave of the Nymphs*), *Ad Marcellam* (*Letter to Marcella*).

Porphyry, *On the Life of Plotinus and the Arrangement of his Works*, appears as introduction to all editions of Plotinus. Also edited separately by P. Kalligas (Athens: Akademia Athenôn, 1991); and as *Vie de Plotin* by L. Brisson (Paris: Belles Lettres, 1972) with a volume of Études Préliminaires (1982).

Proclus, *Commentary on First Alcibiades*, ed. with French trans. A.-B. Segonds, 2 vols (Paris: Belles Lettres, 1986).

Proclus, *Commentary on Republic* (*In Platonis Rem Publicam Commentarii*), ed. W. Kroll, 2 vols (Leipzig: Teubner, 1899–1901)

Proclus, *Commentary on Timaeus* (*In Platonis Timaeum Commentaria*), ed. E. Diehl, 3 vols (Leipzig: Teubner, 1903).

Proclus, *Elements of Theology*, ed. and trans. E.R. Dodds (Oxford: Clarendon Press, 1963).

Proclus, *In Platonis Cratylum Commentarium*, ed. G. Pasquali (Leipzig: Teubner, 1908).

Proclus, *Lezioni sul Cratilo di Platone*, ed. F. Romano (Catania: University of Catania Press, 1989).

Proclus, *Platonic Theology* (*Théologie Platonicienne*), ed. H.-D. Saffrey and L.G. Westerink, 6 vols (Paris: Belles Lettres, 1968–2003).

Prolegomena to Plato, ed. G.L. Westerink, French trans. J. Trouillard (Paris: Belles Lettres, 1990).

Septuaginta, ed. A. Rahlfs and R. Hanhart (Stuttgart: Deustche bibelgesellschaft, 2012).

Sextus Empiricus, ed. and trans. R.G. Bury, 4 vols (Cambridge, MA: Loeb Classical Library).

Socrates Scholasticus, *Church History* (*Kirchengeschichte*), ed. G.C. Hansen (Berlin: Akademie der Wissenschaft, 1995).

Tatian, *Oratio ad Graecos*, ed. and trans. M. Whittaker (Oxford: Clarendon Press, 1982).

Tertullian, *Opera*, ed. A Gerlo, 2 vols (Turnhout: Brepols, 1954).

Theodoret, *Church History* (*Kirchengeschichte*), ed. L. Parmentier and G.C. Hansen (Berlin: Akademie der Wissenschaft, 1998).

Theophilus of Antioch, *Ad Autolycum*, ed. and trans. R.M. Grant (Oxford: Clarendon Press, 1970).

Virgil, *Opera*, ed. R.A.B. Mynors (Oxford: Clarendon Press, 1969).

Scholarly Literature

Adam, J., ed. (1938), *The Republic of Plato* (Cambridge: Cambridge University Press).

Anatolios, K. (1998), *Athanasius. The Coherence of his Thought* (New York: Routledge).

Armstrong, A.H. (1960), 'The Background of the Doctrine that the Intelligibles are not Outside the Intellect', in *Entretiens Hardt V: Les Sources de Plotin* (Geneva: Fondation Hardt), 393–425.

Ashton, J. (1994), *Reading John* (Oxford: Clarendon Press).

Ashwin-Siejkowski, P. (2008), *Clement of Alexandria. A Project of Christian Perfection* (London: Continuum).

Asmis, E. (1991), 'Philodemus' Poetic Theory and *On the Good King according to Homer*', *Classical Antiquity* 10, 1–45.

Asmis, E. (1992), 'Plato on Poetic Creativity', in R. Kraut (ed.), *The Cambridge Companion to Plato* (Cambridge: Cambridge University Press), 335–364.

Austin, J.L. (1979), 'The Line and the Cave in Plato's *Republic*', in his *Philosophical Papers* (Oxford: Clarendon Press), 288–304.

Baert, B. (2004), *A History of Holy Wood. The Legend of the True Cross in Word and Image* (Leiden: Brill).

Bagnall, R. (2009), *Early Christian Books in Egypt* (Princeton, NJ: Princeton University Press).

Ball, D.M. (1996), *The 'I Am' Sayings in John* (Sheffield: Sheffield University Press).

Balthasar, H.U. von (1982), *The Glory of the Lord*, vol. 1 (Edinburgh: T. and T. Clark).

Bandt, C. (2007), *Der Traktat 'Vom Mysterium der Buchstaben'* (New York and Berlin: De Gruyter).

Barnes, T.D. (2010), *Early Christian Hagiography and Roman History* (Tübingen: Mohr Siebeck).

Barr, J. (1993), *Biblical Faith and Natural Theology* (Oxford: Clarendon Press).

Barth, K. (1975), *Church Dogmatics*, 1.1: *The Doctrine of the Word of God*, trans. G. Bromiley and T.F. Torrance (Edinburgh: T. and T. Clark).

Baur, F.C. (1932), *Apollonius von Tyana und Christus* (Tübingen: Fues).

Beall, S. (1993), 'Word-painting in the *Imagines* of the Elder Philostratus', *Hermes* 121, 350–363.

Beck, R. (2006), *The Religion of the Mithras Cult in the Roman Empire* (Oxford: Oxford University Press).

Behr, J. (2004), *The Nicene Faith*, part 1 (New York: St Vladimir's Seminary).

Bendinelli, G. (1997), *Il commentario a Matteo di Origene* (Rome: Pontifical Institute).

Bennett, C. (1988), 'The Conversion of Vergil: The *Aeneid* in Augustine's Confessions', *Revue des Etudes Augustiniennes* 34, 47–69.

Bidez, J. (1913), *Vie de Porphyre* (Ghent).

Bieler, L. (1935–1936), *Theios Aner. Das Bild des göttlichen Menschen in Spätantike und Frühchristentum*, 2 vols (Vienna: Hofels).

Bockmuehl, M. (1997), 'The "Form of God" (Philippians 2.6): Variations on a Theme of Jewish Mysticism', *Journal of Theological Studies* 48, 1–23.

Bowden, H. (2011), *Mystery Cults of the Ancient World* (Princeton, NJ: Princeton University Press).

Bowie, E.L. (1978), 'Apollonius of Tyana: Tradition and Reality', in W. Haase (ed.), *Aufstieg und Niedergang der römischen Welt* 2.16.2, 1652–1699.

Boyarin, D. (2001), 'The Gospel of the Memra: Jewish Binitarianism and the Prologue to John', *Harvard Theological Review* 94, 244–284.

Brakke, D. (2011), *The Gnostics* (Cambridge, MA: Harvard University Press).

Brown, P. (2007), 'The Comic Socrates', in M.B. Trapp (ed.), *Socrates from Antiquity to the Enlightenment* (Aldershot: Ashgate), 1–16.

Bultmann, R. (1965), *Theology of the New Testament*, vol. 2 (London: SCM).

Burkert, W. (1989), *Ancient Mystery Cults* (Cambridge, MA: Harvard University Press).

Burnaby, J. (1938), *Amor Dei: A Study of the Religion of St Augustine* (London: Hodder and Stoughton).

Bussanich, J. (1996), 'Plotinus' Metaphysics of the One', in L. Gerson (ed.), *The Cambridge Companion to Plotinus* (Cambridge: Cambridge University Press), 38–65.

Calame, C. (1995), *The Craft of Poetic Speech in Ancient Greece*, trans. J. Orion (Ithaca, NY: Cornell University Press).

Cameron, Averil (1992), 'The Language of Images: The Rise of Icons and Christian Representation', in D. Wood (ed.), *The Church and the Arts* (Oxford: Blackwell), 1–42.

Cameron, Averil and S. Hall (eds and trans.) (1999), *Eusebius: Life of Constantine* (Oxford: Clarendon Press).

Charalabopoulos, N. (2001), 'The Metatheatrical Reader of Plato's *Protagoras*', in F. Budelmann and P. Michelakis (eds), *Homer, Tragedy and Beyond* (London: Institute of Classical Studies), 149–178.

Charles-Murray, M. (1977), 'Art and the Early Church', *Journal of Theological Studies* 28, 303–345.

Charlesworth, J. (1983), *Old Testament Pseudepigrapha*, vol. 1 (Peabody, MA: Hendrickson).

Charrue, J.-M. (1978), *Plotin, lecteur de Platon* (Paris: Université de Paris X, Nanterre).

Cherniss, H. (1962), *Aristotle's Criticism of Plato and the Academy* (New York: Russell and Russell).

Clark, E. (1992), *The Origenist Controversy: the Cultural Construction of an Early Christian Debate* (Princeton, NJ: Princeton University Press).

Clark, G. (2007), 'Augustine's Porphyry', in G. Karamanolis and A. Sheppard (eds), *Studies on Porphyry* (London: British Institute of Classical Studies), 127–140.

Classen, C.J. (2002), *Rhetorical Criticism of the New Testament* (Leiden: Brill).

Clay, D. (1983), *Lucretius and Epicurus* (Ithaca, NY: Cornell University Press).

Cornford, F. (1997), *Plato's Cosmology: The Timaeus of Plato* (Indianapolis: Hackett).

Corrigan, K. (2009), *Evagrius and Gregory* (Aldershot: Ashgate).

Crombie, I. (1963), *An Examination of Plato's Doctrines*, vol. 2 (London: Routledge and Kegan Paul).

Cross, R.C and A.D. Woozley (1964), *Plato's Republic. A Philosophical Commentary* (Oxford: Clarendon Press).

Daniélou, J. (1977), *The Origins of Latin Christianity*, trans. J.A. Baker (London: Dartman, Longman and Todd).

Darcus, S. M. (1977), '*Daimôn* Parallels the Holy *phrên* in Empedocles', *Phronesis* 22, 175–190.

Davies, M. and J. Kithintamby (1986), *Greek Insects* (London: Duckworth).

Davies, W.D. (1955), *Paul and Rabbinic Judaism* (London: SPCK).

Dawson, D. (1992), *Allegorical Readers and Cultural Revision in Ancient Alexandria* (Berkeley: University of California Press).

Dawson, D. (1997), 'Allegorical Reading and the Embodiment of the Soul in Origen', in L. Ayres and G. Jones (eds), *Christian Origins* (London: Routledge), 26–46.

De Angelis, F. and B. Garstad (2006), 'Euhemerus in Context', *Classical Antiquity* 25, 211–242.

Dechow, J.F. (1988), *Dogma and Mysticism in Early Christianity. Epiphanius of Salamis and the Legacy of Origen* (Leuven: Peeters).

Deck. A.N. (1967), *Nature, Contemplation and the One* (Toronto: University of Toronto Press).

De Clerq, V.C. (1954), *Ossius of Cordova* (Washington, DC: Catholic University Press of America).

De Lange, N. (1976), *Origen and the Jews: Studies in Jewish–Christian Relations in Third-Century Palestine* (Cambridge: Cambridge University Press).

De Lubac, H. (1959), *Exégèse Médiévale. Les quatre sens de l'Écriture*, part 1, vol. 1 (Paris: Aubier).

Derrett, J.M.D. (1989), 'Ὁ ΚΥΡΙΟΣ ἘΒΑΣΙΛΕΥΣΕΝ ἌΠΟ ΤΟΥ ΞΥΛΟΥ', *Vigiliae Christianae* 43, 378–392.

Derrida, J. (1981), 'Plato's Pharmacy', in *Dissemination*, trans. B. Johnson (Chicago: University of Chicago Press), 61–171.

Detienne, M. (1979), *Dionysus Slain*, trans. L. and M. Mueller (Baltimore, MD: Johns Hopkins University Press).

Deuse, W. (2010), 'Plutarch's Eschatological Myths', trans. H.G. Nesselrath and D.A. Russell, in H.G. Nesselrath (ed.), *Plutarch: On the Daimonion of Socrates* (Tübingen: Mohr Siebeck), 169–197.

Diels, H. (1951), *Die Fragmente der Vorsokratiker*, rev. W. Krantz (Berlin: Weidmann).

Dillon, J.M. (1975a), 'Image, Symbol and Analogy: Three Basic Concepts of Neoplatonic Exegesis', in R. Baine Harris (ed.), *The Significance of Neoplatonism* (Norfolk, VA.: International Society for Neoplatonic Studies), 209–262.

Dillon, J.M. (1975b), 'The Transcendence of God in Philo: Some Possible Sources', in Dillon, *The Golden Chain* (Aldershot: Ashgate, 1990), no. IX.

Dillon, J.M. (1977), *The Middle Platonists* (London: Duckworth).

Dillon, J.M. (1986a), 'Plutarch and Second-Century Platonism', in A.H. Armstrong (ed.), *Classical Mediterranean Spirituality* (New York: Crossroad Publications), 214–229.

Dillon, J.M. (1986b), 'Aisthêtê Noêtê: A Doctrine of Spiritual Senses in Origen and Plotinus', in Dillon, *The Golden Chain* (Aldershot: Ashgate, 1990), no. XIX, 443–455.

Dillon, J.M. (1989), 'Tampering with the *Timaeus*: Ideological Emendations in Plato', *American Journal of Philology* 110, 50–72.

Dillon, J.M. (1990), 'Recycling the Heritage of Moses: Philo's Confrontation with Greek Philosophy', *Studia Philonica* 7, 108–123.

Dillon, J.M. (1996), 'The Formal Structure of Philo's Allegorical Exegesis', in Dillon, *The Great Tradition* (Aldershot: Ashgate, 1997), no. V, 123–131.

Dodd, C.H. (1960), *The Authority of the Bible* (London: Collins).

Dodd, C.H. (1968), *The Interpretation of the Fourth Gospel* (Cambridge: Cambridge University Press).

Dodds, E.R. (1934), 'Notes on the ΠΕΡΙ ΨΥΧΗΣ ΑΠΟΡΙΑΙ of Plotinus', *Classical Quarterly* 28, 47–53.

Drake, H.A. (1985), 'Eusebius on the True Cross', *Journal of Ecclesiastical History* 36, 1–22.

Droge, A.J. (1989), *Homer or Moses*? (Tübingen: Mohr Siebeck).

Dunn, J.G. (1989), *Christology in the Making* (London: SCM).

Edwards, M.J. (1988), 'Scenes from the Later Wanderings of Odysseus', *Classical Quarterly* 38, 508–521.

Edwards, M.J. (1990), 'Neglected Texts in the Study of Gnosticism', *Journal of Theological Studies* 41, 26–50.

Edwards, M.J. (1991a), 'Xenophanes Christianus?', *Greek, Roman and Byzantine Studies* 32, 119–128.

Edwards, M.J. (1991b), 'Being and Seeming: Empedocles' Reply', *Hermes* 119, 282–293.

Edwards, M.J. (1992), 'Protagorean and Socratic Myth', *Symbolae Osloenses* 67, 89–102.

Edwards, M.J. (1995), 'Justin's Logos and the Word of God', *Journal of Early Christian Studies* 3, 261–280.

Edwards, M.J. (1997), 'Precursors of Origen's Hermeneutic Theory', *Studia Patristica* 29, 232–237.

Edwards, M.J. (2000), 'Clement of Alexandria and his Doctrine of the Logos', *Vigiliae Christianae* 54, 159–177.

Edwards, M.J. (2003), 'Origen on Christ, Tropology and Exegesis', in G. Boys-Stones (ed.), *Metaphor, Allegory and the Classical Tradition* (Oxford: Oxford University Press), 235–256.

Edwards, M.J. (2006), 'Gospel and Genre: Some Reservations', in B. McGing and J. Mossman (eds), *The Limits of Ancient Biography* (Swansea: University of Wales), 150–162.

Edwards, M.J. (2009a), 'The Figure of Love in Augustine and in Proclus the Neoplatonist', *Downside Review* 127(448), 197–214.

Edwards, M.J. (2009b), *Catholicity and Heresy in the Early Church* (Aldershot: Ashgate).

Eichrodt, W. (1967), *Theology of the Old Testament*, vol. 2, trans. J.A. Baker (London: SCM).

Elsner, J. (1997), *Art and the Roman Viewer. The Transformation of Art from Paganism to Christianity* (Cambridge: Cambridge University Press).

Elsner, J. (2006), 'Perspectives in Art', in N. Lenski (ed.), *The Cambridge Companion to the Age of Constantine* (Cambridge: Cambridge University Press), 255–277.

Feldman, A. (1927), *The Parables and Similes of the Rabbis* (Cambridge: Cambridge University Press).

Finan, T.F. (1992), 'Modes of Vision in St Augustine: *De Genesi ad Litteram* xii', in T.F. Finan and V. Twomey (eds), *The Relation between Neoplatonism and Christianity* (Dublin: Four Courts), 141–154.

Fine, G. (1984), 'Separation', *Oxford Studies in Ancient Philosophy* 2, 31–87.

Fine, G. (1986), 'Immanence', *Oxford Studies in Ancient Philosophy*, supplementary volume, 71–97.

Fine, G. (1995), *On Ideas. Plato's Criticism of Aristotle's Theory of Forms* (Oxford: Clarendon Press).

Fitzmeyer, J. (1987), 'The Resurrection of Jesus Christ according to the New Testament', *The Month* 258, 402–425.

Flacelière, R. (1965), *Greek Oracles* (London: Elek Books).

Fortna, R.T. (1988), *The Fourth Gospel and its Predecessors* (Philadelphia, PA: Fortress).

Frede, D. (1992), 'The Cognitive Role of *Phantasia* in Aristotle', in M. Nussbaum and A.O. Rorty (eds), *Essays on Aristotle's* De Anima (Oxford: Clarendon Press), 279–295.

Frede, M. (2006), 'The Early Christian Reception of Socrates', in L. Judson and V. Karasmanes (eds), *Remembering Socrates: Philosophical Essays* (Oxford: Oxford University Press), 188–201.

Freedman, H. (1977), *The Classic Midrash*, vol. 1 (New York: Soncino).

Friedländer, P. (1958), *Plato. An Introduction*, trans. H. Meyendorff (New York: Bollingen).

Funghi, M.S. (1997), 'The Derveni Papyrus', in A. Laks and G. Most (eds), *Studies in the Derveni Papyrus* (Oxford: Clarendon Press), 24–39.

Gadamer, H.-G. (1986), *The Idea of the Good in Platonic and Aristotelian Philosophy* (New Haven, CT: Yale University Press).

George, A. (trans.) (1999), *The Epic of Gilgamesh* (Harmondsworth: Penguin).

Ginzberg, L. (1998), *Legends of the Jews*, vol. 1, trans. H. Szold (Baltimore, MD: Johns Hopkins University Press).

Gioia, L. (2008), *The Theological Epistemology of Augustine's De Trinitate* (Oxford: Clarendon Press).

Glasson, T.F. (1974–1975), 'Two Notes on the Philippians Hymn (2.6–11)', *New Testament Studies* 21, 133–139.

Goodenough, E.R. (1988), *Jewish Symbols in the Greco-Roman Period*, abridged by J. Neusner (Princeton, NJ: Bollingen).

Goodman, M.D. (2003), 'The Jewish Image of God in Late Antiquity', in R.L. Kalmin and S. Schwartz (eds), *Jewish Culture and Society under the Roman Empire* (Leuven: Peeters), 133–147.

Gordon, C.H. and G.A. Rendburg (1997), *The Bible and the Ancient Near East* (New York: Norton).

Grabar, A. (1968), *Christian Iconography* (Princeton, NJ: Bollingen).

Graham, D.W. (ed. and trans.) (2010), *The Texts of Early Greek Philosophy*, 2 vols (Cambridge: Cambridge University Press).

Graziosi, B. (2001), 'Competition in Wisdom', in F. Budelmann and P. Michelakis (eds), *Homer, Tragedy and Beyond* (London: Institute of Hellenic Studies), 57–74.

Green, E.B. (2010), *Christianity in Ancient Rome. The First Three Centuries* (Edinburgh: T. and T. Clark).

Griffiths, J. (ed.) (1864), *Certain Sermons and Homilies* (London: SPCK).

Griffiths, J.G. (ed. and trans.) (1970), *Plutarch's* De Iside et Osiride, with commentary (Cardiff: University of Wales Press).

Grigg, R. (1977), 'Constantine the Great and the Cult without Images', *Viator* 8, 1–32.

Hadot, P. (1981), 'Ouranos, Kronos and Zeus', in H.J. Blumenthal and R.A. Markus (eds), *Neoplatonism and Early Christian Thought* (Aldershot: Ashgate), 124–134.

Halperin, D. (1992), 'Plato and Erotics of Narrativity', *Oxford Studies in Ancient Philosophy*, supplementary volume, 89–129.

Halfwassen, J. (1992), *Der Aufstieg zum Einen. Untersuchungen zu Platon und Plotin* (Stuttgart: Teubner).

Hanby, M. (2003), *Augustine and Modernity* (London: Routledge).

Hanson, R.P.C. (1959), *Allegory and Event. A Study of the Sources and Significance of Origen's Interpretation of Scripture* (Richmond, VA.: John Knox).

Harder, R. (1936), 'Eine neue Schrift Plotins', *Hermes* 71, 1–10.

Harvey, S.A. (2006), *Scenting Salvation: Ancient Christianity and the Olfactory Imagination* (Berkeley: University of California Press).

Havelock, E.A. (1963), *Preface to Plato* (Cambridge, MA: Harvard University Press).

Heath, M. (1989), *Unity in Greek Poetics* (Oxford: Clarendon Press).

Helleman-Elgersma, W. (1980), *Soul-Sisters. A Commentary on Enneads IV.3 (27), 1–8 of Plotinus* (Amsterdam: Rodopi).

Hooker, M. (1967), *The Son of Man in Mark* (London: SPCK).

Horner, T. (2001), *Listening to Trypho; Justin Martyr's Dialogue Reconsidered* (Leuven: Peeters).

Hoskyns, E.C. (1947), *The Fourth Gospel* (London: Faber).

Hunt, E.J. (2003), *Christianity in the Second Century: The Case of Tatian* (Hove: Psychology Press).

Hunter, R. and D.A. Russell (2011), *Plutarch: How to Study Poetry* (Cambridge: Cambridge University Press).

Hurtado, L. (2007), '"Jesus" as God's Name and Jesus as God's Embodied Name in Justin Martyr', in P. Foster and P. Parvis (eds), *Justin Martyr and his Worlds* (Minneapolis: Fortress Press), 128–136.

Imbert, C. (1980), 'Stoic Logic and Alexandrian Poetics', in M. Schofield, M. Burnyeat and J. Barnes (eds), *Doubt and Dogmatism* (Oxford: Clarendon Press), 182–217.

Jonkers, E. (1954), *Acta et Symbola Conciliorum quae Saeculo Quarto habita sunt* (Leiden: Brill).

Jónsson, G.A. (1988), *The Image of God: Genesis 1.26–28 in a Century of Old Testament Research* (Lund: Almqvist and Wiksell).

Jourdain, F. (2003), *Le Papyrus de Derveni* (Paris: Belles Lettres).

Jourdain, F. (2010), 'Le logos de Clément soumis à la question', *Revue d'Etudes Augustiniennes* 56, 135–172.

Kahn, C. (1987), *The Art and Thought of Heraclitus* (Cambridge: Cambridge University Press).

Kahn, C. (1997), 'Was Euthyphro the Author of the Derveni Papyrus?', in A. Laks and G. Most (eds), *Studies in the Derveni Papyrus* (Oxford: Clarendon Press), 55–63.

Kaiser, E. (1964), 'Odyssee-Szenen als *Topoi*', *Museum Helveticum* 21, 109–136.

Kamesar, A. (2009), 'Biblical Interpretation in Philo', in A. Kamesar (ed.), *The Cambridge Companion to Philo* (Cambridge: Cambridge University Press), 65–91.

Kannengiesser, C. (1970), 'La date de l'apologie Contre les Païens et Sur l'Incarnation du Verbe', *Revue des Sciences Religieuses* 58, 383–428.

Kee, H.C. (1986), *Medicine, Miracle and Magic in New Testament Times* (Cambridge: Cambridge University Press).

Kermode, F. (1979), *The Genesis of Secrecy. On the Interpretation of Narrative* (Cambridge, MA: Harvard University Press).

Keuls, E. (1978), *Plato and Greek Painting* (Leiden: Brill).

Keyser, E. de (1955), *La significance de l'art dans les* Ennéades de *Plotin* (Louvain: Louvain University Press)

King, C. (2005), *Origen on the Song of Songs as the Spirit of Scripture* (Oxford: Clarendon Press).

Kirk, G.S. (1976), *Homer and the Oral Tradition* (Cambridge: Cambridge University Press).

Klein, M.L. (1980), *The Fragment-Targums of the Pentateuch according to Rabbinic Sources*, vol. 1 (Rome: Pontifical Institute).

Kochan, L. (1997), *Beyond the Graven Image: A Jewish View* (Basingstoke: Macmillan).

Kosman, L.A. (1992), 'Silence and Imitation in the Platonic Dialogues', *Oxford Studies in Ancient Philosophy,* supplementary volume, 73–92.

Kurke, L. (2010), *Aesopic Conversations: Popular Traditions, Cultural Dialogue and the Invention of Greek Prose* (Princeton, NJ: Princeton University Press).

Lamberton, R. (1989), *Homer the Theologian. Neoplatonist Allegorical Reading and the Growth of the Epic Tradition* (Berkeley: University of California Press).

Lane Fox, R. (1986), *Pagans and Christians* (Harmondsworth: Penguin).

Leibowitz, W. (1992), *Judaism, Human Values and the Jewish State* (Cambridge, MA: Harvard University Press).

Lewy, H. (1929), *Sobria Ebrietas. Untersuchungen zur Geschichte der Antiken Mystiken* (Giessen: Töpelmann).

Lloyd, A.C. (1987), 'Plotinus on the Genesis of Thought and Existence', *Oxford Studies in Ancient Philosophy* 5, 475–488.

Löhr, W.A. (1992), 'Gnostic Determinism Reconsidered', *Vigiliae Christianae* 46, 381–390.

Long. A.A. (1996), *Stoic Studies* (Cambridge: Cambridge University Press).

Long, A.A. (1998), 'Plato's Apology for Socrates in the *Theaetetus*', in J. Gentzler (ed.), *Method in Ancient Philosophy* (Oxford: Clarendon Press), 113–136.

Long, A.A. and D. Sedley (1987), *The Hellenistic Philosophers*, vol. 2 (Cambridge: Cambridge University Press).

Louth, A. (1989), *Denys the Areopagite* (London: Geoffrey Chapman).

Louth, A. (2002), *John of Damascus. Tradition and Originality in Byzantine Theology* (Oxford: Clarendon Press).

Louth, A. (2007), *Origins of the Christian Mystical Tradition* (Oxford: Clarendon Press).

Ludlow, M. (2000), *Universal Salvation* (Oxford: Clarendon Press).

McCabe, M.M. (1992), 'Myth, Allegory and Argument in Plato', in A. Barker and M. Warner (eds), *The Language of the Cave*, Apeiron 25(4), 47–69.

Maijer, P.A. (1992), *Plotinus on the Good or the One (Enneads VI.9). An Analytical Commentary* (Amsterdam: Gieben).

Mancini, A. (1976), 'Sulle opere polemiche di Colote', *Croniche Ercolanesi* 6, 61–67.

Markschies, C. (2000), 'New Research on Ptolemaeus Gnosticus', *Zeitschrift für Antikes Christentum* 4, 225–254.

Markus, R.A. (1996), *Signs and Meanings: World and Text in Ancient Christianity* (Liverpool: Liverpool University Press).

Marxsen, W. (1978), *The Resurrection of Jesus of Nazareth*, trans. M. Kohl (London: SCM).

May, G. (2004), *Creatio ex Nihilo*, trans. A.S. Worrall (Edinburgh: T. and T. Clark).

Millbank, J. (1997), *The Word Made Strange* (Oxford: Blackwell).

Minns, D. and P. Parvis (eds and trans.) (2009), *Justin, Philosopher and Martyr: Apologies* (Oxford: Clarendon Press).

Moore, G.F. (1922), 'Intermediaries in Jewish Theology', *Harvard Theological Review* 15, 41–85.

Moore, G.F. (1958), *Judaism in the First Centuries of the Christian Era*, vol. 1 (Cambridge, MA: Harvard University Press).

Moravcsik, J. (1982), 'Noetic Aspiration and Artistic Inspiration', in J. Moravcsik and P. Temko (eds), *Plato on Beauty, Wisdom and the Arts* (Totowa, NJ: Rowman and Littlefield), 28–46.

Mortley, R. (1992), 'The Name of the Father Is the Son: *Gospel of Truth* 28', in R.T. Wallis and J. Bregman (eds), *Neoplatonism and Gnosticism* (Albany: SUNY), 239–252.

Mossman, J. (1991), 'Plutarch's Use of Statues', *Bulletin of the Institute of Classical Studies* supplement 58, 98–119.

Most, G. (1989), 'Cornutus and Stoic Allegoresis: A Preliminary Report', *Aufstieg und Niedergang der römischer Welt* II.36.3, 2014–2065.

Moule, C.F. (1965), *The Gospel According to St Mark* (Cambridge: Cambridge University Press).

Mueller, I. (1992), 'Mathematical Method and Philosophical Truth', in R. Kraut (ed.), *The Cambridge Companion to Plato* (Cambridge: Cambridge University Press), 170–200.

Nadich, J. (1994), *The Legends of the Rabbis*, 2 vols (Northvale, NJ: Aronson).

Nasrallah, L. (2005), 'Mapping the World: Justin, Tatian, Lucian and the Second Sophistic', *Harvard Theological Review* 98, 283–314.

Nasrallah, L. (2010), *Christian Responses to Roman Art and Architecture* (Cambridge: Cambridge University Press).

Nehamas, A. (1975), 'Plato on the Imperfection of the Sensible World', *American Philosophical Quarterly* 12, 105–117.

Neuschäfer, B. (1987), *Origenes als Philologe* (Basel: Reinhardt).

Neusner, J. (1991), *Symbol and Theology in Early Judaism* (Minneapolis: Fortress Press).

Newman, F. (1882), *The Soul, Its Sorrows and Its Aspirations* (London: Trübner).

Nussbaum, M. (1986), *The Fragility of Goodness* (Cambridge: Cambridge University Press).

Nygren, A. (1953), *Eros and Agape*, trans. P.S. Watson (London: SCM).

O'Donovan, O. (1980), *The Problem of Self-Love in Augustine* (New Haven, CT: Yale University Press).

Orbe, A. (1991), 'Origen y los Monarguianos', *Gregorianum* 72, 39–72.

Ouspensky, L. (1992), *Theology of the Icon*, vol. 1 (New York: St Vladimir's Seminary).

Owen, G.E.L. (1965), 'The Platonism of Aristotle', *Proceedings of the British Academy* 50, 125–150.

Owen, G.E.L. (1971), 'Plato on Not-Being', in G. Vlastos (ed.), *Plato I: Metaphysics and Epistemology* (Garden City: Doubleday), 223–267.

Pagels, E. (1973), *The Johannine Gospel in Gnostic Exegesis: Heracleon's Commentary on John* (Nashville: Abingdon Press).

Palmer, J. (2009), *Parmenides and Presocratic Philosophy* (Oxford: Clarendon Press).

Pépin, J. (1970), 'Plotin et le mirror de Dionysus', *Revue Internationale de Philosophie* 92, 304–320.

Pfeiffer, R. (1968), *History of Classical Scholarship. From the Beginnings to the End of the Hellenistic Age* (Oxford: Clarendon Press).

Phillimore, J.S. (trans.) (1912), *In Honour of Apollonius of Tyana* (Oxford: Clarendon Press).

Pickstock, C. (1998), *After Writing: the Liturgical Consummation of Theology* (Oxford: Wiley Blackwell).

Plested, M. (2005), *The Macarian Legacy* (Oxford: Clarendon Press).

Pollard, T.E. (1958–9), 'The Exegesis of Scripture in the Arian Controversy', *Bulletin of the John Rylands Library* 41, 414–429.

Quispel, G. (1980), 'Ezekiel 1:26 in Jewish Mysticism and Gnostis', *Vigiliae Christianae* 34, 1–13.

Radice, R. (2009), 'Philo's Theology and Theory of Creation', in A. Kamesar (ed.), *The Cambridge Companion to Philo* (Cambridge: Cambridge University Press), 124–145.

Rahner, K. (1979), 'The Spiritual Senses according to Origen', *Theological Investigations* 16 (New York: Seabury), 81–103.

Reale, G. (1997), *Toward a New Interpretation of Plato*, trans. J. Catan (Washington, DC: Catholic University Press of America).

Reitzenstein, R. (1904), *Poimandres* (Leipzig: Teubner).

Ricoeur, P. (1977), *The Rule of Metaphor*, trans. R. Czerny et al. (London: Routledge and Kegan Paul).

Riedweg, C. (1987), *Mysterienterminologie bei Platon, Philon und Klemens von Alexandrien* (Berlin: De Gruyter).

Ringgren, H. (1966), *Israelite Religion*, trans. D. Green (London: SPCK).

Rist, J.M. (1964), *Eros and Psyche. Studies in Plato, Plotinus and Origen* (Toronto: University of Toronto Press).

Rist, J.M. (1967), *Plotinus: The Road to Reality* (Cambridge: Cambridge University Press).

Rist, J.M. (1973), 'The One of Plotinus and the God of Aristotle', *Review of Metaphysics* 27, 75–87.

Rist, J.M. (1981), 'The Importance of Stoic Logic in the Contra Celsum', in H. Blumenthal and R.A. Markus (eds), *Neoplatonism and Early Christian Thought* (London: Variorum), 64–78.

Ritter, A.M. (1994), *Pseudo-Dionysius Areopagita, Über die Mystischen Theologie und Briefe* (Stuttgart: Hiersemann).

Robertson, D. (2008), *Word and Meaning in Ancient Alexandria* (Aldershot: Ashgate).

Robin, L. (1964), *La théorie platonicienne de l'amour* (Paris: Presses Universitaires de France).

Robinson, H. (1991), 'Form and the Immateriality of the Intellect from Aristotle to Aquinas', *Oxford Studies in Ancient Philosophy*, supplementary volume, 207–226.

Robinson, J.A.T. (1983), 'The Relation of the Prologue to the Gospel of John', *New Testament Studies* 9, 128–129.

Robinson, J.M. (ed.) (1990), *The Nag Hammadi Library* (San Francisco: Harper).

Robinson, R. (1984), *Plato's Earlier Dialectic* (Oxford: Clarendon Press).

Rorem, P. (1993), *Pseudo-Dionysius: A Commentary on the Texts and an Introduction to Their Influence* (New York: Oxford University Press).

Rosenstock, B. (1997), 'From Counter-Rhetoric to Askêsis: How the Phaedo Rewrites the Gorgias', in B.D. Schildgen (ed.), *The Rhetoric Canon* (Detroit: Wayne State University Pres), 83–106.

Runia, D. (1993), *Philo in Early Christian Literature* (Assen: Van Gorcum).

Runia, D. (1995), 'Philonic Nomenclature', in Runia, *Philo and the Church Fathers* (Leiden: Brill), 25–53.

Runia, D. (1999), 'A Brief History of the Term *kosmos noêtos* from Plato to Plotinus', in J. Cleary (ed.), *Traditions of Platonism: Essays in Honour of John Dillon* (Aldershot: Ashgate), 151–172.

Runia, D. (2010), 'Early Alexandrian Theology and Plato's Parmenides', in J. Turner and K. Corrigan (eds), *Plato's* Parmenides *and Its Heritage*, vol. 2 (Atlanta, GA: Society of Biblical Literature), 175–188.

Saffrey, H.-D. (1971), 'Abamon, pseudonyme de Jamblique', in R.B. Palmer and R. Hamerton-Kelly (eds), *Philomathes. Studies in the Humanities in Memory of Philip Merlan* (The Hague: Martinus Nijhoff), 227–239.

Sanday, W.M. (1911), *Christologies Ancient and Modern* (Oxford: Clarendon Press).

Schäferdiek, K. (1980), 'Zur Verfasserschaft und Situation der Epistola ad Constantiam de imago Christi', *Zeitschrift für Kirchengeschichte* 91, 177–186.

Schillebeeckx, E. (1974), *Jesus: An Essay in Christology*, trans. H. Hoskins (Harmondsworth: Penguin).

Scholem, G. (1995), *Major Trends in Jewish Mysticism* (New York: Schocken Books).

Scott, G.A. (2002), *Does Socrates Have a Method? Rethinking the Socratic Elenchus* (University Park: Pennsylvania State University Press).

Seaford, R. (1984), '1 Corinthians xiii.12', *Journal of Theological Studies* 35, 117–120.

Sedley, D. (1999), 'The Ideal of Godlikeness', in G. Fine (ed.), *Plato 2: Ethics, Politics, Religion and the Soul* (Oxford: Clarendon Press), 309–328.

Sheppard, A. (1980), *Studies on the Fifth and Sixth Essays of Proclus'Commentary on the Republic* (Göttingen: Vandenhoeck and Ruprecht).

Smith, A. (1996), 'Eternity and Time', in L. Gerson (ed.), *The Cambridge Companion to Plotinus* (Cambridge: Cambridge University Press), 196–216.

Smith, A. (2004), 'Plotinus on Ideas between Plato and Aristotle', in A.L. Pierris (ed.), *Aristotle on Plato: The Metaphysical Question* (Patras: Institute for Philosophical Research), 93–108.

Smith, M. (2002), *The Early History of God* (Dearborn, MI: Dove).

Smulders, M. (1944), *La doctrine trinitaire de S. Hilaire de Poitiers* (Rome: Gregorian University).

Staehle, K. (1931), *Die Zahlenmystik bei Philon von Alexandreia* (Leipzig: Teubner).

Starobinski-Safran, E. (1978), 'Exode 3.14 dans l'exégèse de Philon d'Alexandrie', in P. Vignaux (ed.), *Dieu et l'être* (Paris: Études Augustiniennes), 47–55.

Stead, G.C. (1980), 'In Search of Valentinus', in B. Layton (ed.), *The Rediscovery of Gnosticism*, vol. 1 (Leiden: Brill), 75–95.

Stead, G.C. (1988), 'Athanasius' Earliest Written Work', *Journal of Theological Studies* 39, 76–91.

Steel, C. (2010), 'Proclus', in L. Gerson (ed.), *The Cambridge History of Philosophy in Late Antiquity*, vol. 2 (Cambridge: Cambridge University Press), 630–651.

Steenberg, M. (2004), 'Children in Paradise: Adam and Eve as "Infants" in Irenaeus of Lyons', *Journal of Early Christian Studies* 12, 1–22.

Stock, B. (1998), *Augustine the Reader: Meditation, Self-Knowledge and the Ethics of Interpretation* (Cambridge, MA: Harvard University Press).

Straw, C. (1999), 'Martyrdom', in A. Fitzgerald (ed.), *Augustine through the Ages* (Grand Rapids, MI: Eerdmans), 538–542.

Svenbro, J. (1988), *Phrasikleia. An Anthropology of Writing in Ancient Greece*, trans. J. Lloyd (Ithaca, NY: Cornell University Press).

Swift, J. (1976), *Gulliver's Travels and Other Writings*, ed. L. Landa (Oxford: Oxford University Press).

Szlezák, T. A. (1993), *Platon Lesen* (Stuttgart: Fromann-Holzboog).

Tarrant, H. (1993), *Thrasyllan Platonism* (Ithaca, NY: Cornell University Press).

Taylor, C.C.W. (1980), '"All Perceptions are True"', in M. Schofield, M. Burnyeat and J. Barnes (eds), *Doubt and Dogmatism* (Oxford: Clarendon Press), 105–124.

Tecusan, M. (1992), 'Speaking about the Ineffable: Plato's Use of Imagery', in A. Barker and M. Warner (eds), *The Language of the Cave, Apeiron* 25(4), 69–87.

Thümmel, H.-G. (1992), *Die Frühgeschichte der Östkirchlichen Bilderlehre* (Berlin: Akademie Verlag).

Trapp, M. (1997), *Maximus of Tyre: The Philosophical Orations* (Oxford: Clarendon Press).

Tuckett, C.M. (ed.) (1983), *The Messianic Secret* (Philadelphia: Fortress Press).

Turcan, R. (1975), *Mithras Platonicus: Recherches sur l'Hellénization Philosophique de Mithra* (Leiden: Brill).

Tzamalikos, P. (2006), *Origen: Cosmology and Ontology of Time* (Leiden: Brill).

Tzamalikos, P. (2007), *Origen: Philosophy of History and Eschatology* (Leiden: Brill).

Urbach, E.E. (1975), *The Sages* (Cambridge, MA: Harvard University Press).

Vaggione, R. (2000), *Eunomius of Cyzicus* (Oxford: Clarendon Press).

Van der Horst, P. (1972), 'Can a Book End with *gar*? A Note on Mark xvi.8', *Journal of Theological Studies* 23, 121–124.

Van der Poll, C. (2001), 'Homer and Homeric Interpretation in the Protrepticus of Clement of Alexandria', in F. Budelmann and P. Michelakis (eds), *Homer, Tragedy and Beyond* (London: Institute of Classical Studies), 179–200.

Van Unnik, W.C. (1973), *Sparsa Collecta III* (Leiden: Brill).

Vaught, C.G. (2005), *Access to God in Augustine's Confessions 10–13* (Albany, NY: State University Press of New York).

Vaux, R. de (1961), *Ancient Israel: its Life and Institutions*, trans. J. McHugh (London: Dartman, Longman and Todd).

Veilleux, A. (1982), *Pachomian Koinonia*, vol. 3: *Instructions, Letters and Other Writings of Saint Pachomius and his Disciples* (Kalamazoo, MI: Cistercian Publications).

Verdenius, W.J. (1971), 'Plato's Doctrine of Artistic Imitation', in G. Vlastos (ed.), *Plato* (Garden City, NY: Doubleday), 259–275.

Vermes, G. (1995), *The Dead Sea Scrolls in English* (Harmondsworth: Penguin).

Vlastos, G. (1963), 'On Plato's Oral Doctrine', *Gnomon* 41, 641–650.

Vlastos, G. (1965), 'A Metaphysical Problem in Plato', in R. Bambrough (ed.), *New Essays on Plato and Aristotle* (London: Routledge and Kegan Paul), 1–19.

Vlastos, G. (1983), 'The Socratic Elenchus', *Oxford Studies in Ancient Philosophy* 1, 27–58.

Von Rad, G. (1966), *Genesis* (London: SCM).

Von Rad, G. (1972), *Wisdom in Israel* (London: SCM).

Walzer, R. (1949), *Galen on Jews and Christians* (Oxford: Clarendon Press).

Watson, G. (1966), *Stoic Theory of Knowledge* (Belfast: Queen's University Press).

Watson, G. (1988), *Phantasia in Classical Thought* (Galway: University of Galway Press).

Weedon, T.J. (1968), 'The Heresy that Necessitated Mark's Gospel', *Zeitschrift für Neutestamentarische Wissenschaft* 59, 145–158.

Wellhausen, J. (1957), *Prolegomena to the History of Ancient Israel* (Cleveland, OH: Meridian).

West, M.L. (1966), *Hesiod: Theogony* (Oxford: Clarendon Press).

West, M.L. (1983), *The Orphic Poems* (Oxford: Clarendon Press).

Westermann, C. (1974), *Creation*, trans. J. Scullion (London: SPCK).

Whitaker, C.W.A. (1996), *Aristotle's* De Interpretatione (Oxford: Clarendon Press).

Whittaker, J. (1969a), 'Ammonius on the Delphic E', *Classical Quarterly* 19, 185–192.

Whittaker, J. (1969b), 'Epekeina nou kai ousias', *Vigiliae Christianae* 23, 91–104.

Wilberding, J. (2004), 'Prisoners and Puppeteers in the Cave', *Oxford Studies in Ancient Philosophy* 27, 117–139.

Wrede, W. (1971), *The Messianic Secret* (Cambridge: James Clarke).

Young, F.M. (1997), *Biblical Exegesis and the Formation of Christendom* (Cambridge: Cambridge University Press).

Young, F.M. (2011), 'God's Image: The "Elephant in the Room" in the Fourth Century?', in A. Brent and M. Vinzent (eds), *Studia Patristica* 50 (Leuven: Peeters), 57–72.

Zachhuber, J. (2000), *Human Nature in Gregory of Nyssa* (Leiden: Brill).

Zanker, G. (1981), '*Enargeia* in the Ancient Criticism of Poetry', *Rheinisches Museum* 124, 297–311.

Index